English Words

Francis Katamba

London and New York

First published 1994
by Routledge
11 New Fetter Lane, London EC4P 4EE

Simultaneously published in the USA and Canada
by Routledge
29 West 35th Street, New York, NY 10001

Phototypeset in Baskerville by Intype, London

Printed and bound in Great Britain by Clays Ltd, St Ives plc.

British Library Cataloguing in Publication Data
A catalogue record for this book is available from the British Library.

Library of Congress Cataloging in Publication Data
Katamba, Francis
English words / Francis Katamba
p. cm.
Includes bibliographical references.
1. English language – Lexicology. I. Title
PE1571.K38 1994
423'.028 – dc20   93–33393

ISBN 0–415–10467–X (hbk)
ISBN 0–415–10468–8 (pbk)

English Words

'The air is always thick with our verbal emissions. There are so many things we want to tell the world. Some of them are important, some of them are not. But we talk anyway. A life without words would be a horrendous privation.'

(from the Introduction)

Words and language, keys to human identity, are fascinating subjects. The aim of this book is to arouse curiosity about English words and about the nature of language in general, especially among students who are not intending to specialise in linguistics.

The book covers a wide range of topics, including the structure of words, the meaning of words, how their spelling relates to pronunciation, how new words are manufactured or imported from other languages, and how the meaning of words changes with the passage of time. It also investigates how the mind deals with words by highlighting the amazing intellectual feat performed routinely when the right word is retrieved from the mental dictionary during conversation. Words of all sorts are examined – from great poetry, nonsense verse and journalism to advertising. It is demonstrated that in their very different ways they are all worthy of serious study.

This textbook is an accessible descriptive introduction, suitable for students of English language and communication, showing how the nature of words can be illuminated by insights from a broad range of areas of linguistics and related subjects.

Francis Katamba is Lecturer in Linguistics at Lancaster University. His publications include *Morphology* (1993) and *Introduction to Phonoi*

To
Janet,
Francis and Helen

Contents

Preface

This book developed out of a course on English words that I have taught at Lancaster over the last few years. It is intended to arouse curiosity about English words and about language in general, especially among students who are not intending to specialise in linguistics.

Is it not strange that we spend so many of our waking hours talking and yet we know so little about words? Putting words under a microscope and peering at them seems to be a dead boring and absolutely unrewarding subject. Most people know more about sport, cars, computers, gardening, virtually about anything than they know about words. If you are one of them, then read on.

This book was written for you. It is intended to disabuse you of the false impression that investigating words is tedious, dry and totally unenjoyable. *English Words* takes you on a voyage of discovery during which you find out how words are structured, how they convey meaning, how their spelling relates to pronunciation, how new words are manufactured, how the meaning of words changes as time passes and how words are imported from other languages. Finally, in the concluding chapter we marvel at the ability you and I have to store tens of thousands of words in our minds and to retrieve the right words instantaneously in conversation. All this is exciting stuff.

Traditionally, the student is not offered a single course or coursebook that covers all the various topics that I have listed above. My aim in departing from normal practice by covering such a wide range of topics in one book is to provide a synthesis of what linguists and students of neighbouring disciplines such as psychology have found out about words. So, this book gives a panoramic view of words in the English language. I think there is some virtue in making sure that students do not concentrate so hard on seeing the trees that they miss the forest.

Another feature of the book is that it is primarily a descriptive study of words in the English language. It is only very occasionally that the structure of words in other languages is discussed.

No previous knowledge of linguistics is assumed. I keep linguistic theory and jargon mostly in the background and focus on the description. Studying the contents of this book will not turn you into a morphologist, but it will teach you a lot of things about English.

Your involvement in learning about English words is important. You will not be invited to watch all the interesting things about words from a distance as a mere spectator. Plenty of examples and exercises are provided for you to do some of the investigations yourself.

It is my pleasure to thank many people who have helped me in various ways during the preparation of this book. First, I acknowledge the help of my family. The writing and preparation of the book would have been an even more arduous task without their constant support and active help in hunting for examples and illustrations.

I am also grateful to various other people whose comments, advice and support have been very useful. I thank Claire L'Enfant, Senior Editor at Routledge, who started it all when she invited me to undertake this project and would not take no for an answer. In addition, I would like to thank the editorial and design staff at Routledge, in particular Beth Humphries and Emma Cotter for their advice and help in the preparation of this book. Next, I would like to thank in a special way first-year undergraduates on *Course LING 152: English Words* at Lancaster over the last couple of years who have been such co-operative, critical and really excellent guinea pigs.

I am also grateful to a number of colleagues and friends. I thank Jenny Thomas, Mick Short and Keith Brown, who commented on part of an early draft. And I thank Ton That Ai Quang from whom I received the Vietnamese data. Finally, above all, I am indebted to Dick Hudson and an anonymous American reader who went through the entire manuscript thoroughly and provided numerous useful comments and suggestions on matters of substance and presentation. The book is much better in every way than it would otherwise have been without their assistance. Any imperfections that still remain are my responsibility.

Francis Katamba
Lancaster, 1993

Acknowledgements

'Appellation controlée'. In *40 Ans de politiques*. Musée des Arts Décoratifs. Paris: Flammarion.

Auden, W. H. 'Musée des Beaux Arts'. In W. H. Auden (1968) *Collected Poems*. Edited by Edward Mendelson. London: Faber.

Bliss, A. J. (1966) *Dictionary of Foreign Words and Phrases in Current English*. London: Routledge & Kegan Paul.

Burns, R. (1786) 'Address to the devil' in W. Beattie and H. W. Meikle (eds) *Poems and Songs of Robert Burns*. Harmondsworth: Penguin.

Carroll. L. (1982) *Alice's Adventures in Wonderland and Through the Looking-Glass*. Harmondsworth: Penguin Books. First published in 1865 and 1872 respectively. Illustration of Humpty Dumpty (from p. 270) and the quotation (from p. 274).

Chaucer, G. (1964) *The Canterbury Tales*, edited by A. Hieatt and C. Hieatt. New York: Bantam Books.

Chirol, L. (1973) *Les 'mots français' et le mythe de la France en anglais contemporain*. Paris: Éditions Klincksieck.

Cole, W. and U. and Ungerer, T. (1978) *Oh, What Nonsense! A Collection of Nonsense Verse*. London: Methuen.

Crystal, D. (1987) *The Cambridge Encyclopaedia of Language*. Cambridge: Cambridge University Press.

Dahl, R. (1982) *The BFG*. Harmondsworth: Puffin Books. BGF text and cartoon.

Eliot, T. S. (1963) *Collected Poems (1963)*. London: Faber & Faber. 'Rhapsody on a Windy Night' (1954).

English children's rhyme 'Beg parding' in W. Cole (1968) *Oh, What Nonsense*, London: Methuen, p. 85.

Fantoni, B. (1984) *Private Eye's Colemanballs 2*. London: *Private Eye*/André Deutsch.

Gairdner, J. (ed.) (1983) *The Paston Letters*. Gloucester: Alan Sutton. Vol. 2, pp. 46–8.

Gleason, H. A. (1961) *An Introduction to Descriptive Linguistics*. New York: Holt, Rinehart & Winston. 2nd edition, p. 414.

Hopkins, G. M. (1970) 'Spring and Fall' in W. H. Gardner and N. H.

MacKenzie, *The Poems of Gerald Manley Hopkins*. Oxford: Oxford University Press.

James, Henry, *Portrait of a Lady*. Harmondsworth: Penguin, p. 5.

Kwik Fit advert in *Lancaster Citizen Newspaper* 24 June 1993.

Lawrence, D. H. (1960) 'Love among the Haystacks' (1930) in *Love among the Haystacks and Other Stories*. Harmondsworth: Penguin, p. 13; London: Methuen, p. 85.

Milligan, S. 'Questions, Quistions & Quostions' in W. Cole (1972) *Oh, That's Ridiculous*. London: Methuen, pp. 16–17.

Mr. Punch's Victorian Era (1888) 'Humble Pie' (1872). London: Bradbury, Agnew.

Mr. Punch's Victorian Era (1888) 'Chef Sauce' (1872). London: Bradbury, Agnew.

Opie, I. and Opie, P. (1980) *A Nursery Companion*. Oxford: Oxford University Press.

Philips, M. 'Another day, another scandal'. *The Guardian*, 16 January 1993, p. 24.

Sampson, G. (1985) *Writing Systems: A Linguistic Approach*. London: Hutchinson, p. 195, Figure 31.

Shakespeare, W. *The Oxford Shakespeare: Complete Works*. Oxford: Oxford University Press. Quotations from: *Henry V*, IV, iii. *Romeo and Juliet*, II, ii. *Sonnet 69*. *The Tempest*, Epilogue.

Sheridan, R. B. *The Rivals* in C. Price (ed.) (1975) *Sheridan Plays*. London: Oxford University Press. I, ii.

Standens advert. *What Hi-Fi*, June 1993, p. 138. Reproduced by courtesy of Standens (Tonbridge) Limited.

Vidal, J. 'The big chill'. An extract from *The Guardian*, 19 November 1992.

Winchester, S. (1993) *The Guardian* (Saturday magazine), 12 June, p. 27.

Young, J. and Young, P. (1981) *The Ladybird Book of Jokes, Riddles and Rhymes*. Loughborough: Ladybird Books, pp. 40, 57.

Yves St. Laurent advertisement. *The Guardian* (Saturday magazine), 30 June 1992.

Abbreviations

Adj.	Adjective
Adv.	Adverb
Af.	Affix
Ag.	Agent
BVS	Basic verbal suffix which is normally -*a*
Class.	Classifer
Det.	Determiner
FLH	Full Listing Hypothesis
Fr.	French
habit.	Habitual
indic.	Indicative mood
Instr.	Instrumental case
ME	Middle English
N	Noun
NP	Noun Phrase
Obj.	Object
OE	Old English
OED	*Oxford English Dictionary*
ON	Old Norse
3p.	3rd person singular
P	Pronoun
part.	Participial mood
Pat.	Patient
Pl./pl.	Plural
PP	Prepositional phrase
Pres.	Present
RP	Received Pronunciation
S	Sentence
1s.	1st person singular

Sing./sg.	Singular
Subj.	Subject
V	Verb
V_{en}	Verb ending in -en (past participle)
V_{ing}	Verb ending in -ing (present participle)
VP	Verb phrase
WP	Word-and-paradigm

Key to symbols used

1. SYMBOLS FOR PHONEMES

A key word for each phoneme is given, first in ordinary spelling and then in phonemic transcription. The phonemic transcription represents the pronunciation in British Received Pronunciation.

Vowels

ɪ	sit	/sɪt/		i:	seed	/si:d/
e	set	/set/		ɑ:	bar	/bɑ:r/
æ	sat	/sæt/		ɔ:	saw	/sɔ:/
ʌ	mud	/mʌd/		u:	zoo	/zu:/
ɒ	dog	/dɒg/		ɜ:	fur	/fɜ:/
ʊ	good	/gʊd/				
ə	send<u>er</u>	/sendə/				
	<u>a</u>bove	/əbʌv/				
eɪ	eight	/eɪt/		əʊ	low	/ləʊ/
aɪ	pie	/paɪ/		aʊ	town	/taʊn/
ɔɪ	toil	/tɔɪl/				
ɪə/	beer	/bɪə/				
eə	bare	/beə/				
ɔə	bore	/bɔə/				
ʊə	boor	/bʊə/				

Consonants

p	pan	/pæn/	f	fan	/fæn/
b	ban	/bæn/	v	van	/væn/
t	tan	/tæn/	θ	thin	/θɪn/
d	did	/dɪd/	ð	then	/ðen/
k	kit	/kɪt/	s	seal	/si:l/
g	get	/get/	z	zeal	/zi:l/
			ʃ	ship	/ʃɪp/
tʃ	chest	/tʃest/	ʒ	measure	/meʒə/
dʒ	jest	/dʒest/	h	hop	/hɒp/
m	mail	/meɪl/			
n	nail	/neɪl/			
ŋ	long	/lɒŋ/			
l	leap	/li:p/			
r	rip	/rɪp/			
j	yes	/jes/			
w	win	/wɪn/			

2. NON-PHONEMIC SYMBOLS

ʔ   Glottal stop as in *water* /wɔ:ʔə/ as said in accents where between vowels the *t* 'can be swallowed'.

ɫ   Dark 1.

l̥   Clear 1.

ı   (Under a consonant) syllabic consonant as in kettle [ketl̩].

3. OTHER SYMBOLS

ā   The symbol ⁻ over a vowel indicates that it is a long vowel.

·   A raised dot indicates that the preceding vowel is stressed (in examples from *OED*).

<   Is derived from.

>   Becomes, develops into.

ˈ   Marks main stress on the following syllable.

ı   Secondary stress.

*   An asterisk shows that a given form is disallowed.

/ /   Slashes indicate a *broad* or phonemic transcription which only shows phonemes.

[ ]   Square brackets indicate a *narrow* (i.e. detailed) transcription that shows allophones.

~   This indicates that forms alternate.
→   Rewrite as; or becomes (depending on context).
( )   Optional items are put in parenthesis.

4. SMALL CAPITALS

Small capitals are used for technical terms when first introduced and occasionally thereafter to highlight their technical sense.

Chapter 1

Introduction

1.1 WHY STUDY WORDS?

Imagine a life without words! Trappist monks opt for it. But most of us would not give up words for anything. Every day we utter thousands and thousands of words. Communicating our joys, fears, opinions, fantasies, wishes, requests, demands, feelings – and the occasional threat or insult – is a very important aspect of being human. The air is always thick with our verbal emissions. There are so many things we want to tell the world. Some of them are important, some of them are not. But we talk anyway – even when we know that what we are saying is totally unimportant. We love chitchat and find silent encounters awkward, or even oppressive. A life without words would be a horrendous privation.

It is a cliché to say that words and language are probably humankind's most valuable single possession. It is language that sets us apart from our biologically close relatives, the great primates. (I would imagine that many a chimp or gorilla would give an arm and a leg for a few words – but we will probably never know because they cannot tell us.) Yet, surprisingly, most of us take words (and more generally language) for granted. We cannot discuss words with anything like the competence with which we can discuss fashion, films or football.

We should not take words for granted. They are too important. This book is intended to make explicit some of the things that we know subconsciously about words. It is a linguistic introduction to the nature and structure of English words. It addresses the question 'what sorts of things do people need to know about English words in order to use them in speech?' It is intended to increase the degree of sophistication with which you think about words. It is designed to give you a theoretical grasp of English word-formation, the sources of English vocabulary and the way in which we store and retrieve words from the mind.

I hope a desirable side effect of working through *English Words* will be the enrichment of your vocabulary. This book will help to increase, in a very practical way, your awareness of the relationship between words. You will be equipped with the tools you need to work out the meanings of unfamiliar words and to see in a new light the underlying structural patterns in many familiar words which you have not previously stopped to think about analytically.

For the student of language, words are a very rewarding object of study. An understanding of the nature of words provides us with a key that opens the door to an understanding of important aspects of the nature of language in general. Words give us a panoramic view of the entire field of linguistics because they impinge on every aspect of language structure. This book stresses the ramifications of the fact that words are complex and multi-faceted entities whose structure and use interacts with the other modules of the grammar such as PHONOLOGY, the study of how sounds are used to represent words in speech, SYNTAX, the study of sentence structure, and SEMANTICS, the study of meaning in language.

In order to use even a very simple word, such as *frog*, we need to access various types of information from the word-store which we all carry around with us in the MENTAL LEXICON or DICTIONARY that is tucked away in the mind. We need to know:

[1.1] (i) its shape, i.e. its PHONOLOGICAL REPRESENTATION/frɒg/ which enables us to pronounce it, and its ORTHOGRAPHIC REPRESENTATION *frog*, if we are literate and know how to spell it (see the Key to symbols used on page xix);

(ii) its grammatical properties, e.g. it is a noun and it is countable – so you can have one *frog* and two *frogs*;

(iii) its meaning.

But words tend not to wear their meaning on their sleeve. Normally, there is nothing about the form of words that would enable anyone to work out their meaning. Thus, the fact that *frog* refers to one of these 🐸 simply has to be listed in the lexicon and committed to memory by brute force. For the relationship between a LINGUISTIC SIGN like this word and its meaning is ARBITRARY. Other languages use different words to refer to this small tailless amphibian. In French it is called (*la*) *grenouille*. In Malay they call it *katak* and in Swahili *chura*. None of these words is more suited than the others to the job of referring to this small reptile.

And of course, within a particular language, any particular pronunciation can be associated with any meaning. So long as speakers accept that sound–meaning association, they have a kosher word. For instance, *convenience* originally meant 'suitability' or 'commodiousness' but in the middle of the nineteenth century a new meaning of 'toilet' was assigned to it and people began to talk of 'a public convenience'. In the early 1960s the word acquired the additional new meaning of 'easy to use, designed for hassle-free use' as in *convenience food.*

We are the masters. Words are our servants. We can make them mean whatever we want them to mean. Humpty Dumpty had all this worked out. The only thing missing from his analysis is the social dimension. Any arbitrary meaning assigned to a word needs to be accepted by the speech community which uses the language. Obviously, language would not be much use as a means of communication if each individual language user assigned a private meaning to each word which other users of the language did not recognise. Apart from that, it is instructive to listen in on the lesson on the nature of language that Humpty Dumpty gave to Alice (see overleaf).

Let us now consider one further example. All competent speakers of English know that you can add -*s* to a noun to indicate that it refers to more than one entity. So, you say *cat* when referring to one and *cats* if there is more than one. If you encountered in the blank in [1.2a] an unfamiliar word like *splet* (which I have just made up), you would automatically know from the context that it must have the plural form *splets* in this position since it is specified as plural by *all*. Further, you would know that the plural of *splet* must be *splets* (rather than *spletren* by analogy to *children* or *spleti* by analogy to *stimuli*). You know that the majority of nouns form their plural by adding the regular plural suffix or ending -*s*. You always add -*s* unless express instructions are given to do otherwise. There is no need to memorise separately the plural form of most nouns. All we need is to know the rule that says 'add -*s* for plural'. So, without any hesitation, you suffix -*s* to obtain the plural form *splets* in [1.2b]:

[1.2] a. We put all the big _____ on the table.

 b. We put all the big *splets* on the table.

'As I was saying, that *seems* to be done right – though I haven't time to look it over thoroughly just now – and that shows that there are three hundred and sixty-four days when you might get un-birthday presents –'

'Certainly,' said Alice.

'And only *one* for birthday presents, you know. There's glory for you!'

'I don't know what you mean by "glory",' Alice said.

Humpty Dumpty smiled contemptuously. 'Of course you don't – till I tell you. I meant "there's a nice knock-down argument for you!" '

'But "glory" doesn't mean "a nice knock-down argument",' Alice objected.

'When *I* use a word,' Humpty Dumpty said in rather a scornful tone, 'it means just what I choose it to mean – neither more nor less.'

'The question is,' said Alice, 'whether you *can* make words mean so many different things.'

'The question is,' said Humpty Dumpty, 'which is to be master – that's all.'

(Carroll 1982: 274)

The study of word-formation and word-structure is called MOR-
PHOLOGY. Morphological theory provides a general theory of word-
structure in all the languages of the world. Its task is to characterise
the kinds of things that speakers need to know about the structure
of the words of their language in order to be able to use them to
produce and to understand speech.

We will see that in order to use language, speakers need to have
two types of morphological knowledge. First, they need to be able
to analyse existing words (e.g. they must be able to tell that *frogs*
contains *frog* plus *-s* for plural). Usually, if we know the meanings
of the elements that a word contains, it is possible to determine
the meaning of the entire word once we have worked out how the
various elements relate to each other. For instance, if we examine
a word like *nutcracker* we find that it is made up of two words,
namely the noun *nut* and the noun *cracker*. Furthermore, we see
that the latter word, *cracker* is divisible into the verb *crack* and
another meaningful element *-er* (roughly meaning 'an instrument
used to do X'), which, however, is not a word in its own right.
Numerous other words are formed using this pattern of combining
words (and smaller meaningful elements) as seen in [1.3]:

[1.3] [[tea]Noun – [strain-er]]Noun
[[lawn]Noun – [mow-er]]Noun
[[can]Noun – [open-er]]Noun

Given the frame [[_____]Noun – [_____er]] Noun, we can fill
in different words with the appropriate properties and get another
compound word (i.e. a word containing at least two words). Try
this frame out yourself. Find two more similar examples of compound words formed using this pattern.

Second, speakers need to be able to work out the meanings of
novel words constructed using the word-building elements and
standard word-construction rules of the language. Probably we all
know and use more words than are listed in dictionaries. We can
construct and analyse the structure and meaning of old words as
well as new ones. So, although many words must be listed in the
dictionary and memorised, listing every word in the dictionary is
not necessary. If a word is formed following general principles, it
may be more efficient to reconstitute it from its constituent elements
as the need arises rather than permanently commit it to memory.
When people make up new words using existing words and word-
forming elements, we understand them with ease – providing we

know what the elements they use to form those words mean and providing the word-forming rules that they employ are familiar. This ability is one of the things explored in morphological investigations.

In an average week, we are likely to encounter a couple of unfamiliar words. We might reach for a dictionary and look them up. Some of them may be listed but others might be too new or too ephemeral to have found their way into any dictionary. In such an event, we rely on our morphological knowledge to tease out their meanings. If you heard someone describe their partner as 'a great list maker and a ticker-off', you would instantly know what sort of person the partner was – although you almost certainly have never encountered the word *ticker-off* before. And it is certainly not listed in any dictionary. The *-er* ending here has the meaning of 'someone who does whatever the verb means'. Given the verb *tick-off*, a *ticker-off* must be a person who *ticks off*. Similarly, if you know what established words like *handful*, *cupful* and *spoonful* mean, you are also able to figure out the meanings of novel words like *fountain-penful* (as in *a fountain-penful of ink*) or *hovercraftful* (as in *hovercraftful after hovercraftful of English shoppers returned from Calais loaded down with cigarettes, cheese and plonk*). Virtually any noun denoting a container can have *-ful* added to it in order to indicate that it is 'full of something'.

To take another example, a number of words ending in *-ist*, many of which have come into use in recent years, refer to people who discriminate against, or hold negative views about, certain less powerful subgroups in society, e.g. *racist*, *sexist*. Anyone who knows what *racist* and *sexist* mean, given the right context should have no difficulty in understanding the nature of discrimination perpetrated by people who are described using the novel words *ageist*, *sizist* and *speechist*. *Ageism* is discrimination on grounds of (old) age – for instance, denying employment to people over the age of 60; *sizism* is discrimination (usually against fat people) on grounds of size and *speechism* is discrimination against people with speech impediments like stuttering.

Did you notice how I exploited your tacit knowledge of the fact that words ending in *-ist* and *-ism* complement each other? You were glad to accept *ageism*, *sizism* and *speechism* because you know that corresponding to an adjective ending in *-ist* there will normally be a noun ending in *-ism*. This is important. It shows that you know that certain word-forming bits go together – and others do not. I suspect that you would reject putative words like *agement, *sizement and *speechment. (An asterisk is used conventionally to indicate that a form is disallowed.) In word-formation it is not a case of anything goes.

A challenging question which morphology addresses is, 'how do speakers know which non-occurring or non-established words are permissible and which ones are not?' Why are the words *fountainpenful, hovercraftful* and *speechist* allowed while *agement, *speechment and *sizement* are not?

Morphological theory provides a general theory of word-formation applicable to any language but, as mentioned earlier, this book focuses on word-formation in English. Its objective is to provide a description of English words designed to make explicit the various things speakers know, albeit in an unconscious manner, about English words. The emphasis will be on the description of English words rather than the elaboration of morphological theory. So, data and facts about English words are brought to the fore and the theoretical and methodological issues are kept in the background for the most part. The use of formal notation has also been kept to a minimum in order to keep the account simple.

1.2 OVERVIEW OF COMING CHAPTERS

At the very outset we need to establish the nature of the subject we are going to be examining. So, Chapter 2 discusses the nature of words. Then the next three chapters delve deep inside words and investigate their internal structure. In the process, traditional morphological concepts of structural linguistics are introduced and extensively exemplified.

Morphology is not a stand-alone module. After the introductory chapters, in Chapter 6 you are introduced to a theory where morphology is an integral part of the LEXICON or DICTIONARY. This chapter focuses on the interaction of phonology and morphology in word-formation.

Chapter 7 explores the relationship between words in speech and in writing. What is the relationship between saying words and writing them down? Is writing simply a mirror of speech – and an apparently distorting one in the case of English?

The following chapter continues the discussion of the role of the lexicon. It attempts to answer questions like 'what is the lexicon for?' 'What items need to be listed in the dictionary?' 'What is the difference between idioms (like *to nail one's colours to the mast*) and syntactic phrases (like *to nail a notice to the door*)?' The next two chapters highlight the fact that the English word-store is vast and infinitely expandable. First, in Chapter 9 we consider the ways in which, using the internal resources of the language, speakers are able to produce an indefinitely large number of words. In Chapter 10 attention shifts to the expansion of English vocabulary through the importation of countless words from other languages. The story of imported words is in many ways also the story of the contacts that speakers of English have had with speakers of other languages over the centuries.

Most of the space in this book is devoted to an examination of the structure of English words. But the analysis of word-structure is seen not as an end in itself, but rather as a means to an end. And that end is to understand what it means to *know* a word. What sorts of information about words do you need to have in order to use them in communication? So the final chapter is devoted to the MENTAL LEXICON. It addresses the question, 'how is it that people are able to store a vast number of words in the mind and to retrieve the right one so fast in communication?' We will see that words are not piled in a muddle in the mind. Rather, the mental lexicon is very highly organised. This concluding chapter will also pull together the various strands developed in the earlier chapters.

I have already stressed the point that morphology is not a self-contained module of language. Any discussion of word-formation touches on other areas of linguistics, notably phonology and syntax, so I have provided a key to the list of pronunciation symbols at the beginning of the book. I have also included at the end a glossary of linguistic terms (many of them from other branches of linguistics) which might be unfamiliar. But still I may have missed out some terms. If you encounter any unfamiliar technical terms that are not explained in this book, I suggest that you consult a good dictionary of linguistics like Crystal (1991). Sometimes it is useful to present data using phonetic notation. A key to the phonetic symbols used is to be found on pp. xix–xx.

After this introductory chapter, all chapters contain exercises. Several of the analytical exercises require you to look up words and parts of words in a good dictionary like the *Oxford English Dictionary*. Acccss to such a dictionary is essential when you study this book. This is a practical way of learning about the structure of English words (and may also be a useful way of enriching your vocabulary).

Chapter 2

What is a word?

2.1 INTRODUCTION

Often we find it very difficult to give a clear and systematic account of everyday things, ideas, actions and events that surround us. We just take them for granted. We rarely need to state in an accurate and articulate manner what they are really like. For instance, we all know what a game is. Yet, as the philosopher Wittgenstein showed, we find it very difficult to state explicitly what the simple word *game* means.

The same is true of the term *word*. We use words all the time. We intuitively know what the words in our language are. Nevertheless most of us would be hard pushed to explain to anyone what kind of object a word is. If a couple of Martian explorers (with a rudimentary understanding of English) came off their space-ship and stopped you in the street to enquire what earthlings meant by the term WORD what would you tell them? I suspect you might be somewhat vague and evasive. Although you know very well what words are, you might find it difficult to express explicitly and succinctly what it is that you know about them.

The purpose of this chapter is to try to find an answer to the question: what is a word? It is not only Martian explorers curious about the way earthlings live who might want to know what words are. We too have an interest in understanding words because they play such an important role in our lives. As we saw in the last chapter, it is impossible to imagine human society without language. And equally, it is impossible to imagine a human language that has no words of any kind. It is impossible to understand the nature of language without gaining some understanding of the nature of words. So, in this chapter we will clarify what we mean when we use the term 'word'. This clarification is essential if our investigations are to make any headway for, as you will see presently, we mean quite a few very different things when we talk of words.

A standard definition of the word is found in a paper written in 1926 by the American linguist Leonard Bloomfield, one of the greatest linguists of the twentieth century. According to Bloomfield, 'a minimum free form is a word'. By this he meant that the word is the smallest meaningful linguistic unit that can be used on its own. It is a form that cannot be divided into any smaller units that can be used independently to convey meaning. For example *child* is a word. We cannot divide it up into smaller units that can convey meaning when they stand alone.

Contrast this with the word *childish* which can be analysed into *child-* and *-ish*. While the *child* bit of *childish* is meaningful when used on its own (and hence is a word), the same is not true of *-ish*. Although according to the *Oxford English Dictionary* (*OED*) *-ish* means something like 'having the (objectionable) qualities of' (as in *mannish*, *womanish*, *devilish*, *sheepish*, *apish* etc.), there is no way we can use it on its own. If some shouted to you in the street, 'Hey, are you *-ish*?' you might smile bemusedly and think to yourself, 'Isn't he weird!' In the next chapter we will take up the question of what to do with pieces of words that cannot be used meaningfully on their own. But for the moment we will focus exclusively on words.

2.2 WORDS ARE LIKE LIQUORICE ALLSORTS

When we talk of words we do not always mean exactly the same thing. Like liquorice allsorts, words come in all sorts of varieties. We will start our discussions by distinguishing the different senses in which we use the term 'word'.

2.2.1 Word-forms

Let us use the term WORD-FORM to describe the physical form which realises or represents a word in speech or writing. Consider the words in the following extract from T. S. Eliot's poem:

[2.1] Half-past one,
         The street-lamp sputtered,

> The street-lamp muttered,
> The street-lamp said, 'Regard that woman
> Who hesitates towards you in the light of the door
> Which opens on her like a grin . . .
> ('Rhapsody on a windy night' in Eliot 1963)

In written English, words are easy to recognise. They are preceded by a space and followed by a space. Using this criterion, we can say that there are thirty-one words (i.e. word-forms) in the extract from 'Rhapsody'. We will call word-forms like these which we find in writing ORTHOGRAPHIC WORDS. If you look again at the extract, you might wonder if some of the hyphenated orthographic words are 'really' individual words. Many people would hyphenate *half-past* as Eliot does but not *street-lamp*. They would write *street lamp* as two separate words, with a space between them. What would you do?

The use of hyphens to indicate that something is a complex word containing more than one word-like unit is variable, largely depending on how transparent the compound nature of a word is. Shakespeare wrote *today* as *to-day* and *tomorrow* as *to-morrow*:

[2.2] a. To-morrow, Caesar,
> I shall be furnished to inform you rightly . . .
> > *(Antony and Cleopatra*, I, iv)

   b. O! that we now had here
> But ten thousand of those men in England
> That do not work to-day.
> > *(Henry V*, IV, iii)

Hyphenating *to-day* and *to-morrow* is less common now, probably because most speakers are unaware of the compound nature of these words. *Today* comes from Old English *tō dæg* 'to + day' and *tomorrow* is from Middle English *to mor(e)we* (i.e. to (the) morrow) – *to-* can be traced back ultimately to a form that meant 'this' in Indo-European. Note in passing that three major periods are distinguished in the history of the English language: Old English (conventionally abbreviated as OE) was spoken *c*.450–1100; Middle English (conventionally abbreviated as ME) was spoken *c*.1100–1500 and Modern English from 1500 to the present.

Generally, the use of the hyphen in such words that are no longer seen as compounds is in decline. The hyphen tends to be mostly used in compounds that are regarded as fairly new words.

Many well-established words that are transparently compounded, e.g. *schoolboy*, are normally written without a hyphen. Of course, judgements as to what is an established word vary greatly. There are few firm rules here. For instance, in the *OED* both *seaway* and *sea-way* are shown to be accepted ways of writing the word pronounced as /siːweɪ/. Similarly, the compilers of the *OED* show variation in the way they enter both hyphenated *first-rate* and *first rate* written as two words separated by a space.

Interestingly, hyphenation is also used creatively to indicate that an idea that would normally be expressed by a phrase is being treated as a single word for communicative purposes because it has crystallised in the writer's mind into a firm, single concept. Thus, for example, the expression *simple to serve* is normally a phrase, just like *easy to control*. But it can also be used as a hyphenated word as in *simple-to-serve recipe dishes (M&S Magazine* 1992: 9). Similarly, on page 48 of the same magazine, the writer of an advertising feature uses the phrase 'fresh from the farm' as a hyphenated word in 'fresh-from-the-farm eggs'. But for creative hyphenation you are unlikely to find anything more striking than this:

[2.3] On Pitcairn there is little evidence of the *what-we-have-we-hold*, *no-surrender*, the *Queen's-picture-in-every-room* sort of attitude.

Simon Winchester in *The Guardian* magazine, 12 June 1993: 27; (italics added to highlight the compounds)

What we have established is that as a rule, orthographic words have a space on either side of them. But there are cases where this simple rule of thumb is not followed. There is a degree of flexibility in the way in which words are written down: being, or not being, separated by a space is in itself not a sure sign of word status. Some orthographic words which are uncontroversially written as one unit contain two words within them. They are compound words like *firstrate*, *seaway*, *wheelbarrow* and *teapot*. Furthermore, there are forms like *they're*, *hadn't* and *I'm* which are joined together in writing yet which are not compound words. When you scratch the skin, you see immediately that *they're*, *hadn't* and *I'm* are really versions of the pairs of words *they are*, *had not* and *I am*. Our theory needs to say something about awkward customers like these. Since the issues they raise are complex, we will postpone discussion of them until sections (4.3) and (8.3). Finally, there are words which are compounded (and maybe hyphenated as in [2.3]) as a one-off to crystallise a particular meaning.

So far we have only considered orthographic words, i.e. recognisable physical written word-forms. Obviously, words as physical objects exist not only in writing, but also in speech. We will now briefly turn to word-forms in spoken language. We will refer to them as PHONOLOGICAL WORDS.

The challenge of word recognition arises in an even more obvious way when we consider speech. Words are not separated distinctly from each other. We do not leave a pause between words that could be equated to a space in writing. (If we did that, conversation would be painfully slow! Just try speaking to one of your friends today leaving a two-second gap between words. See how they react.) In normal speech words come out in a torrent. They overlap. Just as droplets of water cannot be seen flowing down a river, individual words do not stand out discretely in the flow of conversation. So they are much harder to isolate than words in writing. None the less, we are able to isolate them. If you heard an utterance like:

[2.4] The cat slept in your bed.
       /ðə kæt slept ɪn 'jɔː bed/
       (Note: '' shows that the following syllable is stressed;
              phonemic transcription is written between slant lines.)

you would be able to recognise the six phonological words that have been written in PHONEMIC TRANSCRIPTION (which shows the PHONEMES, i.e. the sounds that are used to distinguish the meanings of words) although what you hear is one continuous stream of sound. For purely practical reasons, throughout the book, unless otherwise stated, phonemic transcriptions and references to pronunciation will be based on RECEIVED PRONUNCIATION (RP), the prestige accent of standard British English – the variety popularly known as the Queen's English or BBC English.

An intriguing question that linguists and psychologists have tried to answer is: how do people recognise words in speech? We will address this question in detail in section (11.2.1) below. For now let us simply assume that phonological words can be identified. Our present task will simply be to outline some of their key properties. To do this it will be useful to distinguish between two types of words: the so-called CONTENT WORDS and FUNCTION WORDS. Content words are the nouns, verbs, adjectives and adverbs which contain most of the REFERENTIAL (or COGNITIVE MEANING) of a sentence. This roughly means that they name individuals and predicate of them certain properties. They tell us, for instance, what happened or who did what to whom, and in what circumstances. An example will make the point clear. In the old days, when people sent telegrams, it was content words that were mainly (or exclusively) used. A proud parent could send a message like *Baby girl arrived yesterday* which contained two nouns, a verb and an adverb. Obviously, this is not a well-formed, grammatical sentence. But its meaning would be clear enough.

Function words are the rest – prepositions, pronouns, conjunctions, articles and so on. They have a predominantly grammatical role. A telegram containing only the words *She it and for us* would convey little idea of what the intended interpretation was. This is not to say that function words are superfluous. Without them sentences are usually ungrammatical. A sentence like **Nelly went town* which lacks the preposition *to* is not permitted. We have to say *Nelly went to town*.

In English, content words have this property: one of their syllables is more prominent than the rest because it receives MAIN STRESS. This is seen in the words below where the syllable with main stress is preceded by '':

[2.5]	*Initial stress*	*Medial stress*	*Final stress*
	'acrobat	a'nnoying	ca'hoots
	'kingfisher	de'molish	gaber'dine
	'patriarchate	Chau'cerian	hullaba'loo

Main stress can fall on only one syllable in a word. The location of main stress is part of the make-up of a word and is not changed capriciously by individual speakers. You cannot decide to stress *hullabaloo* on the penultimate syllable on a Monday (*hulla'baloo*), on the antepenultimate syllable on a Tuesday (*hu'llabaloo*), on the initial syllable on a Wednesday ('*hullabaloo*) and on the final syllable for the rest of the week (*hullaba'loo*).

However, in some cases, if we wish to contrast two related words, we can shift stress from its normal position to a new position. This can be seen in '*vendor* and *ven'dee* which normally are stressed on the first and second syllable respectively. But if the speaker wants to contrast these two words both words might be stressed on the final syllable as I heard an estate agent do in a radio interview.

[2.6] It is *ven`dor*, not the *ven`dee* who pays that tax.

This example illustrates well the point that a word is allowed just one stress. Stress can be shifted from one syllable to another, but a word cannot have two main stresses. We could not have **`ven`dor* and **`ven`dee* where the two syllables received equal stress. Stress has to do with relative prominence. The syllable that receives main stress is somewhat more prominent than the rest, some of which may be unstressed or weakly stressed. By contrast, function words are normally unstressed. We can say *Nelly went to town* with no stress on *to* unless we wish to highlight *to* for contrastive purposes, e.g. *Nelly went to town and not far away from town*).

It is easy to see how stress can function as a valuable clue in determining whether two content words are a single compound word or two separate words. The nouns *street* and *lamp* are both stressed when they occur in isolation. But if they appear in the compound *`street-lamp*, only the first is stressed. The stress on *lamp* is suppressed.

Stress is not the only phonological clue. In addition to stress, there are rules regulating the positions in which various sounds may occur in a word and the combinations of sounds that are permissible. These rules are called PHONOTACTIC RULES. They can help us to know whether we are at the beginning, in the middle or at the end of a word. A phonological word must satisfy the requirements for words of the spoken language. For instance, while any vowel can begin a word, and most consonants can appear alone at the beginning of a word, the consonant [ŋ] is subject to certain restrictions. (This consonant is spelled *ng* as in *long* (see the Key to symbols used on p. xix). In English words [ŋ] is not allowed to occur initially although it can occur in other positions. Thus, [ŋ] is allowed internally and at the end of a word as in [lɒŋɪŋ] *longing* and [lɒŋgə] *longer*. But you could not have an English word like *ngether* *[ŋeðə], with [ŋ] as its first sound. However, in other languages this sound may be found word-initially as in the Chinese name Nga [ŋa] and the Zimbabwean name Nkomo [ŋkomo].

There are also phonotactic restrictions on the combination of consonants in various positions in a word in the spoken language. As everyone knows, English spelling is not always a perfect mirror of pronunciation. So when considering words in the spoken language it is important to separate spelling from pronunciation (cf.

Chapter 7). You know that *He is knock-kneed* is pronounced /hɪ ɪz nɒk niːd/ and not */he ɪs knɒk kniːd/. A particular combination of letters can be associated with very different pronunciations in different words or in different positions in the same word. The spelling *kn* is pronounced /kn/ at the end of a word, as in /beɪkn/, but at the beginning of a word as in *knee* and *knock* the /k/ is dropped and only the *n* is sounded. Similarly, other stop-plus-nasal combinations like *tm* /tm/ and *dn* /dn/ are allowed at the end of a word (e.g. *bottom* /bɒtm/ and *burden* /bɜːdn/) but these consonant clusters are not permitted at the beginning of a word. Putative words like */tmɪs/ (**tmiss*) and */dnel/ (**dnell*) are just impermissible. In the spoken language we recognise as English words only those forms that have the right combination of sounds for the position in the word where they occur.

Moreover, even when a sound or combination of sounds is allowed, often a somewhat different pronunciation is used depending on the position in which it occurs in a word. This can be seen in the pronunciation of the *l* sound in standard British English (RP) in different positions in a word. Compare the initial *l* with the final *l* in the following:

[2.7]

Word-initial clear *l* [l]	*Word-final dark* *l* [ɫ]	*Pre-consonantal dark* *l* [ɫ]
labour lead loft	spill smell fulfil	milk salt belt quilt
lend let lick leaf	cool bull sprawl	spoilt colt wild

The *l* sound is always made with the blade of the tongue against the teeth-ridge, with the sides lowered to allow air to escape. But there is a subtle difference. When *l* is in word-final position or when it is followed by another consonant (as it is in the last two columns), besides the articulatory gestures mentioned above, the back of the tongue is also simultaneously raised towards the soft palate (or velum). This type of *l* is called dark or velarised *l* (ɫ). But when *l* is at the beginning of a word, no velarisation takes place. This latter type of *l* is called clear or non-velarised *l* ([l]). Thus, the kind of *l* we hear gives an indication of where in a word it appears.

Do not fail to note the use of square brackets. They are used to enclose ALLOPHONES, i.e. variants of a phoneme. Allophones are different sounds, e.g. [l] and [ɫ], that occur in different contexts which all represent the same phoneme /l/.

With regard to spelling too, the situation is not chaotic, although admittedly the relationship between letters and phonemes is not always straightforward, as *knee* being pronounced /ni:/ demonstrates. We recognise as English words only those orthographic words that conform to the spelling conventions of English. If, for example, you saw the word *zvroglen* you would treat it as a foreign word. The letter combination *zvr* is not English. There is no way a word in English could start with those letters.

Let me summarise. One sense in which we use the term 'word' is to refer to WORD-FORMS. If we are thinking of the written language, our word-forms are ORTHOGRAPHIC words. These are easily recognised. They normally have a space before and after them. By contrast, in normal spoken language our word-forms are PHONO-LOGICAL words. These are more difficult to identify because they are not discrete entities that can be neatly picked off one by one. None the less, phonological words can be identified on the basis of their phonological characteristics such as stress and phonotactic properties.

2.2.2 Words as vocabulary items

We need to distinguish between words in the sense of word-form as opposed to words as vocabulary items. Let us revisit the examples in [2.2.1] on pp. 11–12. If we are considering word-forms, we can see that the hyphenated word-form *street-lamp* occurs three times. So if we were counting different word-forms, we would count *street-lamp* three times. However, if we were counting distinct words, in the sense of distinct VOCABULARY ITEMS we would only count it once.

The distinction between word-forms and vocabulary items is important. Very often, when we talk about words what we have in mind is not word-forms, but something more abstract – what we will refer to here as LEXEMES (i.e. vocabulary items). Anyone compiling a dictionary lists words in this sense. So, although the word-forms in each of the columns in [2.8] below are different, we do not find each one of them given a separate entry in an English dictionary. The first word in each column is listed under a heading of its own. The rest may be mentioned under that heading, if they do not follow a regular pattern of the language – e.g. *write, written* (past participle), *wrote* (past tense). But if they do follow the general pattern (e.g. *washes, washing, washed; smile, smiling, smiled*) they will be left out of the dictionary altogether. Instead, the grammar will be expected to provide a general statement to the effect that verbs take an *-ing* suffix, which marks progressive aspect, and an *-ed* suffix that marks both the past tense and the past participle, and so on.

[2.8] | WASH | TAKE | BRING | WRITE |
| --- | --- | --- | --- |
| wash | take | bring | write |
| washes | takes | brings | writes |
| washing | taking | bringing | writing |
| washed | took | brought | wrote |
| washed | taken | brought | written |

In [2.8] each lexeme (i.e. vocabulary item) that would be entered in a dictionary is shown in capital letters and all the different word-forms belonging to it are shown in lower-case letters.

The examples in [2.8] are all verbs. But, of course, lexemes can be nouns, adjectives or adverbs as well. In [2.9] you will find examples from these other word classes.

[2.9] | *Noun* | *Adjective* | *Adverb* |
| --- | --- | --- |
| a. | MATCH | KIND | SOON |
| | match | kind | soon |
| | matches | kinder | sooner |
| | | | |
| b. | GOOSE | BAD | WELL |
| | goose | bad | well |
| | geese | worse | better |

In [2.9] we have three pairs of lexemes: the nouns, *match* and *goose*; the adjectives *kind* and *bad*; and adverbs *soon* and *well*. In each case the word-forms belonging to each lexeme in [2.9a] follow a general pattern for words of their type and need not be listed in the dictionary. But all the ones in [2.9b] are irregular and must be listed in the dictionary.

The lexeme is an abstract entity that is found in the dictionary and that has a certain meaning. Word-forms are the concrete objects that we put down on paper (orthographic words) or utter (phonological words) when we use language. The relationship between a lexeme and the word-forms belonging to it is one of REALISATION or REPRESENTATION or MANIFESTATION. If we take the lexeme *write* which is entered in the dictionary, for example, we can see that it may be realised by any one of the word-forms *write*, *writes*, *writing*, *wrote* and *written* which belong to it. These are the actual forms that are used in speech or appear on paper. When

you see the orthographic words *written* and *wrote* on the page, you
know that although they are spelt differently they are manifestations of the same vocabulary item WRITE.

The distinction between word-forms and lexemes which I have
just made is not abstruse. It is a distinction that we are intuitively
aware of from an early age. It is the distinction on which word-
play in puns and in intentional ambiguity in everyday life depends.
At a certain period in our childhood we were fascinated by words.
We loved jokes – even awful ones like [2.10]

[2.10]

'Waiter, do you serve shrimps?'
'We serve anyone, sir.
We don't mind what size you are!'

Source: J. and P. Young (1981) *The Ladybird
Book of Jokes, Riddles and Rhymes.*

The humour, of course, lies in recognising that the word-form
shrimp can belong to two separate lexemes whose very different and
unrelated meanings are none the less pertinent here. It can mean
either 'an edible, long, slender crustacean' or 'a tiny person' (in
colloquial English). Also, the word *serve* has two possible interpretations. It can mean 'to wait upon a person at table' or 'to dish
up food'. Thus, word-play exploits the lexical ambiguity arising
from the fact that the same word-form represents two distinct
lexemes with very distinct meanings.

In real-life communication, where potential ambiguity occurs we generally manage to come to just one interpretation without too much difficulty by selecting the most appropriate and RELEVANT interpretation in the situation. Suppose a 20-stone super heavy-weight boxer went to Joe's Vegetarian Restaurant and asked the waiter for a nice shrimp curry and the waiter said in reply, 'We don't serve shrimps', it would be obvious that it was shrimps in the sense of crustaceans that was intended. If, on the other hand, a little man, barely 5 feet tall and weighing a mere 7 stone, went to a fish restaurant and saw almost everyone at the tables around him tucking into a plateful of succulent shrimps, and thought that he would quite fancy some himself, he would be rightly offended if the waiter said 'We do not serve shrimps.' It is obvious in this situation that shrimps are on the menu and are dished up for consumption. What is not done is serve up food to people deemed to be puny.

Source: What HI-FI? June 1993.

Puns are not restricted to jokes. Many advertisements like that for Standens rely on puns for their effect. Given the context, it is obvious that *sound* is meant to be read in more than one sense here.

Serious literature also uses this device. For instance, the First World War poet Siegfried Sassoon gives the title 'Base details' to the poem in which he parodies cowardly generals who stay away at the base, at a safe distance from the action, and gladly speed young soldiers to their death at the front. The word-form *base* in the title represents two distinct lexemes here whose meanings are both relevant: (i) *Base details* are details of what is happening at the *base* (Noun) (meaning 'military encampment'), and (ii) *Base details* are particulars of something that is *base* (Adjective) (meaning 'reprehensibly cowardly, mean etc.').

The term HOMONYM is used to denote word-forms belonging to distinct lexemes that are written and pronounced in the same way. There are separate dictionary entries for such words. *Shrimp* and *base* are examples of homonyms. But perhaps they are not so obvious. Better examples of homonyms are shown in [2.11].

[2.11] a. *bat:bat* (Noun) 'a small flying mammal'
            bat (Noun) 'a wooden implement for hitting a ball in cricket'
        b. *bar:bar* (Noun) 'the profession of barrister'
            bar (Noun) 'a vertical line across a stave used to mark metrical accent in music'
            bar (Verb) 'to obstruct'
        c. *fair:fair* (Adjective) 'beautiful, attractive'
            fair (Noun) 'holiday'

By contrast, word-forms may have the same pronunciation but different spellings and meanings. Such forms are called HOMOPHONES. See this example from a joke book:

[2.12] Why does the pony cough?
        Because he's a little hoarse.

                                    (Young and Young 1981: 57)

The joke is a pun on /hɔːs/, the pronunciation of the two lexemes represented in writing by *horse* and *hoarse*. Other examples of homophones include *tail* ~ *tale*, *sail* ~ *sale*, *weather* ~ *whether*, *see* ~ *sea*, *read* ~ *reed*, *reel* ~ *real*, *seen* ~ *scene*, *need* ~ *knead*.

Conversely, it is also possible to have several closely related meanings that are realised by the same word-form. The name for this is POLYSEMY. Often you find several senses listed under a single heading in a dictionary. For instance, under the entry for the noun *force*, the *OED* lists over ten senses. I have reproduced the first six below:

[2.13] 1. Physical strength. Rarely in *pl.* (= Fr. *forces* – 1818.)
2. Strength, impetus, violence, or intensity of effect ME.
3. Power or might; esp. military power ME. b. In early use, the strength (of a defensive work etc.). Subseq., the fighting strength of a ship. 1577.
4. A body of armed men, an army. In *pl.* the troops or soldiers composing the fighting strength of a kingdom or a commander ME. b. A body of police; often absol. *the force* = policemen collectively. 1851.
5. Physical strength or power exerted on an object; *esp.* violence or physical coercion. ME.
6. Mental or moral strength. Now only, power of effective action, or of overcoming resistance. ME.

The line that separates polysemy from homonymy is somewhat blurred because it is not altogether clear how far meanings need to diverge before we should treat words representing them as belonging to distinct lexemes. In [2.13], it is not entirely clear that the sixth sense of the noun *force* is not sufficiently removed from the other meanings to merit an entry of its own. The other meanings all show a reasonably strong family resemblance. But mental or moral strength shows a somewhat weaker relationship.

In the *OED*, there is a separate entry for the lexeme *force*, the verb. It is considered a different lexeme because it has a different meaning and belongs to a different word-class, being a verb and not a noun. Belonging to different word-classes is an important consideration in determining whether separate dictionary entries are needed.

In real-life communication, the lack of a one-to-one match between lexemes and word-forms does not necessarily cause ambiguity. In context, the relevant meaning is normally easy to determine. But there are cases where it is not. For instance, the homonymy of *bat* in [2.14] can cause semantic confusion:

[2.14] I saw a *bat* under the tree.

It could be a *bat* with which you play cricket or a small, flying mammal. This is a case of LEXICAL AMBIGUITY. We have in this sentence a word-form that represents more than one lexeme with a meaning that is quite plausible. It is not possible to determine the right interpretation of the sentence without looking at the wider context in which it appears.

We have established that the relationship between a word-form and the meaning that it represents is a complex one. This is exploited not only in literature and word-play as we saw above but also in the language of advertising. For instance, a recent British Gas newspaper advertisement for gas heating said:

[2.15] You will warm to our credit. It's free.

This advertisement exploits the lexical ambiguity that is due to the fact that *warm (to)* can mean 'become enthusiastic' or 'experience a rise in temperature'. Next time you look at an advertisement, see whether it exploits any of the relationships between lexemes and word-forms that we have examined.

2.2.3 Grammatical words

Finally, let us consider the word from a grammatical perspective. Words play a key role in syntax. So, some of their properties are assigned taking into account syntactic factors. Often words are required to have certain properties if they serve certain syntactic purposes. Thus, although in [2.16a] we have the same sense of the same lexeme (*play*) realised by the same word-form (*played*), we know that this word does at least two quite different grammatical jobs in the sentence of which it is a part:

[2.16] a. She played the flute.   b. She took the flute.
        She has played the flute.   She has taken the flute.

If you compare the sentences in [2.16] above, you will see that in [2.16a] the verb *play* is realised by the word-form *played* regardless of whether it simply indicates that the action happened in the past as in the first example or that an action was (recently) completed as in the second example. Contrast this with the situation in [2.16b] where these two grammatical meanings are signalled by two different forms. *Took* indicates that the action happened in the past while *taken* (after *has/had*) indicates that the action is complete. In *She played the flute* and *She took the flute* the words *played* and *took* are described grammatically as the 'past tense forms of the verbs *play* and *take*'. By contrast, in *She has played the flute* and *She has taken the flute* we describe *played* and *taken* as the 'past participle' of *play* and *take*.

Linguists use the term SYNCRETISM to describe situations such as that exemplified by *played* where the same word-form of a lexeme is used to realise two (or more) distinct grammatical words that are represented separately in the grammatical representations of words belonging to some other comparable lexemes. The phenomenon of syncretism is one good reason for distinguishing between word-forms and grammatical words. It enables us to show that words belonging to the same lexeme and having the same form in speech and writing can still differ.

A further example should make the ideas of grammatical words and syncretism even clearer. Consider the verbs in the following sentences:

[2.17] a. You hit me. (= you hit me some time in the past)
or
(= you hit me habitually)
b. You cut it. (= you cut it some time in the past)
or
(= you cut it habitually)

As the paraphrases show, the word-form *hit* belonging to the lexeme *hit* can represent either the present tense or the past tense form of the verb. In other words, there is syncretism. We have two different grammatical words *hit* [+verb, +present] and *hit* [+verb, +past] but a single word-form. The same analysis also applies to *cut*. It can represent either the present or past tense of the verb *cut*.

Syncretism is not limited to verbs. It can apply to other word classes (e.g. nouns) as well:

[2.18] (a) The wolf killed a sheep and one deer.
(b) The wolf killed two sheep and three deer.

In these two sentences, although the word-form *sheep* belongs to the same lexeme and is unchanged in form, we know that its grammatical value is not the same. In [2.18a] it realises the word with the grammatical properties of noun and singular, but in [2.18b] it represents a plural form. Likewise, the same word-form *deer* represents a singular noun in [2.18a] and a plural noun in [2.18b].

What can we say about the word as an entity that functions as a grammatical unit in the syntax of a language? As mentioned already, the (grammatical) word is normally defined as the MINIMAL

FREE FORM that is used in the grammar of a language. Let us now put some flesh on this terse and somewhat cryptic statement.

By free form we mean an entity that can stand on its own and act as a free agent; it is an element whose position in a sentence is not totally dictated by other items. In order to explain what 'freedom' means in this context, we need to take on board two ancillary ideas: POSITIONAL MOBILITY and STABILITY. Although words are not the smallest grammatical units used to construct sentences (see the discussion of morphemes in the next chapter), at the level of sentence organisation the rules of sentence formation treat words as unanalysable units. Often it is possible to change the order in which words appear in a sentence and still produce a well-formed sentence. Words enjoy considerable positional mobility. However, the elements inside a word do not enjoy such mobility. While syntactic rules can transport words to new places in a sentence, they cannot shift in the same way elements that are found inside words. Moving words around in the following produces grammatical sentences with basically the same meaning, but with somewhat different emphasis:

[2.19] a. This old industrialist revisited Lancaster, fortunately.
        b. Fortunately, this old industrialist revisited Lancaster.
        c. Lancaster, this old industrialist revisited, fortunately.
        d. Fortunately, Lancaster was revisited by this old industrialist.

Evidently, the position of words in a sentence is not rigidly fixed. They can, and often do, get moved around if the communicative needs of the speaker or writer require it. However, the interior of a word is a no-go area for syntactic rules. They are strictly barred from manipulating elements found inside a word. As far as syntax is concerned, words are indivisible units that cannot be split and whose internal units are inaccessible (cf. Bauer 1988, Matthews 1991, Lyons 1968, Di Sciullo and Williams 1987).

The word as a grammatical unit shows stability (or INTERNAL COHESION). The order of elements inside a word is rigidly fixed. If the elements of a sentence are shifted, certain meaningful units (in this case *re-visit-ed* and *fortun-ate-ly*) all move *en bloc*, and their order always remains unchanged. The internal structure of the word cannot be tampered with. We are not allowed to perform operations that would yield words like **ed-visit-re*, **ate-fortune-ly* etc. We will return to this point on p. 33 below.

The definition of the word includes the term 'minimal' for a good reason. This is intended to separate words from phrases like *this old industrialist*. Like words, phrases can occur in isolation and they can be moved from one position to another (as we have seen in [2.19]). But the expression *this old industrialist* is not a minimal form since it contains smaller forms capable of occurring independently namely, *this*, *old* and *industrialist*. Furthermore, the sequence *this old industrialist* does not have the kind of internal cohesion found in words. It can be interrupted by other words e.g. *this wealthy old industrialist*; *this very wealthy, old, benevolent industrialist*.

The assumption that the grammatical word is 'a minimum free form' works well as a rule of thumb. But it encounters difficulties when confronted by a COMPOUND WORD like *wheelbarrow* which contains the words *wheel* and *barrow* which can stand alone. In such cases it is clear that the word is not the smallest meaningful unit that can be used on its own. It is for this reason that the definition of the word as the unit on which purely syntactic operations can be performed is preferable. In the case of compounds this definition works. The interior of a compound is a syntactic no-go area. Syntactic rules are not allowed to apply separately to words that make up a compound. Thus, for example although the nouns *wheel* and *barrow* can be modified by the adjective *big* ([*big barrow*], [*big wheel*]), and although we can talk of [*big wheelbarrow*], in which case *big* modifies the entire compound, there is no possibility of saying *wheel* [*big barrow*], with the adjective only modifying the second element of the compound word.

2.3 SUMMARY

In this chapter we have established that normally, the term 'word' is used ambiguously. To avoid the ambiguity, we need to distinguish between three different types of word: (i) a word-form (i.e. a particular physical manifestation of one or more lexemes in speech or writing); (ii) a vocabulary item (i.e. lexeme); and (iii) a unit of grammatical structure that has certain morphological and syntactic properties.

We will revisit the distinction between lexemes, grammatical words and word-forms mainly in Chapters 7 and 11. In Chapter 7 our main concern will be the realisation of words in speech and in writing. In Chapter 11 we will show that this distinction is not an artefact of the linguist's analysis. Rather, it is a distinction that is well supported by studies in the way in which we store words in the mind and retrieve them for use in communication in real life.

In the coming chapters, in cases where the relevant sense of the term 'word' is clear from the context I will not spell out whether it is the word as a vocabulary item, grammatical word, phonological or orthographic form that is being dealt with. But where it is not clear, I will indicate the sense in which I am using this term. We are now in a position to consider in detail the internal structure of words. That is the task of the next chapter.

EXERCISES

1. Comment on the problems you encounter in determining the number of words in the following nursery rhyme. Relate your answer to the different senses in which the term 'word' is used.

> The grand old Duke of York
> He had ten thousand men.
> He marched them up to the top of the hill,
> Then he marched them down again.
>
> When they were up, they were up,
> And when they were down, they were down,
> And when they were only half way up
> They were neither up nor down.

2. Find and analyse at least three examples of advertisements that exploit the homonymy, polysemy or homophony of words.

3. Which ones of the italicised word-forms in the following sentences belong to the same lexeme? What difficulties, if any, have you come across in determining whether word-forms belong to the same lexeme?

   a. She *saw* him *saw* through that plank of wood.
   b. *Bill* will pay the *bill*.
   c. I saw *Farmer* near your *farm* again this morning.
   d. Jan looked *pale* when she walked towards the *pail*.
   e. I am *sick* of your claiming to be *sick* all the time.
   f. I was looking at the *book* when she *booked* the ticket.

4. Using at least two fresh examples, show how syncretism can

be used to support the distinction between word-forms and grammatical words.

5. This is the beginning of W. H. Auden's poem 'Musée des Beaux Arts'.

> About suffering they were never wrong,
> The Old Masters . . .

These lines can be paraphrased as 'The Old Masters were never wrong about suffering.'

Referring to the definition of the word given in this chapter, explain why it is correct to regard *suffering* as a word but incorrect to treat *about suffering* also as a word.

Chapter 3

Close encounters of a morphemic kind

3.1 THE QUEST FOR VERBAL ATOMS

We saw in the last chapter that the word is the smallest meaningful unit of language that can function independently in the grammar. A word can be used on its own, without appending it to some other unit. Thus, in the word *childish* we can isolate *child* and use it on its own because it is a word in its own right. But we cannot use -*ish* as a stand-alone unit, for -*ish* is not a word.

While recognising that words are the smallest meaningful units which function independently in the grammar, we also need to recognise that words can be decomposed into smaller units that are also meaningful. Our task in this chapter is to explore the internal structure of words in order to gain some understanding of the basic units which are used to form words.

3.2 CLOSE MORPHOLOGICAL ENCOUNTERS: ZOOMING IN ON MORPHEMES

Originally 'morphology' meant the study of biological forms. But nineteenth-century students of language borrowed the term and applied it to the study of word-structure. In linguistics MOR-PHOLOGY is the study of the formation and internal organisation of words.

Let us begin our morphological analysis by considering half a dozen words (not altogether randomly chosen):

[3.1] hope soon mend boil safe leaf word elephant

Obviously all the words in [3.1] have a meaning, but lack internal structure. We cannot identify any smaller units that are themselves meaningful which occur inside them. If a Martian stopped you in a street near the local zoo and enquired what *phant* in *elephant* or *ho* in *hope* means, you would think she was asking a most bizarre question that did not merit an answer. Or you might condescendingly explain that, of course, in each case the whole word means something, but its parts cannot be said to mean anything on their own. Though somewhat puzzled, the Martian might accept your explanation.

But, being the persistent type, let us suppose she enquired further whether the words in [3.2] were also indivisible into smaller meaningful units:

[3.2] childish hopeless sooner mended elephants re-boil unsafe ex-wife

You would have to give a different answer. You would need to tell your interrogator, who by now would be getting increasingly bewildered, that the words in [3.2] can be divided into smaller units of meaning as shown in [3.3]:

[3.3] child-*ish* hope-*less* soon-*er* mend-*ed* elephant-*s* *re*-boil *un*-safe *ex*-wife

The part of the word that is not italicised can function as an independent word in the grammar. Indeed, each of the non-italicised chunks is a word (i.e. vocabulary item) that is listed as such in the dictionary. By contrast, the italicised bits, though meaningful (and their meanings can be indicated as shown in [3.4]), cannot function on their own in the grammar.

[3.4]	-ish	'having the (objectionable) qualities of'	child-ish = 'having the qualities of a child'
	-less	'without X'	hopeless = 'without hope'
	-er	'more X'	sooner = 'more soon'
	-ed	'past'	mended = 'mend in the past'
	-s	'plural'	elephants = 'more than one elephant'
	re-	'again'	re-boil = 'boil again'
	un-	'not X'	unsafe = 'not safe'
	ex-	'former'	ex-wife = 'former wife'

What we have done to the words in [3.4] can be done to thousands of other words in English. They can be decomposed into smaller units of meaning (e.g. *re-* 'again') or grammatical function (e.g. *-ed* 'past').

The term MORPHEME is used to refer to the smallest unit that has meaning or serves a grammatical function in a language. Morphemes are the atoms with which words are built. It is not possible to find sub-morphemic units that are themselves meaningful or have a grammatical function. Thus, given *-less* or *un-*, it would make no sense to try to assign some identifiable meaning to any part of these forms. Of course, it is possible to isolate the individual sounds /l-ɪ-s/ or /ʌ-n/, but those sounds in themselves do not mean anything.

We have now established that words are made up of morphemes. But how do we recognise a morpheme when we see one? Our definition of the morpheme as the smallest unit of meaning (or grammatical function) will be the guiding principle. Any chunk of a word with a particular meaning will be said to represent a morpheme. That is how we proceeded in [3.3] and [3.4] above.

Morphemes tend to have a fairly stable meaning which they bring to any word in which they appear. If we take *re-* and *un-*, for example, they mean 'again' and 'not' respectively – not just in the words we have listed above, but also in thousands of other words. Usually morphemes are used again and again to form different words. Thus *re-* meaning 're-do whatever the verb means' can be attached before most verbs to yield a new word with a predictable meaning (e.g. *re-run*, *re-take*, *re-build* etc.). In like manner, *un-* meaning 'not X' (where X stands for whatever the adjective means) can be attached to various adjectives (e.g. *un-real*, *un-clean*, *un-happy* etc.) to yield a new word with a predictable negative meaning.

The segmentation of words into morphemes is not a trivial and arcane pastime indulged in by linguists to while away the time on a wet Bank Holiday afternoon. It is something that is important for all users of language. During your lifetime, you will probably encounter hundreds of thousands of different words. Many of these words will be new to you. For no matter how extensive your vocabulary is, you will inevitably come across words that are unfamiliar. It is impossible for anyone to know all the words that are found in English.

So, what do you do when faced with an unfamiliar word? Reach for a good dictionary? Perhaps. But this is not always feasible. Nor is it always necessary. Very often you just figure out what the

strange word means using the context, together with your knowledge of the meaning of the morphemes which the word contains.
You normally do this subconsciously. What we are doing here is
making explicit your tacit knowledge of word-structure.

Imagine this scenario. In 1992, a newspaper report on the war
in the Bosnian republic states that what we are witnessing is the
Lebanonisation of Bosnia. Suppose you have not encountered the
word *Lebanonisation* before. Would you understand what the writer
is saying? Probably you would – without looking it up in any
dictionary. How would you do it? The answer is simple. By using
your knowledge of the world – in particular history (*Balkanisation*)
– and your knowledge of current affairs (the civil war in Lebanon)
plus your knowledge of the principles of word-formation you are
able to work out the meaning of *Lebanonisation*.

Let us focus on principles of word-formation. You know that
-ize/-ise is used when talking about nations to mean 'to make X',
e.g. from *America* we get *Americanise*, from *Korea* we get *Koreanise*,
from *Kenya* we get *Kenyanise* etc. By attaching *-(an)ise* we turn a
noun into a verb. So, given the noun *Lebanon* we can form the verb
Lebanonise. Next, from the verb *Lebanonise*, we can create a new
noun by adding *-ation* (which forms nouns of action).

If you know that various warlords created warring fiefdoms that
destroyed the Lebanese state during the civil war that raged in
Lebanon in the 1970s and 1980s, you will know that the Croats,
Muslims and Serbs engaged in the Bosnian conflict risk doing the
same to the Bosnian state in the 1990s. *Lebanonisation* is the act of
'turning a country into another Lebanon'. Thus, our knowledge
of word-structure contributes to our understanding of the meaning
of unfamiliar words.

We have demonstrated that words can be decomposed into morphemes. Now we are going to see that words have INTERNAL STRUC-
TURE. A simple way of showing this is to analyse words like *uncanny*
and *unhappy*. From these words we can derive *uncannier* and *unhappier*. If you analyse *unhappier*, you will see that extracting the correct
meaning 'more [not happy]' (i.e. sadder) rather than the incorrect
one 'not [more happy]' (i.e. not happier) depends on the way we
group together the morphemes. In the first analysis where *unhappier*
is interpreted as *sadder*, the meaning 'not' conveyed by *un-* is bracketed together with *happy* [unhappy] as one unit and this is intensi-
fied by the *-er* suffix. In the alternative second analysis, *happy* and
-er are bracketed together as a unit [happier] (i.e. more happy)

which then is negated by [un-] to give 'not more happy', which is incorrect. When someone is *unhappier*, it does not mean they are simply less happy, it means rather that they are not happy at all. They are sad. This shows that morphemes in a word with several morphemes may be grouped together in different ways for semantic purposes. The way in which this is done has semantic consequences. Conceivably, morphemes could be thrown together higgledy-piggledy to form a word. So long as you had the right morphemes, a well-formed word would pop out. But that is definitely not the case. Words have internal structural groupings, as we have seen.

Furthermore, the sequencing of morphemes in a word may be subject to restrictions. Take a word like *ungovernability* which contains four morphemes, namely *un-*, *govern*, *abil*, *ity*. Everyone who knows this word knows that these four morphemes must appear in the order in [3.5a]. Any other order is strictly forbidden:

[3.5]   a.   un-govern-abil-ity
        b.   *govern-abil-un-ity
        c.   *ity-un-abil-govern
        d.   *abil-un-ity-govern
        e.   *un-govern-ity-abil etc.

Clearly, knowing a word means not just knowing the morphemes it contains, but also the rigid order in which they are allowed to appear. We will return to this point in section (4.4).

To sum up the discussion so far, words are built using morphemes. If we know how morphemes are used to form words, we do not need to be unduly flustered when we come across a strange word. Usually it is possible to work out the meaning of a strange word if it contains familiar morphemes.

3.3 MORPHEMES AND THEIR DISGUISES

The identification of morphemes is not altogether straightforward. This is because there is no simple one-to-one correspondence between morphemes and the speech sounds that represent them. In this section we will attempt to unravel the complexities of the relationship between morphemes and the actual forms (sounds of groups of sounds) by which they are manifested in speech.

3.3.1 Allomorphs: morph families

Any physical form that represents a morpheme is called a MORPH. The forms *-ish, -less, -er, -ed, -s, re-, un-* and *ex-* in [3.4] on p. 31 are all morphs. Morphological analysis begins with the identification of morphs, i.e. forms that carry some meaning or are associated with some grammatical function. In *asparagus* there is just one morph but in all the words in [3.4] there are two.

It is important not to confuse morphs with SYLLABLES. When we talk of morphs we have in mind sounds that can be related to a particular meaning or grammatical function (e.g. plural or past tense). However, when we talk of syllables all we have in mind are chunks into which words can be divided for the purposes of pronunciation.

This is not an abstruse distinction. We are not being pedantic. It is a distinction that matters to ordinary people because human languages are organised in such a way that the construction of units that are meaningful is normally in principle separate from the construction of strings that are pronounceable. Thus, for rhythmical effect, nursery rhymes often use nonsense syllables like '*Deedle, deedle*' in '*Deedle deedle dumpling my son John*' which do not represent anything meaningful.

Alternatively, a sound representing a morpheme may not be a syllable in its own right, e.g. by itself, the *-s* which represents the plural morpheme is not a syllable. The word *cats* has two morphemes, *cat* and *-s*, but it is all just one syllable. The single syllable *cats* realises two morphemes. The converse situation, where several syllables realise a single morpheme, is equally possible. Thus, the trisyllabic and quadrisyllabic word-forms *elephant* and *asparagus* both realise just a single morpheme.

The nature of the relationship between sounds and morphemes is intriguing. At first sight, it might look reasonable to assume that morphemes are made up of PHONEMES. We might be tempted to think that *cat*, the English morpheme with the meaning 🐱 is made up of the phonemes /kæt/. But we have several kinds of evidence showing that this is not the case.

First, if morphemes were *made up* of phonemes, a given morpheme would be uniquely associated with a given phonological representation. In reality, the same morpheme can be realised by different morphs (i.e. sounds or written forms). Morphs which realise the same morpheme are referred to as ALLOMORPHS of that morpheme.

The INDEFINITE ARTICLE is a good example of a morpheme with more than one allomorph. It is realised by the two forms *a* and *an*. The sound at the beginning of the following word determines the allomorph that is selected. If the word following the indefinite article begins with a consonant, the allomorph *a* is selected, but if it begins with a vowel the allomorph *an* is used instead:

[3.6] a. a dictionary   b. an island
           a boat   an evening
           a pineapple   an opinion
           a leg   an eye
           a big (mat)   an old (mat)
           a dull (song)   an exciting (finish)

Hence the incorrectness of the sentence marked with an asterisk in [3.7]:

[3.7] a. I spent *an* evening with them.
           *I spent *a* evening with them.
       b. I spent *the* evening with them.

Allomorphs of the same morpheme are said to be in COMPLEMEN-TARY DISTRIBUTION. This means that they do not occur in identical contexts and therefore they cannot be used to distinguish meanings. In other words, it is impossible to have two otherwise identical utterances that differ in their meanings depending on the allomorph of a morpheme that is selected. So, because *a* and *an* both realise the same indefinite article morpheme, it is impossible to have two sentences like those in [3.7a] above which are identical in all ways, except in the choice of *a* or *an*, but mean different things.

Complementary distribution presupposes the more basic notion of DISTRIBUTION. Distribution is to do with establishing facts about the occurrence of allomorphs of a particular morpheme. It is concerned with establishing the contexts in which the morpheme which we are investigating occurs and the allomorphs by which it is realised in those different contexts. In other words, by distribution we mean the total set of distinct linguistic contexts in which a given form appears, perhaps in different guises. For instance, the indefinite article has the distribution: *a* before consonants (e.g. *a tree*) and *an* before vowels (e.g. *an eagle*).

As mentioned already, such functionally related forms which all represent the same morpheme in different environments are called allomorphs of that morpheme. Another way of putting it is that allomorphs are forms that are phonologically distinguishable which, none the less, are not functionally distinct. In other words, although they are physically distinct morphs with different pronunciations, allomorphs do share the same function in the language.

An analogy might help to clarify this point. Let us compare allomorphs to workers who share the same job. Imagine a job-share situation where Mrs Jones teaches maths to form 2DY on Monday afternoons, Mr Kato on Thursday mornings and Ms Smith on Tuesdays and Fridays. Obviously, these teachers are different individuals. But they all share the role of 'maths teacher' for the class and each teacher only performs that role on particular days. Likewise, all allomorphs share the same function but one allomorph cannot occupy a position that is already occupied by another allomorph of the same morpheme. To summarise, we say that allomorphs of a morpheme are in complementary distribution. This means that they cannot substitute for each other. Hence, we cannot replace one allomorph of a morpheme by another allomorph of that morpheme and change meaning.

For our next example of allomorphs we will turn to the plural morpheme. The idea of 'more than one' is expressed by the plural morpheme using a variety of allomorphs including the following:

[3.8]   *Singular*   *Plural*
   a. rad-ius   radi-i
      cactus   cact-i
   b. dat-um   dat-a
      strat-um   strat-a
   c. analys-is   analys-es
      ax-is   ax-es
   d. skirt   skirt-s
      road   road-s
      branch   branch-es

Going by the orthography, we can identify the allomorphs *-i, -a, -es* and *-s*. The last is by far the commonest: see section (7.3).

Try and say the batch of words in [3.8d] aloud. You will observe that the pronunciation of the plural allomorph in these words is variable. It is [s] in *skirts*, [z] in *roads* and [ɪz] (or for some speakers [əz]) in *branches*. What is interesting about these words is that the selection of the allomorph that represents the plural is determined by the last sound in the noun to which the plural morpheme is appended. We will return to this in more depth in section (5.2).

We have already seen, that because allomorphs cannot substitute for each other, we never have two sentences with different meanings which solely differ in that one sentence has allomorph X in a slot where another sentence has allomorph Y. Compare the two sentences in [3.9]:

[3.9] a. They have two cats   b. They have two dogs
          [ðeɪ hæv tu: kæt-s]   [ðeɪ hæv tu: dɒg-z]
          *[ðeɪ hæv tu: kæt-z]   *[ðeɪ hæv tu: dɒg-s]

We cannot find two otherwise identical sentences which differ in meaning simply because the word *cats* is pronounced as [kæt-s] and *[kæt-z] respectively. Likewise, it is not possible to have two otherwise identical sentences with different meanings where the word *dogs* is pronounced as [dɒgz] and *[dɒgs]. In other words, the difference between the allomorphs [s] and [z] of the plural morpheme cannot be used to distinguish meanings.

3.3.2 Contrast

Different morphemes CONTRAST meanings but different allomorphs do not. If a difference in meaning is attributable to the fact that one minimal meaningful unit has been replaced by another, we identify the morphs involved as manifestations of distinct morphemes. So, in [3.7] on p. 36 the indefinite article realised by *a* or *an* is a distinct morpheme from the definite article realised by *the* since a semantic difference is detectable when *a* or *an* is replaced with *the*.

A further example of contrast is given in [3.10]:

[3.10] a. I unlocked the door.   b. She is untidy.
           I re-locked the door

The two sentences in [3.10a] mean very different things. Since they are identical except for the fact that where one has *un-* the other has *re-*, the difference in meaning between these two sentences is due to the difference in meaning between the morphemes realised by *re-* (meaning 'do again') and *un-* (meaning 'reverse the action').

Now, contrast the *un-* of *unlocked* with the *un-* of *untidy*. In both cases we have the same morph *un-* (which is spelt and pronounced in exactly the same way). But it is obvious that *un-* represents different morphemes in these two word-forms. In *I unlocked the door* the morph *un-* found in *unlocked* realises a reversive morpheme which is attached to verbs – it reverses the action of locking. But in *untidy* it realises a negative morpheme attached to adjectives – *untidy* means 'not tidy'. (If a person is *untidy*, it does not mean that at some earlier point they were tidy and someone has reversed or undone their tidiness.)

If morphemes were made up of phonemes a simple correlation of morphs with morphemes is what we would find. But, in fact, it is quite common for the same phonological form (i.e. morph) to represent more than one morpheme. It is from the context that we can tell which morpheme it represents. This is the second piece of evidence against the assumption that morphemes are composed of phonemes.

The complex relationship between morphemes and the allomorphs that represent them gives us a window through which we can glimpse one of the most fascinating aspects of language: the relationship between FORM and FUNCTION. In linguistics we explore the form of various elements of language structure, e.g. words and sentences, because it is important to know how they are constructed. However, form is not everything. We are also interested in knowing what linguistic elements are used for, what function they serve.

Just consider for a moment this non-linguistic analogy. Imagine a friend returns from a foreign vacation with two beautiful ornamental glass containers with a globular shape and gives one to you as a present and keeps the other for herself. She does not tell you what your present is used for. She uses hers as a vessel for containing wine at the table – she got the idea of buying these containers when she was served wine in a similar container in a fancy restaurant. You do not know this. You look at your present and decide to put it on the table as a container for cut fresh flowers. She calls hers a flagon, for that is what she is using it as. You call yours a vase.

Here are the questions now: are these objects 'flagons' or 'vases'? Which one of you is right? I am not being evasive if I say that both of you are right. For, although the two objects are identical as far as their form, their physical properties, is concerned, they are very different with regard to the functions that they serve in your two households.

There are numerous linguistic parallels. What is physically the same linguistic form can be used to represent distinct morphemes. In order for forms to be regarded as allomorphs belonging to the

same morpheme, it is not sufficient for them to have the same form
– to be pronounced or written in the same way. They must also
have the same grammatical or semantic function. The significance
of this point was hinted at in the discussion of *un-* in *unlocked* and
untidy when we showed that the same morph can represent different
morphemes. It should become even more obvious when you consider the form *-er* in the following:

[3.11] a. think ~ thinker   drive ~ driver
           write ~ writer   sing ~ singer
           sweep ~ sweeper   sell ~ seller
        b. cook ~ cooker   strain ~ strainer
           receive ~ receiver   compute ~ computer
           propel ~ propeller   erase ~ eraser
        c. London ~ Londoner   north ~ northerner
           Iceland ~ Icelander   east ~ easterner
           New York ~ New Yorker Highlands ~ Highlander

The same form, *-er*, represents three different meanings and
hence has to be assigned to three distinct morphemes. In [3.11a]
it forms an agentive noun from a verb, with the meaning 'someone
who does X' (i.e. whatever the verb means). In [3.11b] the same
-er forms an instrumental noun from a verb, with the meaning
'something used to X' (i.e. to do whatever the verb means). Finally,
in [3.11c] the same *-er* form is attached to a noun referring to a
place to mean 'an inhabitant of'.

Clearly, the same form does serve different functions here. So, it
realises different morphemes. This is further evidence that should
quickly disabuse us of the assumption that morphemes are made
up of morphs. Not only can a single morpheme have several allomorphs (as in the case of the plural morpheme), the same morph
(e.g. *-er*) can represent different morphemes. There is no simple
one-to-one matching of morphemes with morphs.

3.4 FREEDOM AND BONDAGE

When we classify morphemes in terms of where they are allowed
to appear, we find that they fall into two major groupings. Some
morphemes are capable of occurring on their own as words, while
other morphemes are only allowed to occur in combination with
some other morpheme(s) but they cannot be used by themselves
as independent words.

Those morphemes that are allowed to occur on their own in sentences as words are called FREE MORPHEMES while those morphemes that must occur in the company of some other morphemes are called BOUND MORPHEMES. In [3.12] the bound morphemes are italicised.

[3.12] pest   pest(i)-*cide*
        modern   *post*-modern-*ist*
        child   child-*ish*
        pack   *pre*-pack-*ed*
        laugh   laugh-*ing*

The free morphemes in [3.12] can all be manipulated by syntactic rules; they can stand on their own as words. By contrast, it is impossible to use the forms -*cide*, *post*-, -*ist*, -*ish*, *pre*-, -*ed* or -*ing*, independently.

So far, all the examples of free morphemes that function as roots that we have encountered have been content words (see p. 14). However, not all free morphemes are content words. Some are employed to indicate grammatical functions and logical relationship rather than to convey lexical or cognitive meaning in a sentence. Hence such words are called FUNCTION WORDS. They include words such as the following:

[3.13] articles: *a/an*, *the*
        demonstratives: e.g. *this*, *that*, *these* and *those*
        pronouns: e.g. *I*, *you*, *we*, *they*; *my*, *your*, *his*, *hers*,
                                who etc.
        prepositions: e.g. *in*, *into*, *on to*, *at*, *on* etc.
        conjunctions: e.g. *and*, *or*, *but*, *because*, *if* etc.

In ordinary language use such words are extremely common. But on their own they would not convey a lot of information. If you received a telegram like *But it my on to the in* you might suspect that the sender either had a strange sense of humour or was not mentally sound.

3.5 SOUND SYMBOLISM: PHONAESTHEMES AND ONOMATOPOEIA

In the vast majority of words, the relationship between sound and meaning is arbitrary (see p. 2). There is no reason why a particular sound, or group of sounds, should be used to represent a particular word, with a particular meaning. If someone asked you what [b] in *bed* or [str] in *strange* meant, you would think they were asking a very odd question. As a rule, sounds *qua* sounds do not mean anything.

However, the general principle that says that the link between sound and meaning in words is arbitrary is occasionally dented. This happens in two sets of circumstances. First, certain individual sounds, or groups of sounds, which do not represent a specific enough meaning to be called morphs nevertheless appear to be vaguely associated with some kind of meaning. Such sounds are called PHONAESTHEMES.

As our first example of a phonaestheme, let us take the RP vowel [ʌ] (which is historically descended from [ʊ], the vowel that is still used in words like *dull* and *hut* in the north of England). This phonaestheme is found in words associated with various kinds of dullness or indistinctness, e.g. *dull, thud, thunder, dusk, blunt, mud, slush, sludge, slump* etc. Obviously, the vowel [ʌ] *per se* does not mean 'dull'. If it did, *dim* which contains the vowel [ɪ] would not be a virtual synonym for *dull*.

Many words which mean 'to talk indistinctly' contain one or more occurrences of the labial consonant [m], which is made with the lips firmly closed, preventing clear articulation. That way, the very act of pronouncing the word iconically mimics a key aspect of its meaning. You can see this if you watch yourself in a mirror saying words like *mumble, murmur, mutter, muted, grumble* etc. It is probably not an accident that these words also contain the phonaestheme [ʌ]. Similarly, the sound [ʌmp] (spelled *-ump*) as in *clump, dump, bump, lump* and *hump* is often found at the end of words which are associated with heaviness and clumsiness although no one would wish to suggest that *-ump* in itself represents the ideas of heaviness and clumsiness. Interestingly, here again we have the vowel [ʌ] followed by the labial consonants [mp].

Observe also that whereas [ʌ] tends to have associations of heaviness or dullness, the high front vowels [iː] and [ɪ] frequently occur as phonaesthemes in words associated with smallness, as in *wee, teeny-weeny, lean, meagre, mini, thin* and *little*. (The fact that *big* has the opposite meaning just goes to show that phonaesthemes only represent a tendency.)

Second, and more importantly, in addition to phonaesthemes, there are onomatopoeic words in which a direct association is made between the sounds of a word-form and the meaning that it

On the Ning Nang Nong

On the Ning Nang Nong
Where the cows go Bong!
And the Monkeys all say Boo!
There's a Nong Nang Ning
Where the trees go Ping!
And the tea pots Jibber Jabber Joo.
On the Nong Ning Nang
All the mice go Clang!
And you just can't catch 'em when they do!
So it's Ning Nang Nong!
Cows go Bong!
Nong Nang Ning!
Trees go Ping!
Nong Ning Nang!
The mice go Clang!
What a noisy place to belong,
Is the Ning Nang Ning Nang Nong!
                    SPIKE MILLIGAN

represents. In cases of ONOMATOPOEIA, the sounds (*qua* sounds and
not as morphs) symbolise or reflect some aspect of the meaning of
the word that they represent. So, if speakers of any language want

an onomatopoeic word for the noise a cat makes, they will not choose a noise like *bimbobam* – except, perhaps, in the land of the Ning Nang Nong.

The words for sounds made by various animals e.g. *neigh, miaow, moo* etc. are the most obvious examples of onomatopoeia. But there are others such as *roar, crack, clang, bang, splash, swish, whoosh, buzz, hiss, cheep, bleep, gurgle, plop* and *plod*. In the case of onomatopoeic words, the relationship between sound and meaning is to some extent ICONIC. The sounds mimic an aspect of the meaning of the linguistic sign much in the same way that this iconic sign for a restaurant   ¶   represents, more or less directly, the meaning 'restaurant'. This symbol is still conventional to some degree. To people who eat with chopsticks, it might not be immediately obvious why this sign represents a restaurant (rather than a cutlery shop), but once it is pointed out the link can be seen quite easily.

Onomatopoeic words are iconic in so far as they directly reflect some aspect of the meaning of what they stand for. So, conventionally in English cows go 'moo' and horses go 'neigh' and bees go 'buzz'. That is why Spike Milligan's nonsense poem 'On the Ning Nang Nong' is bizarre.

To be onomatopoeic, the sound must imitate to some degree an aspect of the noise made by the bird or animal. But exactly what is imitated will vary from language to language. An English cock will say *cockadoodledoo*, a Russian cock *kukuriku* and in Uganda it may say *kookolilookoo*. (These differences are not attributable to dialectical variation among the males of the *Gallus domesticus* species.) Onomatopoeic words are not purely and simply formed by mimicking precisely the meanings that they convey. To some extent onomatopoeic words are also moulded by linguistic convention. That is why in different places in the world different onomatopoeic words may be used for the same animal or bird noise.

3.6 VERBAL BLUEPRINTS

Linguistic theory incorporates the hypothesis that there are universal principles of grammar that regulate the amount of variation in linguistic structure across languages. In the last section we saw the marginal role played by sound symbolism in word-formation. This does not obscure the fact that normally languages form words by using sounds in a non-imitative way. There is an overriding tendency for the relationship between sounds and meanings to be arbitrary. Normally there is no reason why a particular morpheme is realised by any particular sounds. The choice of the allomorph or allomorphs that represent a particular morpheme is arbitrary.

Obviously, as everyone knows, all languages do not have the same words. Since virtually any arbitrary match of sound and meaning can produce a word, it is not surprising that words vary greatly in their structure across languages. But this does not mean that chaos reigns. The ways in which morphs are used to form words is regulated by general principles. So, the amount of cross-linguistic variation in word-formation falls within certain broad parameters. It is as if there is a menu of blueprints for word-formation from which all languages make their selections:

[3.14] (i) ISOLATING (or analytic) languages
       (ii) AGGLUTINATING languages
       (iii) INFLECTING (or synthetic) languages
       (iv) POLYSYNTHETIC languages

No language makes all its choices from just one part of the menu. To varying degrees all languages make mixed choices. The idea of this menu is to indicate the predominant word-formation tendencies, if they exist. In the subsections below we shall consider in turn examples of the different morphological types.

3.6.1 Tiny words (isolating languages)

In an archetypical isolating language the word is virtually indistinguishable from the morpheme, for every word contains just one morpheme. Every morpheme is a free morpheme. There are no bound morphemes. Vietnamese comes close to this ideal:

[3.15] *Vietnamese*
       a. Tôi đá   đã   qua' bóng vā hắn đấm đã   tôi
          I   kick past class. ball and he punch past me
          'I kicked the ball and he punched me.'
       b. Chúng tôi mua đã   gạo
          Pl.   I   buy past rice
          'We bought the rice.'

Typically, the words are short and contain just one morpheme each. Almost every concept is expressed by a separate word. Look again, for example, at the treatment of past tense in verbs (e.g. *punched*, *bought*) and the plurality of *we* (plural plus first person).

3.6.2 Get the glue (agglutinating languages)

In an ideal agglutinating language most words contain more than one morpheme and the morphemes are realised by morphs arranged in rows like corn on the cob. The morphs can be neatly picked off, one by one. Swahili is a good example of an agglutinating language as you can see:

[3.16] a. ni-ta-pik-a
        I-future-cook-BVS
        'I will cook'

     b. a-li-tu-pik-i-a
        s/he-past-us-cook-for-BVS
        's/he cooked for us'

     c. tu-li-wa-lim-ish-a
        we-past-them-cultivate-cause-BVS
        'we made them cultivate'

Note: BVS = basic verbal suffix which is normally *-a*

In a Swahili word, it is normally possible to say which morph represents which morpheme. Most morphs only represent one morpheme at a time and do not FUSE with adjacent morphemes, as, say, plural marking does in *leaves* where it is partly signalled by the suffix *-es* /-ɪz/ and partly by the change of the /f/ of *leaf* to /v/. It is as if the word is contructed by gluing together separable, discrete morphs.

3.6.3 Labyrinthine words (synthetic languages)

In a SYNTHETIC LANGUAGE a word normally contains more than one morpheme. In this respect synthetic languages resemble agglutinating languages. However, whereas in an agglutinating language the morphemes and the morphs that realise them are arranged in a row one after the other, the morphs of a synthetic language are to a considerable extent fused together and cannot be separated neatly one from the other. Furthermore, the morphemes themselves are not arranged in a row. Rather, they are all thrown together in a big pot like pot-pourri. It is impossible to separate the different strands.

Latin is a classic example of an inflecting language. Any attempt to segment Latin words into morphs in such a way that each morph is associated uniquely with a particular morpheme very

soon runs into trouble. You can see this for yourself if you attempt
to segment the various word-forms of the nouns *mēnsa* 'table' and
flōs 'flower' into their constituent morphs and try to match those
morphs with the corresponding morphemes:

[3.17] a.

Case	Singular	Plural	b.	Singular	Plural
Nominative	mēns*a*	mēns*ae*		flōs	flōr*ēs*
Accusative	mēns*am*	mēns*as*		flōr*em*	flōr*ēs*
Genitive	mēns*ae*	mēns*arum*		flōr*is*	flōr*um*
Dative	mēns*ae*	mēns*īs*		flōr*i*	flōr*ibus*
Ablative	mēns*ā*	mēns*īs*		flōr*e*	flōr*ibus*

We could say that *mens* means '*table*' and that *flōs-* and *flōr-* mean
'flower' and the rest marks case and number of the noun. There
is a general and historical rule in Latin that gets /s/ pronounced
as [r] when it occurs between vowels. That is why instead of *flōs*
we get *flōr* everywhere except in the nominative singular. But what
of the rest? In each case the ending realises two morphemes simultaneously: number and case. For instance, *-as* in *mēnsas* marks both
accusative and plural and *-em* in *flōrem* marks accusative case and
singular number. The same kind of analysis applies to the other
endings.

That it would be futile to try and separate the morphs representing different morphemes is even clearer in the Latin verb. Take
monēre 'to advise', for example, which has forms that include:

[3.18] a. mone*ō* 'I advise'   b. mone*or* 'I am being advised'
         monē*s* 'you advise'   monē*ris* 'you are being advised'
         monē*mus* 'we advise'   monē*mur* 'we are being advised'

Let us attempt to isolate morphs and morphemes. Having separated out *monē* as the part representing the morpheme 'advise' we
might identify the underlined part of the word, *-o*, *-s*, *-mus*, *-or*,
-mur etc. as representing number, person (I, you etc.) as well as
voice, i.e. active in [3.18a] and passive in [3.18b]. Segmentation
would not work. The mapping of morphemes on to morphs is not
one-to-one as in Swahili. We have in each case just one form *-o*,
-s etc. representing several morphemes all at once. Morphs which
simultaneously realise two or more morphemes are called PORTMAN-
TEAU MORPHS (i.e. 'suitcase morphs'). For example, *-mur* in *monēmur*
is a portmanteau morph since it signals first person, plural, present
tense and passive.

[3.19] Portmanteau morph: -mur

Morphemes: first person   plural   present tense   passive

In a language of this type the superior analysis, and one that is traditionally preferred, is one where no attempt is made to chop up the word into morphemes and line them up one-to-one with morphs. Instead all the morphological and syntactic properties of the grammatical word should be noted and a statement should be made along these lines: *monēmur* is the first person, plural, present tense, passive verb form of the lexical item *monēre*. In modern linguistics this model is called WORD-AND-PARADIGM or WP for short (cf. Matthews 1991).

3.6.4 Verbal juggernauts (polysynthetic languages)

Finally, there are the so-called polysynthetic languages (or incorporating languages) which have very complex words that are built not only by combining morphemes, but also by implanting words within words. Eskimo is a very good example of a polysynthetic language. For instance, in this language the transitive verb incorporates within it the direct object noun. Consequently, words can be *very* big:

[3.20] a. *kissartumik kavvisurput*   'They drank hot coffee'
            kissartu-mik   kavvi-sur-put
            hot instr.   coffee drink 3p-indic.

        b. *nutaamik piilisiurpunga*   'I am looking for a new car'
            nutaa-mik   piili-siur-punga
            new-instr.   car look for 1s-indic.

        c. *Atuagalliutituqaanngitsunik atuagassa aliqinartaqaaq*
            'There was really nothing to read apart from old copies
            of Atuagalliutit'
            Atuagalliuti -tuqa -a -nngit -su -nik
            Atuagalliutit -old be not intr.-part. instr.-pl.
            atua-ga-ssa
            rcad -pass.-part.

aliqi-nar-ta-qa-aq
lack (-future) be-such-as-to habit.very 3s-indic

Notes: instr.= instrumental case; indic. = indicative mood,
1s = 1st person singular; 3p = 3rd person; pl.=
plural; habit. = habitual; pass. = passive; part. =
participial mood; intr. = intransitive.

(from Fortescue 1984: 83)

The last Eskimo sentence, which has just three word-forms, is
translated in English as 'There was really nothing to read apart
from old copies of Atuagalliutit'. For the sake of clarity each word
is re-written as a grammatical word on a line of its own, complete
with a gloss, to show the complexity.

3.6.5 No thoroughbreds

There are no morphological thoroughbreds. There is no pure isolating, agglutinating, inflecting or polysynthetic language. All languages are to varying degrees mixtures. If we classify a language
as belonging to this or that type, all we are claiming is that it
shows a strong tendency to have words formed in a certain way.

Although we classified Swahili as agglutinating, for instance,
there is not always a one-to-one matching of morphemes with
morphs. In our Swahili data, there are a number of portmanteau
morphs. Thus, morph *tu-* simultaneously represents second person,
subject and plural in *tu-li-wa-lim-ish-a* 'we made them cultivate'.
The same form *-tu-* is again found in *a-li-tu-pik-i-a* 's/he cooked for
us'. Once more it is a portmanteau. But in this case it realises
different morphemes, namely second person, plural and (indirect)
object. Similarly, *wa* is a portmanteau morph. It can represent
either the first person, plural subject (as in *wa-ta-pik-a* 'they will
cook') or the first person plural, object (as in *a-li-wa-lim-ish-a* 's/he
made them cultivate').

We could make the same point about the other examples. For
instance, although Eskimo is polysynthetic, it does have words that
are formed by simple agglutination e.g., *kissartu-mik* 'hot instr.'.

The best we can do with labels like isolating and inflecting is to
capture the dominant word-formation trends in a language. You
may be wondering what we mean by dominant in this context.
How agglutinating, isolating, etc. must a language be for it to be
classified in a particular way? Linguists have attempted to answer

this question by establishing an ISOLATING INDEX which is worked out by calculating the ratio of morphemes to grammatical words in running texts of several thousand words. A prototypical isolating language would always have one morpheme per grammatical word. The closer to this particular idealised language type a given language is, the more isolating it is said to be. At the other extreme we find the polysynthetic languages which approximate an average of four morphemes per grammatical word. Eskimo, with a ratio of 3.72 morphemes per word comes close to this. Sanskrit with a ratio of 2.59 is inflecting. The main difference between inflecting and agglutinating languages is not so much in the ratio of morphemes to grammatical words but in the one-to-one mapping of morphemes on morphs in agglutinating languages as opposed to the one-to-many mapping in inflecting languages.

Let us end the chapter by determining the morphological type to which English belongs. The first thing to note is that English is not a perfect example of any one morphological type. English words can exemplify any of the four types we have described:

[3.21] a. The baby can walk now.
        b. Unfortunately customers wanted pre-packed cigars.
        c. We went.
        d. Potato-picking is back-breaking work.

The baby can walk now exemplifies isolating morphology. With the exception of the portmanteau morph *can*, which realises the morphemes meaning 'able', present tense, each word in this sentence contains only one morpheme.

Contrast that with [3.21b] which illustrates agglutination. Here each word can be neatly divided morphemes that are arranged in a row one after the other. *Un-fortun-ate-ly custom-er-s want-ed pre-pack-ed cigar-s*. There are just over 2.5 morphemes per word on average in this sentence.

Likewise in *We went*, the ratio of morphemes to grammatical words is high. *We* is subject, first person and plural and *went* realises the lexeme 'go' and past tense. Again the average number of morphemes per word exceeds two. But in this case the morphemes are simultaneously realised by portmanteau morphs. This sentence exhibits an inflecting tendency.

An even better example of a portmanteau morph is the verb *is* which represents the morphemes third person, singular, present tense and the lexeme *be*. It is impossible to divide up the word-form *be* and align these different morphemes with chunks of this verb.

In the [3.21d], the key words are *potato-picking* and *back-breaking* which show English behaving like a polysynthetic language by incorporating the object of the verb into the verb itself: *picking* VERB *potatoes* NOUN (OBJ) → *potato-picking* NOUN; *breaking* VERB *backs* NOUN (OBJ) → *backbreaking* (ADJECTIVE). (Subsequently the verb is turned into a noun or adjective.)

English has a bit of everything. However, when large samples of text are examined, it becomes clear that it is basically an isolating language. It has a ratio of 1.68 morphemes per word. Although the lexicon contains innumerable complex words, most words usually found in texts are simple.

3.7 SUMMARY

In this chapter we have established that words have internal structure. They are built using morphemes which are put together following rigid principles that determine how they are arranged. While the elements of a sentence enjoy a considerable degree of mobility the morphemes in a word do not.

A basic distinction was drawn between morphemes that are free and capable of occurring independently as words in their own right, and others that are bound which must always be attached to some other morphemes in words. Bound morphemes are incapable of occurring in isolation as self-standing words and so they cannot be manipulated directly by rules of the syntax.

In doing morphological analysis, the principles of contrast and complementary distribution play a key role. If morphs (i.e. forms) contrast meaning, they represent distinct morphemes. But if morphs cannot contrast meaning, they are grouped together as allomorphs of the same morpheme.

In principle, the relationship between morphemes and morphs is indirect. It involves representation, not composition. Hence, on the one hand the same morph may represent different morphemes and, on the other hand, the same morpheme may be represented by distinct allomorphs.

Normally the relationship between a linguistic sign like a morpheme and its meaning is arbitrary. However, in a minority of cases, sound symbolism (in the shape of phonaesthemes and onomatopoeia) plays a role in word-formation. In such cases the relationship between the sign and its meaning is to some extent iconic.

The structure of words in the languages of the world falls into four broad types: isolating, agglutinating, inflecting and polysynthetic. These types are determined by the patterning of morphemes in word-building. No language is morphologically 'pure'. The classification only indicates the dominant pattern. Thus, although English is mostly an isolating type of language, it exhibits other tendencies as well.

EXERCISES

1. List the meanings associated with the form -er in *teach-er*, *London-er*, *cooker*, *louder* and *chatt-er*. If in doubt, consult a good dictionary.

2. Identify the morphemes in the words below and determine which ones are free, and which ones are bound. In some cases the choice will not be clear-cut. Explain the grounds for your decision.

beds	manly	pedestrian
bedding	mannish	pedal
bedrooms	manhood	pedestal
bedfellows	manager	pedate
unenthusiastically	managers	biped
servility	management	tripod
servant	mismanaged	millipede
server	foothold	centipede
servitor	footpaths	expedition
served	footlights	expedite
services	footman	impede
servicing	footsteps	impediment

3. Use the data below to explain the difference between syllables and morphemes.

> Those parts of thee that the world's eye doth view
> Want nothing that the thought of hearts can mend;
> All tongues (the voice of souls) give thee that due,
> Utt'ring bare truth, even so as foes commend.
>
> (from Shakespeare, Sonnet 69)

4. Illustrating your answer with the italicised words below, explain

the difference between *lexeme* and *word-form*; *morpheme* and *allo-morph*:

> The boy in the green *jumper* is a *better jumper* than his brother who was the school champion last year. Each of his first two *jumps* so far have been *higher* than his brother ever *jumped*.

5. Study the passage below with which Henry James's novel, *The Portrait of a Lady* begins and answer the questions which follow.

> Under certain circumstances there are few hours in life more agreeable than the hour dedicated to the ceremony known as afternoon tea. There are circumstances in which, whether you partake of the tea or not – some people of course never do – the situation is in itself delightful. Those that I have in mind in beginning to unfold this simple history offered an admirable setting to an innocent pastime. The implements of the little feast had been disposed upon the lawn of an old English country house in what I should call the perfect middle of a splendid summer afternoon.

   a. Identify the bound morphemes contained in the words in the above passage. Comment on any words that cannot be segmented uncontroversially.
   b. Identify all the portmanteau morphs and the morphemes that they represent.
   c. Select a word that illustrates each of the following morphological types: isolating, agglutinating and inflecting. Justify your selection.
   d. Identify the compound words in the text. Show the word-class to which each one of them belongs.
   e. If we assumed that this passage is representative of the language, what morphological type would it indicate that English belongs to? Is it inflecting, agglutinating or isolating?

Chapter 4

Building words

4.1 WORDS AND JIGSAWS

In this chapter we shall group morphemes into four broad categories on the basis of how they function in word-building. Just as anyone putting together a jigsaw must realise that the different pieces go in positions where their shape fits, anyone putting together words must also realise that the various morphemes available in a language can only be used in certain places where they fit.

4.2 KNOW THE PIECES OF THE JIGSAW

We established in Chapter 3 that words have internal structure. What we shall do in this section is to consider in some detail the various elements used to create that structure. We will begin with a discussion of roots and affixes. This will be followed by conversion and compounding.

4.2.1 Roots are the core

A ROOT is a morpheme which forms the core of a word. It is the unit to which other morphemes may be added, or looked at from another angle, it is what remains when all the affixes are peeled away. All roots belong to one of the LEXICAL CATEGORIES, i.e. they belong to the word classes of noun, verb, adverb or adjective. Here are some examples:

[4.1]	*Noun*	*Adjective*	*Verb*	*Adverb*
	bell	big	bring	now
	child	black	eat	soon

tree	good	love	here
lamp	clean	sit	then
light	high	speak	there
lion	strong	think	very

We saw in the last chapter that many words contain a free morpheme which may occur on its own, with nothing appended to it. The vast majority of root morphemes that are capable of appearing on their own are CONTENT WORDS, i.e. nouns, verbs, adjectives and adverbs (see section 2.2.1).

We also saw that there are very many morphemes which are always kept in bondage. These are the bound morphemes, which are totally barred from occurring independently. Many roots fall into this category. Examples of BOUND ROOTS are provided below. In each case the root is italicised and separated from the rest of the word (which may contain one or more morphemes).

[4.2]	*santc-* 'holy'	*vir-* 'man'	*tox-* 'poison'	*loc-* 'place'
	sanct-ify	*vir*-ile	*tox*-in	*loc*-al
	sanct-um	*vir*-il-ity	*tox*-ic	*loc*-al-ity
	sanct-uary	*vir*-ago	non-*tox*-ic	dis-*loc*-ate
	sanct-ity	trium-*vir*-ate	in-*tox*-ic-ate	*loc*-um

The data in [4.2] illustrate another important point. Some of the forms to which affixes are attached are words in their own right or bound roots which are not words. There is a need for a common term to refer to forms, be they bound roots or self-standing words, to which affixes may be attached. The term BASE is used to meet this need. Any form to which affixes are appended in word-formation is called a base. Bases to which affixes are added can be bare roots like *loc-* in *loc-al*, *loc-um*, *loc-us* or they can be independent words, e.g. *govern* in *governor* and *govern-ment*. They can also be forms which already contain other affixes, e.g. [[*loc-al*]-*ity*], [[*loc-al*]-*ism*].

An issue raised by the segmentation of words into morphemes is what counts as a morpheme. I suspect that *sanct-*, *vir-* and *tox-* do not jump at you as obvious examples of morphemes in the same way that *govern* does because their meanings are not immediately obvious. An etymological dictionary, or a knowledge of Latin, might help to persuade you that these are indeed recognisable morphemes. But your intuitions as a speaker of English would probably not enable you readily to reach that conclusion. So the question arises of how to treat such awkward cases. If a form was recognisable at some time in the past as a morpheme, does that mean that for ever more it should be recognised as a morpheme? Where do we draw the line between forms whose analysis is only of historical or etymological relevance and those whose analysis is well motivated in the synchronic study of the language? We will just note this tricky problem for the moment and defer tackling it until section (6.6).

4.2.2 Affixes are for appending

It is clear that many words are complex. They are made up of a root together with other morphemes. Any morphemes that are appended to the root are called AFFIXES. We shall discuss affixes in a preliminary way in this section and return to them in more detail in section (4.4.1).

Affixes can be attached before or after the base. For instance, using the root *polite* as our base, we can form the new lexical items by adding *-ness* to give *polite-ness* ('the property of being polite') or *-ly* to give *polite-ly* ('in a polite manner'). An affix that is appended after the base (e.g. *-ness* and *-ly*) is called a SUFFIX while an affix that goes before the base, as *im-* does in *im-polite*, is called a PREFIX.

In some languages affixes are not just placed before or after the base. Some are inserted inside it. Such affixes are called INFIXES. Thus, in the Ulwa language of Nicaragua, the portmanteau morph *-ka* representing 'third person, singular, possessive' is placed after the first metrical foot of the word (this roughly means it goes after the second vowel). So *-ka* is a suffix where the base has just two vowels as in [4.3a] and [4.3b]. But it is an infix where the base is longer and contains more than two vowels, as in [4.3c] and [4.3d]:

[4.3] *Base*   *Possessed*
    a. kii   'stone'   kii-*ka*   'his/her stone'
    b. sana   'deer'   sana-*ka*   'his/her deer'
    c. suulu   'dog'   suu-*ka*-lu   'his/her dog'
    d. siwanak   'root'   siwi-*ka*-nak   'his/her root'

(based on McCarthy and Prince 1990)

English has no bound infix morphemes. But this does not mean that it has no infixing whatsoever. In expressive language, whole words can be inserted into other words as infixes as in:

[4.4] My ex-husband now lives in Minne*bloody*sota.

Several more colourful four-letter words could fill the position occupied by *bloody*. Can you think of some?

Furthermore, there is a class of bound morphemes which are attached at the margins of words but which are not affixes. Such morphemes are called CLITICS. They co-habit with a word without getting into a deep relationship with it: clitics retain a degree of independence. For instance, they can easily move from one word to another within a phrase if the syntactic conditions are right. A good example of a clitic in English is the GENITIVE *'s* as in *the professor's car*. It can be attached to whatever noun precedes the last noun of a genitive noun phrase. So we can say *the professor's car* and *the professor of ancient history's car*. Of course, in both cases it is the professor who owns the car but the genitive *'s* is not necessarily attached to *professor*. (See (8.3) for further discussion.)

Up to now all the word-building elements we have encountered have been morphs that represent a morpheme; they have all been entities associated with some meaning. This is not always the case. Sometimes, morphological forms that do not represent any meaning are used in word-building in the same way that blank fillers are put in by a joiner to occupy space when cupboards or doors do not quite fill the entire space available. We will call such 'blanks' FORMATIVES. For instance, the adjective-forming suffix *-al* is attached directly to *region* to form *region-al* and to *politic* to form *political*. However, when *-al* is suffixed to some other bases a bridging formative is needed. Thus, in the case of *contract* we get *contractual*. The meaningless formative *-u-* must intervene between the base *contract* and the suffix *-al*. We cannot just say **contractal*. Similarly, in *maternal* and *paternal* the meaningless formative *-n-* is interposed between the suffix *-al* and the bases *pater* and *mater*. An even better example of a formative is the form *u* in *rivulet*. This *u* is inserted after *river* (and the final *-er* (/ə/ is dropped) before the suffix *-let*, meaning 'small'. Elsewhere, as in *piglet*, the suffix *-let* attaches directly to the root.

4.3 THE MAIN TYPES OF WORD-BUILDING: INFLECTION AND DERIVATION

We have seen above the types of morphemes that are available. Now we will consider how they are deployed. We will see that word-building processes fall into two broad categories: INFLECTION and DERIVATION. Typically inflection contributes a morpheme that is required in order to ensure that the word has a form that is appropriate for the grammatical context in which it is used. For instance, if we have a third person subject, a present tense verb agreeing with it must take the -*s* ending; anything else is forbidden:

[4.5] She run*s* her business very efficiently.
　　　*She run her business very efficiently.
　　　*She running her business very efficiently.

To take another example, a monosyllabic adjective (e.g. *tall*, *nice*, *short* etc.) or a disyllabic adjective with a weak second syllable (e.g. *clever*, *thirsty*, *dirty* etc.) must take the comparative degree of suffix -*er* if it is followed by *than* indicating comparison. Failure to use the -*er* ending results in ungrammaticality:

[4.6] John is tall*er* than Jane.　(*John is tall/tallest than Jane.)
　　　He is dirt*ier* than Robin.　(*He is dirty/dirtiest than Robin.)
　　　I am shorter than you.　(*I am short/shortest than you.)

OBLIGATORINESS is an important feature of inflection. In [4.5] the choice of the verb form ending in -*s* and in [4.6] the choice of the adjective ending in -*er* is not a matter of personal preference. It is mandatory. The application of an inflectional process is automatically triggered if the right syntactic conditions obtain. Can you diagnose what is wrong with the extract from Roald Dahl's *The BFG* – beside the spelling and punctuation? (See also (4.4.1) below for further discussion of inflection.)

I HAS RITTEN A BOOK AND IT IS SO EXCITING NOBODY CAN PUT IT DOWN. AS SOON AS YOU HAS RED THE FIRST LINE YOU IS SO HOOKED ON IT YOU CANNOT STOP UNTIL THE LAST PAGE. IN ALL THE CITIES PEEPLE IS WALKING IN THE STREETS BUMPING INTO EACH OTHER BECAUSE THEIR FACES IS BURIED IN MY BOOK AND DENTISTS IS READING IT AND TRYING TO FILL TEETHS AT THE SAME TIME BUT NOBODY MINDS BECAUSE THEY IS ALL READING IT TOO IN THE DENTIST'S CHAIR. DRIVERS IS READING IT WHILE DRIVING AND CARS IS CRASHING ALL OVER THE COUNTRY. BRAIN SURGEONS IS READING IT WHILE THEY IS OPERATING ON BRAINS AND AIRLINE PILOTS IS READING IT AND GOING TO TIMBUCTOO INSTEAD OF LONDON. FOOT-BALL PLAYERS IS READING IT ON THE FIELD BECAUSE THEY CAN'T PUT IT DOWN AND SO IS OLIMPICK RUNNERS WHILE THEY IS RUNNING.

EVERYBODY HAS TO SEE WHAT IS GOING TO HAPPEN NEXT IN MY
BOOK AND WHEN I WAKE UP I IS STILL TINGLING WITH EXCITEMENT
AT BEING THE GREATEST RITER THE WORLD HAS EVER KNOWN
UNTIL MY MUMMY COMES IN AND SAYS I WAS LOOKING AT YOUR
ENGLISH EXERCISE BOOK LAST NITE AND REALLY YOUR SPELLING IS
ATROSHUS SO IS YOUR PUNTULASHON.

Whereas inflection is driven by the requirement to form a word with the appropriate form in a particular grammatical context, derivation is motivated by the desire to create new lexical items using pre-existing morphemes and words. When you need a new word (in the sense of vocabulary item), you do not usually need to make it up from scratch. It is possible to create new lexical items by recycling pre-existing material. This is derivation. It takes one of three forms: AFFIXATION, CONVERSION or COMPOUNDING.

Derivation enables us to add new lexical items to the OPEN WORD-CLASSES of noun, adjective, verb and adverb. These are the classes that contain the so-called content words (cf. section 2.2.1). We are extremely unlikely to create new words belonging to classes like pronouns, articles or prepositions. Hence these classes are said to be CLOSED. It is extremely unlikely that one fine morning you will wake up with the inspired idea that English needs some new

articles – the same boring *the*, *a/an* have been around too long –
and coin a dozen fresh articles as a public service.

Not everyone would characterise derivation in the way that I
have, contrasting derivation which produces new lexical items with
inflection which produces grammatical words. Many linguists
restrict the term derivation to the creation of new lexical items by
adding affixes (including 'zero' ones: see below p. 94). They
explicitly distinguish it from compounding which combines two
bases containing root morphemes to form a new lexical item.

I prefer a two-way distinction between inflection on the one
hand, and a broadly defined category of derivation on the other,
because it highlights clearly the fact that essentially all word-
formation boils down to one of two things: either the creation of
lexical items, the province of derivation, or the creation of grammatical words, the province of inflection. It should be pointed out,
however, that there are other (marginal) methods of forming lexical
items that fall outside derivation (cf. Chapter 9).

4.4 DERIVATION: FABRICATING WORDS

Most of the words you use in a day have been part of the English
language for a long time. But that does not necessarily mean that
you have memorised all of them. In many cases, and to varying
degrees, we can reconstitute words we encounter as the need arises,
or even occasionally coin new ones. What makes this possible is
our mastery of the rules of word-formation. Confronted with a
complex word, you will often be able to deconstruct it using your
knowledge of word structure.

How can knowledge of word-structure be represented? We can
represent the structure of a complex word such as *teachers*, *American-
isation*, *governmental* and *ungovernability* in two ways. We can use
LABELLED BRACKETS as in [4.7] or a TREE DIAGRAM as in [4.8].
Either way, we want to show which morphemes in the word go
together, and what string of morphemes forms the input to each
word-formation process. Further we need to know the word-class
to which the resulting word belongs.

[4.7] *Labelled brackets*
    $[\text{teach}]_V\text{er}]_N\text{s}]_N$ $[\text{Americ(a)}]_N\text{an}]_{ADJ}\text{is}]_V\text{ation}]_N$
    $[[\text{govern}]_V\text{ment}]_N\text{al}]_{ADJ}$

[4.8] *Tree diagrams*

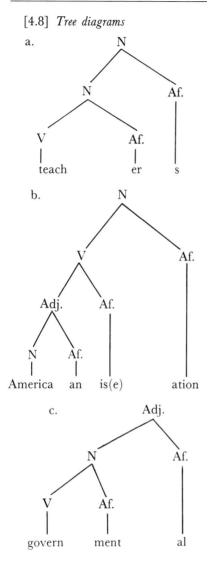

a.

b.

c.

Note: Af.=affix

Many complex words that contain multiple affixes have internal structure. When a base that contains one or more affixes is used as an input to a process that attaches more affixes, certain morphemes go more closely together than others and form a subgrouping.

4.4.1 Affixation: prefixes and suffixes

Probably the commonest method of forming words (in the sense of lexical terms) is by AFFIXATION. Affixes have already been introduced in section (4.2.2). We will now briefly examine their characteristics and return to them in more detail in Chapter 6.

The meanings of many affixes are not altogether transparent. It may be necessary sometimes to look them up in an etymological dictionary (like the *OED* or Skeat 1982). This of course raises questions about what we are doing when we divide words up into morphemes. To what extent is the morphological segmentation of words a historical exercise? In this chapter we will concentrate on the identification of morphemes and leave this awkward question to one side until section (6.6).

It is possible to group together affixes in different ways depending on one's purposes. For instance, we can classify affixes on the basis of their meaning. We can recognise a class of negative prefixes, e.g. *im-* (*im-possible*), *un-* (*un-necessary*), *dis-* (*dis-approve*), *non-* (*non-combatant*) etc. However, that will not be our approach. We will instead group affixes together on the basis of their phonological properties. It has been found very useful to classify affixes on the basis of their phonological behaviour, in particular on the basis of their effects (if any) on stress in the base to which they are attached. It has been shown that affixes fall into two major classes: some are NEUTRAL while others are NON-NEUTRAL in their effects.

Normally, prefixes are stress neutral. Thus, in [4.9] stress falls on the same syllable in the word regardless of their presence or absence. When determining which syllable is going to be the most prominent in the word, these prefixes are not taken into account. It is as though they were invisible.

[4.9] *Stress-neutral prefixes*
    be- (forming derivative verbs with the general meaning of 'around')
       beset, besmear, becloud
    co-/con-/com- 'together'
       co-operate, co-habit, co-appear, co-opt, combine, conspire
    ex- 'former'
       ex-miner, ex-wife, ex-leader, ex-director, ex-pupil, ex-pilot
    mis- 'wrongly, badly'
       mis-understand, mis-manage, mis-read, mis-take, mis-inform, mis-allocate

mal(e)- 'bad(ly)'
malcontent, malpractice, maladjusted, malefactor, mal-
evolent

re- 'again'
re-think, re-take, re-play, re-examine, re-issue

un- 'negative'
unexciting, unhappy, uncomfortable, unwise, unmanage-
able, uncool

dis- 'negative' (with adjectives)
dishonest, dishonourable, discomfortable

dis- 'negative, reversive' (with verbs)
disallow, disagree, disapprove, dislike, disaffirm, disbe-
lieve, disarm

in- 'negative' (with adjectives)
inarticulate, inactive, inept, inevitable, intangible,
innumerable

un- 'negative' (with adjectives)
unoriginal, unusual, unseemly, unripe, unpleasant,
unsavoury, unreliable

un- 'reversive' (with verbs)
undo, unblock, unpack, unravel, unpick, unseat, unroll,
unsaddle

In words of two syllables the initial syllable attracts stress when
the word-form realises a verb, but it repels stress when the word-
form represents a noun or adjective. In the latter case stress falls
on the second syllable. It so happens that in many of these words
there is a prefix but the presence of a prefix is not the vital factor.
It is being disyllabic that counts. Admittedly, historically words
like *preserve* were formed using the prefix *pre-*. But that is no longer
relevant. People generally are unaware of it.

[4.10]   *Stress on prefix Stress on first syllable of the base*

	a. NOUN	VERB
	'conduct	con'duct
	'contract	con'tract
	'convert	con'vert
	'digest	di'gest
	'export	ex'port
	'import	im'port
	'increase	in'crease
	'permit	per'mit

	'preserve	pre'serve
	'project	pro'ject
	'present	pre'sent
	'produce	pro'duce
	'reject	re'ject
	'subject	sub'ject
	'survey	sur'vey
b.	ADJECTIVE	VERB
	'abstract	ab'stract
	'perfect	per'fect
	'present	pre'sent

In some cases, in addition to the stress change, there is also a change in the vowels, e.g. *record* /'rekɔːd/(noun) *record* /rɪ'kɔːd/ (verb). Here we will ignore such phonological changes, which are not important for our present purposes.

What [4.10] shows is that besides having morphological consequences (creating a word belonging to a particular grammatical category), affixation also has phonological consequences. Your knowledge of English word-structure involves knowing the meaning and grammatical class of the words produced using a given affix. (You need to know the grammatical class of the words you form in order to know in what grammatical contexts you can deploy them.) But your knowledge goes further than that. It also includes knowing the pronunciation (and if you are literate, the spelling) of the words formed by attaching that affix so that you can produce the appropriate forms of the words. As you can see by looking back at the extract from *The BFG*, the ability to form, or find in your mental dictionary, the right lexeme is not sufficient. For competent use of the language you also need to produce correct grammatical words and word-forms realising your lexical items.

Next, let us survey derivational suffixes. Coverage is not meant to be comprehensive by any means, but it should be sufficient to provide a reasonably good picture of derivational affixation. In [4.11] I have provided a representative sample of derivational suffixes together with their general meaning, the grammatical class of bases that they attach to and the grammatical class of the resulting word. Discussion of the phonological effects of suffixes will be taken up in Chapter 6.

[4.11] DERIVATIONAL SUFFIXES

a. *Verb → Noun*

-*ation*   'derives nouns of action from verbs':
            don-ation, reconcili-ation, regul-ation, confisc-
            ation, simul-ation

-*ant*   'person that does whatever the verb means':
            inhabit-ant, celebr-ant, protest-ant, occup-ant,
            attend-ant

-*ant*   'instrument that is used to do whatever the
            verb means':
            lubric-ant, stimul-ant, intoxic-ant

-*er*   'person who does whatever the verb means':
            teach-er, runn-er, writ-er, build-er, paint-er

-*er*   'instrument that is used to do whatever the
            verb means':
            cook-er, strain-er, drain-er, pok-er

-*ing*   'act of doing whatever the verb indicates':
            learn-ing, read-ing, writ-ing, sav-ing, rid-ing,
            wait-ing

-*ist*   'derives agent nouns from verbs – one who
            does X':
            cycl-ist, typ-ist, copy-ist

-*ion*   'derives nouns of condition or action from verbs':
            eros-ion (from *erode*), corros-ion (from *corrode*),
            persuas-ion (from *persuade*), radiat-ion, promot-
            ion

-*ment*   'the result or product of the action of the verb;
            the instrument used to perform the action of
            the verb':
            pave-ment, appoint-ment, accomplish-ment,
            govern-ment, pay-ment

-*ery*   'derives nouns indicating a place where ani-
            mals are kept or plants grown':
            catt-ery, pigg-ery, orang-ery, shrubb-ery

-*ery*   'derives nouns indicating place where the
            action specified by the verb takes place':
            bak-ery, cann-ery, brew-ery, fish-ery, refin-ery,
            tann-ery

-*ee*   '(passive) person who undergoes action indi-
            cated by the verb':
            employ-ee, detain-ee, pay-ee, intern-ee

b. *Verb* → *Adj.*

-*ing*   'in the process or state of doing whatever the verb indicates':

        wait-ing (as in *waiting car*) stand-ing (as in *standing passengers*)

-*ise/-ize*   'to bring about whatever the adjective signals':

        real-ise, neutral-ise, fertil-ise, immun-ise

-*ive*   'having the tendency to X; having the quality character of X; given to the action of Xing':

        act-ive, pens-ive, indicat-ive, evas-ive, product-ive, representat-ive

-*able*   'able to be X-ed':

        read-able, govern-able; manage-able, do-able

-*ing*   'the act of doing whatever the verb signifies':

        sail-ing, sing-ing, fight-ing, writ-ing

c. *Noun* → *Verb*

-*ate*   'derives verbs from nouns':

        regul-ate, capacit-ate, don-ate

-*ise/-ize*   'to bring about whatever the noun signals':

        colon-ise, American-ise, computer-ise

-*ise/-ize*   'put in the place or state indicated by the noun':

        hospital-ise, terror-ise, jeopard-ise

d. *Noun* → *Adj.*

-*al*   'pertaining to X':

        autumn-al, dent-al, division-al, reacreation-al, tradition-al, medicin-al

-*ate*   'derives adjectives denoting state':

        intim-ate, accur-ate, obdur-ate

        (There is normally a corresponding noun ending in -*acy*, e.g. intim-acy, accur-acy, obdur-acy.)

-*ish*   'having the (objectionable) nature, qualities or character of X':

        lout-ish, fiend-ish, freak-ish, child-ish, mother henn-ish

-*less*   'without X':

        joy-less, care-less, fear-less, child-less

-ful	'filled with X':
	joy-ful, care-ful, fear-ful, cheer-ful
-(i)an	'associated with whatever the noun indicates':
	Chomsky-an, Dominic-an, suburb-an, Trinidad-(i)an, Canad-(i)an, Ghana-(i)an, reptil-(i)an, mammal-(i)an
-some	'forms adjectives from verbs, having quality X':
	quarrel-some, trouble-some, tire-some.

e. *Adj → Verb*

-ate	'cause to become, do etc. whatever the adjective indicates':
	activ-ate (<active) equ-ate (< equal)
-ise	'cause to become whatever the adjective indicates':
	tranquill-ise, modern-ise, steril-ise, stabil-ise, civil-ise, familiar-ise

f. *Adj → Noun*

-ness	'forms a noun expressing state or condition':
	good-ness, fair-ness, bitter-ness, dark-ness
-ity	'forms a noun expressing state or condition':
	timid-ity, banal-ity, pur-ity, antiqu-ity
-ship	'state or condition of being X':
	hard~hardship
-ery	'having the property indicated by the adjective':
	brav-ery, effront-ery, trick-ery, chican-ery

g. *Adj → Adv.*

-ly	'forms adverbs from adjectives':
	usual-ly, busi-ly, proud-ly, loud-ly, grateful-ly

h. *Noun → Noun*

-aire	'to be possessed of X':
	million-aire, doctrin-aire, solit-aire
-acy	'derives a noun of quality, state or condition from another noun or adjective (normally the base to which it is added also takes the nominal suffix *-ate*)':
	advoc-acy, episcop-acy, intim-acy, accur-acy, obdur-acy

-er	'a person who practises a trade or profession connected to the noun': marin-er, geograph-er, football-er, haberdash-er, hatt-er
-ery	'derives nouns indicating general collective sense "-ware, stuff" ': machin-ery, crock-ery, jewell-ery, pott-ery
-let	'derives a diminutive noun': pig-let, is-let, riv(u)-let
-ling	'derives a diminutive noun from another noun': duck-ling, prince-ling, found-ling
-hood	'quality, state, rank of being X': boy-hood, sister-hood, priest-hood
-ship	'state or condition of being X': king-ship, craftsman-ship, director-ship, steward-ship
-ism	'forms nouns which are the name of a theory, doctrine or practice': femin-ism, capital-ism, Marx-ism, structural-ism
-ist	'adherent to some *-ism*, a protagonist for X, an expert on X' (usually a base that takes *-ist* also takes *-ism*): femin-ist, capital-ist, Marx-ist, structural-ist

i. *Adj → Adj*.

-ish	'having the property of being somewhat X': narrow-ish, blu-ish, pink-ish

j. *Verb → Verb*

-er	'adds frequent or iterative meaning to verbs': chatt-er, patt-er, flutt-er

Having studied [4.11], I suggest that you find one fresh example of a word that contains each of the suffixes listed. Afterwards identify two non-neutral suffixes which affect the location of stress in the base to which they are attached and two neutral ones that do not. This will give you a taste of the challenge posed by suffixes for morphological theory by the interaction between word-formation rules and phonological rules. We will take up that challenge in the next two chapters.

Let us now turn to INFLECTIONAL SUFFIXES. English has not got much inflection, being essentially an isolating language, as noted in section (3.6.5). The little inflection that it has consists of suffixes rather than prefixes. [4.12] contains a sample of common inflectional suffixes.

[4.12] a. *Verbal suffixes* *Function* *Example*

-s	3rd person, singular, present	He snore-s
-ing	progressive aspect (denoting action in progress)	He is snor-ing
-ed	past tense	He snor-ed

b. *Noun suffixes*

-s	noun plural marker	road-s

c. *Adj. suffixes*

-er	comparative adjective/ adverb	slow-er, soon-er
-est	superlative adjective/ adverb	slow-est, soon-est

A base to which inflectional affixes are added is called a STEM. Singling out stems from other bases in this fashion enables us to highlight the distinction between inflection and derivation. This is important, as we will see in Chapter 11, not only for the way linguists describe language but also for the way in which the brain processes words. So the bases in *road-s*, *government-s* and *schoolboy-s* are all stems since they are followed by the plural inflectional suffix-*s*. Of course, the internal structure of these stems is different: *road* is a simple root, *govern-ment* is a complex one, containing as it does the derivational suffix -*ment*; and *school-boy* is also complex since it is a compound word.

Although until now we have treated inflection and derivation separately, it does not mean that they are mutually exclusive. Both derivational and inflectional morphemes may be found in the same word. In that event, derivational morphemes are attached first and any inflectional morphemes are added later, as it were. That is why when both inflectional and derivational morphemes are present, the inflectional morphemes are on the outer fringes of the word, as you can see in [4.13]. In other words, derivation can create the input to inflection. A new lexeme that has been yielded by derivation can subsequently undergo inflection in order to ensure that the word has the appropriate grammatical properties for the syntactic position in which it occurs.

Similarly, if both compounding and inflection take place, as a rule compounding is carried out first. So, the inflectional morpheme is appended on the outer margins to the second element of the compound, which is on the right (cf. [4.14a]). Finally, if a compound stem which includes an affixed base is inflected, as in [4.14b], again the inflectional morpheme appears on the margin, as the element of the word furthest to the right:

[4.13] *Inflection of stems with derivational suffixes*
de-regul-at(e)-*ed* (*de-regul-*ed*-ate)
perfect-ion-ist-*s* (*perfect-*s*-ion-ist)

[4.14] a. *Inflection of compound stems*
bed-room-*s* (*bed-*s*-room)
wind-surf-*ing* (*wind-*ing*-surf)
b. *Inflection of compound stems (including a derived base)*
foot-ball-er-*s* (*foot-*s*-ball-er)
trouble-shoot-er-*s* (*trouble-*s*-shoot-er)

Thus, inflectional morphemes tend to be more peripheral than derivational morphemes in a word, not only in English but also in other languages (see Katamba 1993).

4.4.2 Conversion

In English very often lexical items are created not by affixation but by CONVERSION or ZERO DERIVATION, i.e. without any alteration being made to the shape of the input base. The word-form remains the same, but it realises a different lexical item.

Conversion of verbs into nouns and nouns into verbs is extremely productive in English. Usually the same word-form can be used as a verb or a noun, with only the grammatical context enabling us to know which category it belongs to. Thus, *jump* in the two sentences below is exactly the same in form but it belongs to two different lexemes. In [4.15a] *jump* is the non-finite form of the verb 'jump' while in [4.15b] it is the singular form of the noun *jump*.

[4.15] a. The pig will jump over the stile!
b. What a jump!

In *What a jump!* the verb is converted into a noun by 'zero derivation', i.e. without using any affix. What enables us to know whether the word is a noun or a verb is the position that it occupies in the sentence. If we see the subject *the pig* and the auxiliary verb *will* before the word *jump*, we know it must be a verb. But when *jump* occurs after the indefinite article *a* we know it must be a noun.

In [4.16] I have listed some common examples of forms that are subject to noun-to-verb or verb-to-noun conversion. It is not difficult to think of situations where these words may be used either as nouns or as verbs:

[4.16] | light | bridge | seat | kick |
| --- | --- | --- | --- |
| fish | bus | dog | lift |
| farm | police | smear | finger |
| smell | skin | rain | paper |

Conversion is not restricted to nouns and verbs. Adjectives too can undergo conversion. For instance, the word-form *green* realises an adjective in [4.17a] and a noun in [4.17b]:

[4.17] a. The Green Party had political clout in the 1980s.
b. The Greens had political clout in the 1980s.

Likewise, some adverbs are formed from adjectives without any perceptible change in shape:

[4.18] a. She is a *fast* runner. (*fast* Adj.)
She runs very *fast*. (*fast* Adv.)

Slow has even more possibilities. It can be an adjective, an adverb, a verb or a noun:

[4.19] a. He is a slow bowler. (*slow* Adj.)
b. Go slow. (*slow* Adv.)
c. Slow the car! (*slow* Verb)
d. *Mr Slow* is a popular children's book. (*slow* Noun)

The widespread use of conversion shows the importance of the criterion of syntactic function in determining word-class membership in English. Very often it is by its function rather than by its morphological form that we tell the word-class to which a word belongs.

4.4.3 Compound parade

The third method of forming new lexical items is to use COMPOUND-ING. In this section I will present a brief outline of compounding in English. For more extensive coverage of compounds see Marchand (1969), Adams (1973), Roeper and Siegel (1978), Selkirk (1982), Lieber (1983), Bauer (1983) and Katamba (1993).

As mentioned already, a compound is formed by combining two bases, which may be words in their own right, to form a new lexical item. This is shown in [4.20a] where the two bases are separated by a hyphen:

[4.20] a. shop-steward   ink-pot
           room-mate   road-show
           moon-light   shoe-string
        b. strong-mind=ed   book-sell=er
            old-fashion=ed   market-garden=er
            time-honour=ed   muck-rak=er

As we saw at the end of section (4.4.1), compounding and affixation are by no means incompatible. An affixed base may serve as input to a compounding process, and vice versa. In [4.20b], the suffix is separated by '=' from the base.

Compounds differ in their structure. The majority of English compounds are nouns. Common types of noun compounds include the following:

[4.21]

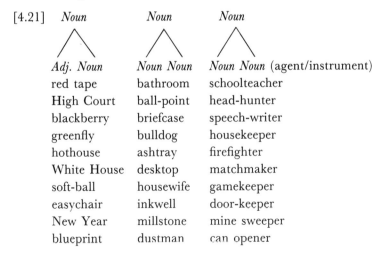

Noun	*Noun*	*Noun*
Adj. Noun	*Noun Noun*	*Noun Noun* (agent/instrument)
red tape	bathroom	schoolteacher
High Court	ball-point	head-hunter
blackberry	briefcase	speech-writer
greenfly	bulldog	housekeeper
hothouse	ashtray	firefighter
White House	desktop	matchmaker
soft-ball	housewife	gamekeeper
easychair	inkwell	door-keeper
New Year	millstone	mine sweeper
blueprint	dustman	can opener

Let us now turn to examples of adjectival compounds. Some are listed in [4.22]:

[4.22]
N+ *Ven*	*Adj.*+ *Ving*	*Adj.*+ *Ven*
crestfallen	hard-working	clear-sighted
waterlogged	good-looking	hard-featured
heartbroken	easygoing	soft-hearted
frost-bitten	fast-growing	new-born

> *Note*: *Ven* is the past participial form of the verb. It is the verb form that ends in -*en* or -*ed* after *has* in, e.g. *It has eaten* or in *It has wounded*.

An interesting property of most compounds is that they are HEADED. This means that one of the words that make up the compound is syntactically dominant. In English the head is normally the item on the right hand of the compound. The syntactic properties of the head are passed on to the entire compound. Thus, in our examples above, if we have a compound like *easychair* which is made up of the adjective *easy* and the noun *chair*, syntactically the entire word is a noun. This applies to all the words in the left-hand column in [4.21].

Furthermore, the syntactic head is usually also the semantic head of the compound. The non-head element in the compound specifies more narrowly some characteristic of the head. So, an *easychair* is a type of *chair*, a *bulldog* is a kind of *dog*, a *bedroom* is a kind of *room* etc. If a compound contains a semantic head, it is called an ENDOCENTRIC COMPOUND.

Unfortunately, at the semantic level headedness is not consistently applied. A minority of compounds have no semantic head. Take *turncoat*, *head-hunter* and *red tape*. *Turncoat* is not a coat at all, but a person. Literally, a *turncoat* is a person who 'turns his or her coat'. But the word is used metaphorically to mean 'renegade'. A *head-hunter* at one time might literally have hunted people for their heads, armed with a bow and arrow, or a heavy club. But today's head-hunters who occupy plush office suites are not hunters who collect heads for trophies. They are simply (peaceful) recruiters of top business executive talent.

Likewise, *red tape* may literally refer to pinkish red tape used to secure legal and bureaucratic documents. But in most uses of that expression today it is more likely to mean obsessive adherence to administrative procedures which gets in the way of positive decision-making and action. Red tape in this sense is not a kind of tape.

Let us now turn to the phonology of compounds. As mentioned in Chapter 2, compounds typically have one word that receives the main word stress while the other word is relatively less prominent. Contrast the stress pattern of the compound nouns in [4.23a] and in the noun phrases containing the same words in [4.23b]:

[4.23] a. *Compound*   b. *Phrase*
            'White 'House   a 'white 'house
            'green 'fly   a 'green 'fly
            'black 'bird   a 'black 'bird

    Note: " ' " = main stress and " ' " = secondary stress

Normally in compound nouns primary stress falls on the first word and the second word gets secondary stress, as in the '*White* '*House* (the residence of the US President in Washington) and the other words in [4.23a]. However, in the phrases in [4.23b] like *a white house* (as opposed to any house that is painted green, purple or pink) both content words receive primary stress, and neither has its stress suppressed.

Another aspect of compounding that has interested linguists in recent years is the place of compounds in the lexicon. The question that has been raised is whether or not compounds should be listed in the dictionary. The consensus is that compounding is very widely and productively used in word-formation and many headed compound words do not need to be listed in the dictionary because their meanings are so transparent that they can be worked out using standard rules in the grammar.

COMPOSITIONALITY holds the key. Normally we can work out the meaning of the whole from the meanings of its parts. If we know the meanings of the smaller units which the larger unit contains, we can work out the meaning of the whole. In syntax we do not need to list sentences with their meanings since they are predictable from the meanings of the words they contain and the grammatical and semantic relationships between them. If we know what the words mean, using our knowledge of syntactic and semantic rules we can work out the meanings of sentences like *The dog chased the cat* and *The cat chased the mouse*; *The unicorn kicked the yeti* and *The yeti was kicked by the unicorn*. Similarly, in morphology, where the meaning of compound words can be predicted with a high degree of accuracy by general rules from the meaning of the elements they contain, we do not need to list them in the dictionary. (See the discussion of compositionality in section (8.1) below.)

Following Selkirk (1982), I shall argue that the same rules that characterise the structure of sentences are used to construct and interpret transparent, compositionally formed compounds such as the those in [4.24]. The examples and the analysis are based on Marchand (1969):

[4.24] a	b	c
watchmaker	fishing rod	writing table
road-sweeper	frying pan	waiting room
bookseller	carving knife	dining room
speech-writer	sewing machine	ironing board

All the examples in [4.24] are DEVERBAL COMPOUND NOUNS, i.e. noun compounds formed from verbs. Their structure is like that of a sentence fragment where the verb is in construction with a noun (or more precisely a NP: noun phrase) which has a very intimate syntactic and semantic relation with it. Semantically, the NP has a role like agent, instrument or patient *vis-à-vis* the verb (cf. Selkirk 1982).

In the *bookseller* type of compound in column a, the NP refers to someone whose role is that of AGENT, i.e. the person who normally does whatever the verb signifies. The head, which is the element on the right in the compound, is a noun derived from a verb by adding the -*er* suffix which forms nouns denoting agents. Corresponding to the compound *bookseller* is the clause 'someone who sells books'; corresponding to *watchmaker* is the clause 'someone who makes watches', etc.

In the *fishing rod* type of deverbal noun compound in column b, the head NP on the right of the compound denotes an INSTRUMENT used to perform whatever action is designated by the verb. The element on the left that tells us in more specific terms about the head is a GERUNDIVE NOUN which is derived from the verb by suffixing -*ing*. A *fishing rod* is in a very literal sense a 'rod used for fishing'. The instrumental interpretation serves us well in the rest of the examples. A *frying pan* is 'a pan used for frying', a *carving knife* is 'a knife used for carving', etc.

The final set of examples found in column c, which includes *writing table*, is similar in structure to the examples in b. Again we have a gerundive noun as the non-head constituent on the left of the compound. What is different here is the semantic relationship between the gerundive and the head NP following it. Whereas in column b the head NP that follows the gerundive functions as the instrument used to do whatever the verb that underlies the gerundive denotes, in column c the head NP indicates the LOCATION where the action or event or state designated by the verb underlying the gerundive takes place. A *writing table* is 'a table at which one writes', a *waiting room* is 'a room where one stays while waiting', etc. There is a sentence which corresponds to each one of these verbal compounds. The reason for this is that verbal compounds are derived from sentences.

Now, the number of grammatical sentences in English (or any other language) is unlimited. So, it would be futile to try to memorise *all* the sentences that are sanctioned by the rules of English grammar. The same is true of verbal compounds, since they have sentences as their source. It would be futile to attempt to list all verbal compounds. So, how do speakers of English cope? The answer is that they do not attempt to memorise all verbal compounds any more than they try to memorise all sentences by brute force. Rather, they master a system of grammatical rules that allows them both to construct and to understand an indefinitely large number of sentences. One refinement is necessary: often the general interpretation of compounds provided by the grammar requires a little fine tuning. For instance, given a deverbal compound noun with a locative meaning, e.g. *waiting room*, the grammar enables us to determine that it is a room where people wait. But it will not enable us to know that it is a room in a public place like a railway station designated especially for that purpose.

A major part of the rule system in the grammar consists of PHRASE STRUCTURE RULES whose job is to define CONSTITUENT STRUCTURE. By constituent structure we mean word groupings that form coherent units called PHRASES on which syntactic rules operate. Some simplified phrase structure rules are shown below.

[4.25] a. S → NP VP
  b. NP → (Det.) N (PP)
  c. VP → V (NP) (PP)
  d. PP → P NP

  Notes: (i) The arrow → is to be interpreted as 'consists of'
    (ii) Parentheses indicate that the presence of an item is optional. The rest of the abbreviations are listed on p. xvii.

Often it is more convenient to show the information conveyed in phrase structure rules using a PHRASE STRUCTURE TREE. Such trees express more explicitly the 'hierarchical' nature of syntactic structure. Syntactic organisation is like Chinese boxes, with smaller units contained in bigger units.

The first three phrase structure rules [4.25] can be re-stated as shown in [4.26].

[4.26]

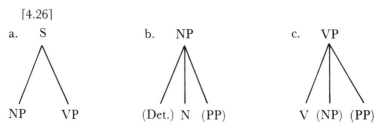

a. S — NP VP
b. NP — (Det.) N (PP)
c. VP — V (NP) (PP)

It says in [4.26a] that a sentence contains two constituents, a NP and a VP; [4.26b] says that a NP can contain a noun on its own or a noun together with either or both a determiner and a PP. In [4.26c] we see that a VP must contain a verb which may be followed by either a NP or a PP, or both a NP and a PP.

In the dictionary, words are entered with a word-class label like N for noun. Adj. for adjective, V for verb and P for preposition. A word belonging to the appropriate class is selected to fill a slot below N, V, P etc. In other words, below N we put a noun, below V we put a verb, and so forth.

We can represent a whole sentence in a tree diagram as shown in [4.27]:

[4.27]

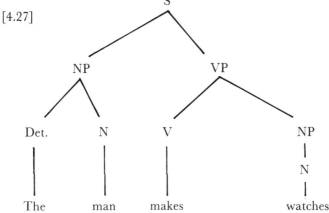

Phrase structure rules and phrase structure trees are not to be seen merely as a statement of the constituent structure of a given sentence but as very general rules for GENERATING, i.e. enumerating, an indefinitely large number of sentences with the same structure. *The man makes watches* is analogous to *The girl loves tennis, The chicken lays eggs, The student hates exams* etc. All these sentences and thousands more are generated by [4.27] if the appropriate words are provided.

At no cost, we can use the rules that produce sentences to produce compound words. Selkirk (1982) has proposed that in morphology we should characterise the structure of compounds by harnessing the phrase structure rules used in syntax. The realisation that compound words share important properties with sentences has important consequences. We can represent the structure of the verbal compounds we have discussed using phrase structure trees:

[4.28]

To conclude, the fact that deverbal compounding usually operates in a predictable way means that it is not necessary to list all the compounds in the lexicon and memorise them. Just as it is possible to use phrase structure rules in syntax to produce an indefinitely large number of sentences, it is also possible, when dealing with lexical items, to use phrase structure rules in morphology to produce an indefinitely large number of compound words. Morphology is no different to syntax in the rules it employs for this purpose.

4.4.4 Wishy-washy words

Sapir (1921: 76) observed that nothing is more natural than the prevalence of REDUPLICATION, the repetition of the base of a word in part or in its entirety. He observed that though rare, reduplication is found in English. It is attested in words such as:

[4.29] pooh-pooh   goody-goody   wishy-washy
       sing-song   roly-poly   harum-scarum

Later on, Thun (1963) showed that reduplication is less marginal than is commonly assumed. He listed and examined about 2,000 reduplicative words in standard English and in various dialects.

The most significant property of reduplicatives (words formed by reduplication) is that word-formation is driven by phonological factors. There are two main types of reduplicatives: RHYME MOTIVATED COMPOUNDS and ABLAUT MOTIVATED COMPOUNDS (cf. Bauer 1983). Rhyme means what it means in poetry: the vowels and any consonant(s) that appear after it in the last syllable are identical while ablaut means a change in the root vowel. (Usually ablaut signals a change in grammatical function, e.g. the *o* ~ *e* alternation in *long* (Adj.) vs. *length* (Noun) marks a difference in word-class.) These labels for the two categories of reduplicative compounds highlight the fact that the repetition of the bases in compounds of this kind involves copying the rhyme in so-called rhyme motivated compounds, and copying the consonants and altering the vowel in ablaut motivated compounds.

Some rhyming compounds are formed by joining bases which are both pre-existing words as in *Black-Jack* and *brain-drain*. Probably more common, however, are rhyming compounds where one or both bases is not an independent word, as in [4.30]:

[4.30] *Rhyme motivated compounds*
       nitwit   helter-skelter   namby-pamby
       titbit   hobnob   higgledy-piggledy
       nitty-gritty   teeny-weeny

Finally, there are ablaut motivated compounds in which one or both bases may not be an independent word:

[4.31] *Ablaut motivated compounds*
       tip-top   riff-raff   ding-dong   shilly-shally
       tick-tock   tittle-tattle   wibble-wobble   dingle-dangle
       ping-pong   dilly-dally   flip-flop

4.5 SUMMARY

In this chapter we have explored the building blocks available for constructing words. We have established that roots are the core units to which different types of affixes can be attached. Affixes that precede the base are called prefixes and those that follow the base are called suffixes. Affixes may be neutral or non-neutral in their effect on the base.

Further, we have seen that word-formation involves two main processes: inflection and derivation. Inflection is motivated by syntax. Inflectional processes assign a stem certain grammatical properties so as to produce a grammatical word that can fit in a given syntactic slot. Derivation is not steered by syntax; its function is to create lexical items. There are three major classes of derivational processes: affixation, conversion and compounding. I have stressed the point that many words have internal structure and can be semantically analysed using compositionality. So the phrase structure rules used in syntax to generate innumerable permissible sentences can also be used to account for the productivity observed in compounding.

Finally, there is a substantial minority of reduplicative compounds which are driven by phonology. Such compounds are typically motivated by either rhyme or ablaut.

EXERCISES

1. Illustrating your answer with fresh examples, explain the following:

   a. morpheme and formative
   b. root, stem, base
   c. neutral vs. non-neutral suffix
   d. inflectional morpheme vs. derivational morpheme
   e. conversion

2. Study the following list of bound roots:

-ceive	-gress	-scribe	-tect
-cur	-ject	-serve	-tract
-duce	-mand	-side	-trude
-fer	-mit	-spect	-vert
-fine	-pand	-spire	-vade
-form	-port	-sumc	-vidc

a. List two different verbs formed by attaching prefixes to each of the above roots.

b. With the help of a good etymological dictionary, work out the meaning of each root.

c. Which of these roots should be recognised as living morphemes in contemporary English? Explain why.

Note: Linguists normally keep totally separate what people know today about their language from what is known about its history and evolution. This is meant to reflect the fact that an infant acquiring the language has no access to its history. The aim of this exercise is to get you to consider some of the problems encountered by a student of English words who tries to enforce the separation of knowledge that contemporary speakers have from knowledge that is of purely historical interest.

3. Draw labelled trees to show the structure of the following words:

motherhood	re-examining	unnaturalness	showmanship
shoemakers	shoplifted	dislocation	range-finder
unputdownable	underprivileged	unclassifiable	worm's eye view

4. a. Provide two fresh examples of different kinds of phonologically motivated word-formation.

b. Explain in detail the main phonological phenomenon that plays a role in the process you have chosen.

Chapter 5

Masquerading allomorphs

5.1 THE RIGHT MASK

We saw in the last chapter that many morphemes have several allomorphs. The question we will address now is this: how is the distribution of those allomorphs determined? In other words, how do speakers select the right allomorph to use in a given situation? (Refer back to section (3.3.1) for a discussion of the idea of distribution.)

We will see that normally the choice of allomorph is not arbitrary. There is a number of general principles that guide speakers in choosing one allomorph rather than another. These factors may be phonological, grammatical or lexical. We will explore these factors in turn.

5.2. PHONOLOGICALLY CONDITIONED ALLOMORPHS

Some morphemes do not have different allomorphs that represent them in different environments. They are like a poor person who has a single outfit that is worn on all occasions. Such morphemes, e.g. *cut* and *day*, are unproblematic. They are realised in the same way, by the same allomorph regardless of where they occur. (I am ignoring very minor, subtle variations in pronunciation.) The dictionary entries of morphemes like these and the actual forms that represent them in different situations do not differ significantly. If all English morphemes were like that, English morphology would be a very dull subject.

In fact, many morphemes have several allomorphs. In the vast majority of cases, the distribution of these allomorphs is determined by phonological factors. For instance, given a base with certain phonetic characteristics, a particular allomorph of the affix morpheme has to be selected. Or, conversely, in some cases when a certain affix is present, a base with particular phonetic characteristics must be selected. This sounds abstract. Let us get down to earth.

A standard example of PHONOLOGICALLY CONDITIONED choice of allomorphs is the regular plural of English nouns. The plural morpheme is represented by -s or -es in the orthography but has three different phonetic manifestations in the spoken language: /s/ as in /hæts/ *hats*, /z/ as in /dʌvz/ *doves*, and /ɪz/ as in /bædʒɪz/ *badges*. Because the alternation between /s/, /z/ and /ɪz/ is regular, we can incorporate a rule in the grammar (and we will be doing that below) which predicts how the plural is realised (cf. section 7.3).

The rules whose job it is to account for the alternations in the representation of morphemes are called MORPHOPHONEMIC RULES. Normally a morphophonemic rule will say, 'Morpheme M is to be realised by allomorph X in this context, by allomorph Y in that context, and by allomorph Z in some other context' etc. The allomorph with the widest distribution is usually taken as the UNDERLYING REPRESENTATION (also called the UNDERLYING FORM or BASE FORM).

At first sight it might seem reasonable to assume that all one needs to do is to provide a list of the allomorphs of a morpheme together with the environments where they are found. Rules may seem to complicate matters gratuitously. However, closer examination of the evidence suggests otherwise. Listing might have some merit but it also has the drawback of failing to show that there is usually a well-motivated phonetic basis to the alternation in the realisation of morphemes. It is important to separate things that belong together for some good reason from things thrown together by chance. My contention is that *normally* the list of allomorphs of a morpheme is not a random collection of morphs. The allomorphs bear a strong phonological resemblance to each other. This is because all the allomorphs of a morpheme are normally derived from a single underlying representation. The underlying representation is the only form that appears in the lexicon. But in the SURFACE REPRESENTATIONS (also called PHONETIC REPRESENTATIONS) the morpheme may be realised by different forms, depending on the context where it occurs. The allomorphs, whose distribution is predictable by rule, are not entered in the lexicon in order to keep dictionary entries simple. The rules express any generalisations that can be made about the distribution of allomorphs.

In the case of the regular English plural, /z/ is the allomorph that occurs in the widest range of environments. It occurs after any vowel and after all voiced consonants except the half-dozen sibilants /s z, ʃ ʒ, tʃ dʒ/. So /z/ is set up as the underlying form. In their underlying representations in the lexicon, all nouns with the regular plural have the /-z/ suffix. But that /z/ appears in the surface representation as /s/, /ɪz/ or /z/ depending on the phonetic properties of the final sound of the stem to which it is suffixed:

[5.1] *Phonologically conditioned allomorphs of the plural morpheme*
  a. Underlying /-z/ is realised as /-s/ in the surface represen-
     tation if a stem ends in a voiceless consonant which is
     not a STRIDENT CORONAL. (A STRIDENT CONSONANT is a
     hissing sibilant. A coronal is a consonant made with the
     tip or the blade of the tongue touching the upper front
     teeth or the part of the roof of the mouth extending up
     to where the soft palate begins).

     This means that /-z/ is realised as /-s/ after /p t k f
     θ/.

	Underlying representation	*Surface representation*
lips	/lɪp-z/	/lɪps/
maps	/mæp-z/	/mæps/
sheets	/ʃiːt-z/	/ʃiːts/
brats	/bræt-z/	/bræts/
mark	/mɑːk-z/	/mɑːks/
leeks	/liːk-z/	/liːks/
serfs	/sɜːf-z/	/sɜːfs/
chief	/tʃiːf-z/	/tʃiːfs/
oaths	/əʊθ-z/	/əʊθs/
moths	/mɒθ-z/	/mɒθs/

  b. Underlying /-z/ is realised as /-z/ in the surface represen-
     tation if a stem ends in a voiced sound which is not a
     strident coronal.

     This means that /-z/ is suffixed after the consonantal
     segments /b d g v ð m n ŋ l r w/ and after any vowel.

	Underlying representation	*Surface representation*
tubs	/tʌb-z/	/tʌbz/
lads	/læd-z/	/lædz/
mugs	/mʌg-z/	/mʌgz/
groves	/grəʊv-z/	/grəʊvz/
lathes	/leɪð-z/	/leɪðz/
brooms	/bru:m-z/	/bru:mz/
tons	/tɒn-z/	/tɒnz/
songs	/sɒŋ-z/	/sɒŋz/
spells	/spel-z/	/spelz/
cars	/kɑ:r-z/ or /kɑ:-z/	/kɑ:rz/ or /kɑ:z/
cows	/kaʊ-z/	/kaʊz/
days	/deɪ-z/	/deɪz/
seas	/si:-z/	/si:z/
shoes	/ʃu:-z/	/ʃu:z/

c. Underlying /z/ is realised as /-ɪz/ in the surface representation if a stem ends in a consonant which is both (i) strident and (ii) coronal. This means that /-ɪz/ is the allomorph selected after the sibilants /s z ʃ ʒ tʃ dʒ/, with /ɪ/ separating the coronal sibilant of the stem from that of the suffix.

We can envisage the sort of analysis below to account for the realisation of this allomorph. I have set it out as a blow-by-blow account for clarity of exposition. But I am not suggesting that these stages need to be gone through one after the other. There is no reason why they should not all happen simultaneously.

(i)   The consonant /z/ is introduced by the morphological rule of plural suffixation, e.g. /læs-z/.

(ii) The vowel /ɪ/ is inserted to separate the strident coronal of the stem from that of the suffix. (English does allow word-final clusters like /ʃs/, /sz/, /ʒz/ etc. when a suffix follows a stem.)
      This gives:
      /læs-z/ → /læs-ɪ-z/

(iii) The selection of /z/ rather than /s/ is a foregone conclusion as now /-z/ is preceded by a vowel, which is voiced. So, we get /læs-ɪ-z/ → /læsɪz/, not */læs-ɪs/.

	Underlying representation	Surface representation
lasses	/læs-z/ → /læs-ɪz/	/læsɪz/
cheeses	/tʃiːz-z/ → /tʃiːz-ɪz/	/tʃiːzɪz/
ashes	/æʃ-z/ → /æʃ-ɪz/	/æʃɪz/
bridges	/brɪdʒ-z/ → /brɪdʒ-ɪz/	/brɪdʒɪz/
finches	/fɪntʃ-z/ → /fɪntʃ-ɪz/	/fɪntʃɪz/
charges	/tʃɑːdʒ-z/ → /tʃɑːdʒ-ɪz/	/tʃɑːdʒɪz/

As [5.1] shows, the selection of allomorph of the plural morpheme is conditioned by phonological considerations. In each case the allomorph selected is one that has the same affinity with the last sound of the stem to which it is suffixed. Ignoring the subtleties of the situation, the essence of the generalisation that we need to capture is this: allomorphs of the plural agree in voicing with the final sound of the stem to which they are attached.

ASSIMILATION is the name given to this kind of 'agreement' which has the effect of making one sound become more like another sound in its neighbourhood. So, voiceless final consonants in the stem require the voiceless fricative allomorph /s/ while voiced final consonants go with the voiced fricative /z/. However, where following this procedure would result in two sibilants being right next to each other, the vowel /ɪ/ (or /ə/ in some dialects) is inserted between the last consonant and the suffix (as in *lasses* /læsɪz/ or /læsəz/). This phenomenon of vowel insertion is also called SCHWA EPENTHESIS (schwa being the name of the vowel /ə/).

Assimilation is normally the reason for the phonological conditioning of allomorphs. A morpheme may have more than one mask. It may masquerade as one of several allomorphs when the sounds that represent it are modified so that they become more like some other sound(s) in the environment where it appears. An allomorph wearing a suitable phonological mask is chosen to suit each set of phonological circumstances.

The phonological modification, as mentioned at the beginning of this chapter, can affect bases as well as affixes. So far we have seen a suffix with several phonologically conditioned allomorphs. Now we will look at bases that change when an affix is attached.

In some nouns which end in a labial or dental voiceless fricative, i.e. /f/ or /θ/ (spelled as *-th* and *-f*), the final consonant gets voiced to /v/ and /ð/ respectively when the plural suffix /-z/ is present. The voicing is much more common with the nouns ending in /f/ than those ending in /θ/.

[5.2]

	Plural	Genitive
wife	wives	wife's
wolf	wolves	wolf's
calf	calves	calf's
thief	thieves	thief's
leaf	leaves	leaf's
life	lives	life's
knife	knives	knife's
sheaf	sheaves	sheaf's

In [5.2] the final sound of the noun stem ending in /f/ shows two contrasting behaviours when /-z/ is suffixed. If the /-z/ represents the plural of the noun as in *wives* (< *wife* (singular)) the final /-f/ changes to /v/. But where the /-s/ represents the genitive morpheme as in *the wife's job*, no such change takes place (**the wive's job*) (cf. Swadesh and Voeglin 1939).

This is typical. The phonological conditioning of allomorphs seldom operates in a manner that is totally predictable on the basis of phonological information alone. It is frequently the case that given precisely the same phonological situation, we can observe differing patterns of phonological behaviour depending on the morphological context in which an allomorph appears. We saw this when we contrasted the voicing of the final /f/ in the plural with the non-application of the voicing rule in the genitive where no change takes place although in both cases as /s/ follows a voiceless fricative.

Let us now briefly turn to nouns ending in the voiceless dental fricative /θ/ (spelled *-th*). The spelling always remains the same, and the pronunciation does not normally change either. It is /θ/ when next to a consonant (as in *lengths, births* etc.). Usually it is also /θ/ after vowels (e.g. *moths, cloths* etc.). But in a few cases, when the final /θ/ is preceded by a vowel, it optionally undergoes voicing. So the words below have two possible plurals:

[5.3]

	Voiceless /θ/	Voiced /ð/
baths	/ba:θs/	/ba:ðz/
youth	/ju:θs/	/ju:ðz/
wreath	/ri:θs/	/ri:ðz/

There is a change in progress in the way nouns ending in /f/ form their plural. However, the direction of change is towards eliminating the allomorph of the root with the sound /v/ so that we only have the /f/ form. *Hooves* and *rooves* are being supplanted by *hoofs* and *roofs* as the plurals of *hoof* and *roof*. There are many nouns ending in /f/ whose last sound never changes in the plural. viz. *chiefs* /tʃiːfs/ (*/tʃiːvz/), *laughs* /lɑːfs/ (*/lɑːvz/), *beliefs* /bɪliːfs/ (*/bɪliːvz/). The ongoing elimination of the /f/ ~ /v/ alternation (in *hooves* etc.) is a way of making a quirky part of the system fall into line.

To sum up, the behaviour of /f/-final nouns illustrates two properties of morphophonemic rules:

(i) Morphophonemic rules tend to be exception ridden. They rarely apply to all forms with the appropriate phonological properties. Much of the morphophonemic alternation reflects incomplete phonological changes in the history of a language. In some respects a language is like an army marching in one direction when the order is given to change direction. Some soldiers fail to hear (or choose to ignore) the order to change direction. Thus, we have seen that some /f/s are phonetically realised as [v] in the plural and others are not.

In this respect morphophonemic rules differ from purely allophonic rules found in phonology. ALLOPHONIC RULES (which have the job of specifying the phonetic realisation of phonemes) apply automatically and blindly wherever the requisite phonetic environment that triggers the alternation is present. For instance, any vowel that appears before a voiced consonant is slightly lengthened. Compare the /e/ in *bet* [bet] with the slightly longer [e·] of *bed* [be·d]. (The raised dot marks this slight lengthening.) The lengthening takes place regardless of which morphemes are represented. It only fails to happen if the phonological circumstances are not right.

(ii) Morphophonemic rules are triggered by the presence of certain morphemes. They are tied rules which are only permitted to operate if certain morphological information sets them off. Thus, for example, in the data in [5.2] above if suffix /-z/ represents the plural morpheme, it assimilates the voicing of the last sound of the stem, but if it represents the genitive, it does not.

5.2.1 Selecting underlying representations

I argued earlier that by setting up a single underlying representation from which different allomorphs of a morpheme are derived by phonological rules we are able to capture generalisations about the phonological behaviour of morphemes. The distribution of the different allomorphs of a morpheme is normally not arbitrary. We saw, for example, that voice assimilation is the principle behind the different allomorph guises adopted by the /-z/ plural suffix. The idea of generality is vital. It is the principle that led us to posit /-z/ as the underlying representation from which the allomorphs /-z/, /ɪz/ and /-s/ are derived.

Often the same phonological factor that determines the morphophonemic alternations of one morpheme is also relevant in alternations of several other morphemes. Therefore what is needed is a solution that enables us to make a general statement of phonological conditioning which is valid for several morphemes. For instance, if you look at the suffix of the third person singular present tense forms of verbs, you will see that it shows exactly the same alternations as the /-z/ plural suffix of nouns. If we made separate statements for these two morphemes we would be missing this generalisation.

[5.4] *Phonologically conditioned allomorphs of the third person singular*

    a. Underlying /-z/ is realised as /-s/ if a stem ends in a voiceless consonant which is not a strident coronal. This means that /-s/ is added after /p t k f θ/.

	Underlying representation		*Surface representation*
skips	/skɪp-z/	→	/skɪps/
lights	/laɪt-z/	→	/laɪts/
likes	/laɪk-z/	→	/laɪks/
laughs	/lɑːf-z/	→	/lɑːfs/
baths	/bɑːθ-z/	→	/bɑːθs/

    b. Underlying /-z/ is realised as /-z/ if a stem ends in a voiced sound which is not a strident coronal. This means that /-z/ is added after the consonantal segments /b d g v m n ŋ l r w/ and after any vowel, e.g.:

	Underlying representation		Surface representation
roams	/rəʊm-z/	→	/rəʊmz/
calls	/kɔ:l-z/	→	/kɔ:lz/
skids	/skɪd-z/	→	/skɪdz/
brags	/bræg-z/	→	/brægz/
sees	/si:-z/	→	/si:z/
shows	/ʃəʊ-z/	→	/ʃəʊz/

c. Underlying /-z/ is realised as /-ɪz/ if a stem ends in a consonant which is both strident and coronal.

This means that /-ɪz/ is added after the consonantal segments /s z ʃ ʒ tʃ dʒ/, with /ɪ/ being inserted to separate coronal sibilants. (See p. 85 above.)

	Underlying representation			Surface representation
misses	/mɪs-z/	→	/mɪs-ɪz/	/mɪsɪz/
wishes	/wɪʃ-z/	→	/wɪʃ-ɪz/	/wɪʃiz/
launches	/lɔ:ntʃ-z/	→	/lɔ:ntʃ-ɪz/	/lɔ:ntʃɪz/
touches	/tʌtʃ-z/	→	/tʌtʃ-ɪz/	/tʌtʃɪz/
cringes	/krɪndʒ-z/	→	/krɪndʒ-ɪz/	/krɪndʒɪz/

The tables in [5.1] and [5.4] are virtually identical. Merely listing separately the allomorphs of the third person singular present tense and those of the plural would fail to show that there is something very predictable and systematic about the distribution of the allomorphs of these morphemes – namely, that they all are subject to voice assimilation. What is required is a general statement to the effect that in English inflectional morphology, a suffix consonant AGREES IN VOICING with the last segment of the stem. But if the last stem consonant is very similar to the suffix consonant (e.g. if both sounds are coronal stridents) insert /ɪ/ to separate them. The importance of voice assimilation will become even clearer when we look at more inflectional suffixes later in this chapter.

5.2.2 Derivations

Underlying representations can be quite different from phonetic representations. To go from UNDERLYING REPRESENTATIONS in the dictionary entries of morphemes to their actual SURFACE (PHONETIC) REPRESENTATIONS which occur in speech, phonological representations of morphemes may go through a metaphorical journey involving modifications at various stages. We will call that journey a DERIVATION. A derivation entails applying phonological rules which, step by step or, more likely, simultaneously, alter the underlying representation and bring it closer and closer to the ultimate surface representation.

As we have already seen, in the case of the /-z/ noun plural and third person verb endings, the derivation involves two rules:

[5.5] a. Rule 1:

/ɪ/ *insertion* (or *schwa epenthesis*)

If the stem-final sound is a strident coronal, insert /ɪ/ after it. (In some dialects, the vowel inserted is /ə/ (e.g. *buses* is pronounced /bʌsəz/). So this rule is also called SCHWA EPENTHESIS.)

b. Rule 2:

Voice assimilation

Make the suffix agree in voicing with the preceding sound if it does not do so already.

(This ensures that the coronal sibilant that is suffixed is voiceless /-s/ after /p t k f θ/, and voiced /-z/ elsewhere.)

Four illustrative examples of derivations are given in [5.6]:

[5.6]

Underlying *representation*	/mæt-z/	/læd-z/	/ʃuː-z/	/pɪtʃ-z/
Rule 1				
/ɪ/ *insertion*	inapplic.	inapplic.	inapplic.	/pɪtʃ-ɪz/
Rule 2				
Voice assimilation	/mæt-s/	inapplic. (Already voiced)	inapplic. (Already voiced)	inapplic. (Already voiced)
Surface *representation*	/mæts/ 'mats	/lædz/ 'lads'	/ʃuːz/ 'shoes'	/pɪtʃɪz/ 'pitches'

The interaction between rules in a derivation is crucially important. Applying the right rules in the wrong order will yield an incorrect output. Here voice assimilation must not apply before /ɪ/ epenthesis or else we will get the incorrect output: /pɪtʃ-z/ → /pɪtʃ-s/ → /pɪtʃ-ɪ-s → /pɪtʃɪs/ → *[pɪtʃɪs].

The account of phonological conditioning motivated by voice assimilation which has been provided for the regular plural (spelt -*s*) can be extended to the regular past tense morpheme (spelt -*ed*) with very little modification (see also section 7.3). The past tense has three allomorphs. Their selection follows very similar principles to those that govern the selection of the allomorphs of the noun plural and the third person singular which we have described:

[5.7] a. After the alveolar stops /t/ and /d/ select /-ɪd/ (or /-əd/ depending on the dialect), e.g. *acted* /æktɪd/, *lifted* /lɪftɪd/, *added* /ædɪd/, *wounded* /wʊndɪd/

b. After any voiceless consonant other than /t/ select /t/, e.g. *taped* /teɪpt/, *fished* /fɪʃt/, *sparked* /spɑːkt/, *minced* /mɪnst/

c. After any vowel or any voiced consonant other than /d/ select /d/, e.g. *tamed* /teɪmd/, *boozed* /buːzd/, *waged* /weɪdʒd/, *cooled* /kuːld/

If the underlying representation of this morpheme is assumed to be /-d/, a derivation featuring two rules we have already used in our treatment of inflectional morphemes, namely /ɪ/ epenthesis and voice assimilation, will account for its surface realisation:

[5.8] a. */ɪ/ epenthesis* (or *schwa epenthesis*)
In order to prevent two alveolar stops from being next to each other, insert /ɪ/ before the suffix /-d/ in cases where the stem ends in one of the alveolar stops /t/ and /d/, e.g., *added* /æd-d// → /æd-ɪd/ → /ædɪd/;
lifted /lɪft-d/ → /lɪft-ɪd/ → /lɪftɪd/

b. *Voice assimilation*
The suffix agrees in voicing with the last sound in the stem to which it is attached,
e.g. *taped* /teɪpd/ → /teɪp-t/ → /teɪpt/;
tamed teɪm-d/ → /teɪm-d/ (no change) /teɪmd/

Note again that assimilation must not apply before epenthesis lest we obtain the incorrect forms * [lɪftɪt] from derivations like /lɪft-d/ → /lɪft-t/ → /lɪftɪt/ → *[lɪftɪt].

With this we will leave phonological conditioning of allomorphs and turn to other factors which determine the distribution of allomorphs.

5.3. PHONOLOGY IN THE SHADE: LEXICAL AND GRAMMATICAL CONDITIONING

The selection of allomorphs of *root morphemes* is sometimes determined not by the phonological environment but rather by the grammatical context in which the morpheme occurs. Different allomorphs of the root may be used depending on the grammatical word of which it forms part. I will illustrate this by contrasting the base form, the past tense form and the past participle form of the following verbs:

[5.9]	*Base*	*Past tense*	*Past participle*
a. jump	He *jump-ed* yesterday.	He has *jump-ed*.
call	He *call-ed* yesterday.	He has *call-ed*.
b. ride	He *rode* yesterday.	He has *ridden*.
drive	He *drove* yesterday.	He has *driven*.
c. sing	He *sang* yesterday.	He has *sung*.
stink	He *stank* yesterday.	He has *stunk*.

In [5.9a] regular verb stems like *jump* remain unchanged in all three columns. The formation of the past tense and the past participle is simply accomplished by the suffixation of *-ed*. This contrasts with the verbs in [5.9b] and [5.9c] where the grammatical word that is realised by the word-form dictates the allomorph of the stem that is used. Thus in [5.9b] we see the base form *ride* (as in *I ride*). But if *ride* is in the past tense, it must be realised as *rode* and if it is the past participle that is required, then the form selected is *ridden*. Similarly, in [5.9c] the base form of *sing* is *sing* (as in *I sing*). But if *sing* is in the past tense, it must be realised as *sang* and if it is the past participle that is required, then the form selected is *sung*, and so on. This is a case of the selection allomorph of the root being solely conditioned by grammatical factors. Hence it is called GRAMMATICAL CONDITIONING.

The converse is also possible. The selection of INFLECTIONAL AFFIXES may be determined by the presence of a particular lexical root morpheme. Hence this is called LEXICAL CONDITIONING. A classic example of this in English is the way in which *ox* forms its plural as *oxen* rather than **oxes*. Phonologically and grammatically comparable words like *fox ~ foxes* and *box ~ boxes* form their plurals using the regular /-z/ suffix. In the grammar and phonology of modern English, there is nothing that explains why *ox* has *oxen* as its plural. The suffix *-en* singles out this particular word. In other words, *-en* is a lexically conditioned allomorph of the plural morpheme.

Our final example involves nouns which remain unchanged in the plural:

5.10 *Singular*: sheep, deer, equipment, aircraft
Plural: sheep, deer, equipment, aircraft

If a farmer said to you: *I have lost just one sheep but my neighbour has lost 200 sheep this year*, you would know that *sheep* is singular in '*one sheep*' but plural in '*200 sheep*' although the same word-form *sheep* is used in both cases. The plural of *sheep* and other words of this ilk is formed by adding a ZERO SUFFIX, as it were. In spite of the absence of any overt number marking, such nouns can function as plurals. A child acquiring English needs to recognise and memorise, word by word, the set of nouns which take zero, rather than the standard /-z/, suffix because the distribution of the zero plural suffix is lexically conditioned.

5.4 MADNESS WITHOUT METHOD: SUPPLETION

Occasionally, there is no method in the madness. This is so in a tiny minority of cases when SUPPLETION takes place. Then the choice of the allomorphs of a root morpheme that serve in different grammatical contexts is phonologically arbitrary: the allomorphs in question bear no phonological resemblance to each other.

That is what happens in the case of the verb *go*, which has *went* as its past tense form and *gone* as its past participle. The forms *good, better* and *best* which belong to the adjective *good* also show suppletion since the relationship between the morphs representing the root morpheme is phonologically arbitrary. It would plainly make no sense to claim that there is a single underlying representation in the dictionary from which *go* and *went* or *good* and *better* are derived. The best we can do is to content ourselves with listing these allomorphs together under the same entry in the dictionary.

Normally, the word-forms representing the same lexeme show some phonetic similarity (see [5.9] for example). However, when suppletion occurs, the word-form that realises a lexeme bears no reasonable resemblance to the other word-forms representing the same lexeme.

Mercifully, the majority of words follow general rules (for example adding the suitable phonologically conditioned allomorph of the plural /-z/ suffix) and word-forms belonging to the same lexeme are phonologically similar to some degree. Acquiring a language for the most part involves working out these general rules rather than using brute force to commit morphemes and their allomorphs to memory.

5.5 SUMMARY

In this chapter we have seen that many morphemes have several allomorphs. The selection of allomorph to use on a given occasion may be conditioned by phonological, grammatical or lexical factors. Normally, phonological conditioning is due to assimilation: the allomorph that occurs in a particular context is the one that is most similar to the sounds found in neighbouring forms. However, the choice of allomorph is sometimes grammatically conditioned. If a root morpheme occurs in a particular grammatical word, then it must have a certain specified allomorph. Or, if an affix morpheme occurs with a given root, it may require the selection of a given affix (lexical conditioning). Very occasionally, allomorphs may be selected arbitrarily (suppletion).

Phonological conditioning is the commonest determinant of the distribution of allomorphs. When allomorphs are phonologically conditioned, we can make general statements about their distribution by positing an underlying representation of the morpheme which is entered in the lexicon from which the various allomorphs are derived by rule.

EXERCISES

1. Using at least one fresh illustrative example, explain:

assimilation	zero suffix
phonological conditioning	grammatical conditioning
underlying representation	lexical conditioning
morphophonemic rule	suppletion
derivation	

2. Make a phonemic transcription of the data below which exemplify the regular allomorphs of the past tense and past participle morphemes:

strapped	shelled	previewed	accented
bewitched	owned	obeyed	courted
attacked	mesmerised	pursued	alluded
quenched	merged	sighed	doubted
based	scrubbed	wooed	advocated
fished	slogged	paid	seeded

a. Write a morphophonemic rule that states the distribution of the different allomorphs of the past tense morpheme.

b. Provide a derivation of *strapped, shelled, previewed, accented* and *seeded*.

3. Make a phonemic transcription of the following words:

imprudent	insane	incalculable	inexpressive
immigrant	ingressive	inject	impregnate
inlet	impel	induction	incarnate
impractical	innumerable	incapable	inarticulate
involuntary	indirectness	inglorious	inorganic
import	intemperateness	incomparable	inalienable
inbred	indoors	imprison	implant

a. With the help of a good dictionary, state the meaning of each prefix morpheme that you can identify.

b. Using your phonemic transcription, list the prefixes together with their allomorphs.

c. Attempt to write morphophonemic rules that make a very general and thorough statement that predicts the distribution of the allomorphs of the prefixes that you have recognised. If you encounter any variation, or any difficulties, comment on them.

4. Study the following words and answer the questions that follow:

alumni	vertebrae	automata
stimuli	larvae	phenomena
loci	algae	criteria

a. All the words above have been imported into English from other languages. With the help of a good dictionary, find out where they came from.

b. Write down the singular form of each noun.

c. Identify the plural suffix in each noun.

d. Determine whether the selection of the appropriate plural allomorph in these words is phonologically, grammatically or lexically conditioned.

Chapter 6

A lexicon with layers

6.1 THE NATURE OF THE LEXICON

This chapter is concerned with the lexicon from the perspective of the linguist constructing a model of language structure rather than the typical lexicographer's dictionary. We will address questions like: What should be included in the lexicon? In what form should it be included? How does the lexicon relate to the rest of the grammar? In Chapter 11 we will return to the lexicon from a different angle. Our concern there will be the MENTAL LEXICON to which language users must have access when constructing and interpreting sentences.

Our examination of the nature of the lexicon here will concentrate on the relationship between phonology and morphology in word-formation. But other matters will not be completely ignored. We will also deal more generally with the role of the lexicon in grammatical theory and how it relates to other modules (cf. section 1.1). This is in keeping with the view of the place of the lexicon in mainstream linguistics today where the interaction of the different modules of the grammar has been an area of major research in recent years.

Everyone agrees that the lexicon must contain a LIST of morphemes and simple words (in the sense of lexemes) because the relationship between their meaning and their form is arbitrary. Unless we are told what a word like *dew* means, we have no way of working out its meaning. All morphemes must also be listed in the lexicon since their meaning is unpredictable (there is no way of predicting what *dew*,-*ity* or -*ism* means).

But it is not necessary to list all the words (i.e. lexical items). As we saw in section (4.4.3) where we discussed compounds, many words have meanings that are COMPOSITIONAL. Compositionality means that the semantic interpretation of a complex semantic unit is predictable from the meaning of its parts. Morphology and the lexicon need to be equipped with rules that allow the creation and analysis of any word that is compositional. If that is done, it is not necessary to list the meanings of words like *smok-er, iron-ing, pre-arrang(e)-ed* and *farm-labour-er* for the meanings of these words can be computed from the meanings of their parts. By the same token, it is not necessary for speakers to memorise the meanings of such words. They can just work them out.

In the theoretical framework that we are using, morphology is part of the lexicon. The lexicon is not a passive list of words and their meanings. It is not simply like an anatomy laboratory where existing words are dissected on a slab into their constituent morphemes, and examined under a microscope. No, in this theory the lexicon is much more than that. It is also a place full of vitality where rules are used actively to create new words. To perform this function, the lexicon must include in dictionary entries these types of information about each simple word and each morpheme:

[6.1]   (i)   its meaning
         (ii) its phonological properties
         (iii) its syntactic properties
         (iv) its morphological properties

The reasons for including these kinds of information in dictionary entries will be made clear below.

6.2 MORPHOLOGICAL INFORMATION IN THE LEXICON

The lexicon needs to contain various kinds of morphological information. Words behave differently in the language depending on the morphological subclasses they belong to. For instance, morphological rules often apply to words marked as belonging to specified subclasses. Thus, with regard to number, in English we need to know whether a particular word is a COUNT NOUN and has a plural form (e.g. *tables, voices, children* etc.) or a NON-COUNT NOUN that has no plural form (e.g. *furniture, gold, music,* etc.). Further, we need to know whether a morpheme is native or of foreign origin as this may affect the range of morphemes that can co-occur with it in words. For example, some affixes borrowed from French (e.g. *-aire* as in *millionaire, communautaire, doctrinaire, solitaire*) only combine with roots adopted from that language.

6.3 SYNTACTIC INFORMATION IN THE LEXICON

We cannot think of word-formation in total isolation from the rest of the grammar. The lexicon is not merely a list of the idiosyncratic syntactic properties of morphemes and lexical items. It is has to be much more than that because much of the syntactic behaviour of words is predictable. For instance, normally if a TRANSITIVE VERB (i.e. a verb that takes a direct object) can occur in sentences like the ones in [6.2a], it can also occur in sentenes like those in [6.2b]:

[6.2]

a. *Active voice*

SUBJECT	VERB	DIRECT OBJECT
The children	saw	the lions.
The thief	stole	his money.
Robin	soaked	the clothes.

b. *Passive voice*

SUBJECT	VERB	BY-NP (AGENT)
The lions	were seen	by the children.
His money	was stolen	by the thief.
The clothes	were soaked	by Robin.

It is not a peculiarity of the verbs *see, steal* and *soak* that they appear in active and passive sentences. This is a general characteristic of English verbs. So it should be captured by a general rule in the lexicon stating that corresponding to a passive sentence there is an active sentence with a transitive verb preceded by the subject and followed by the direct object. In the passive sentence, the NP that would function as the direct object in the active version of the sentence functions as the subject and precedes the verb, while the NP that would be the subject if the sentence were in the active follows the verb and is part of an agent phrase introduced by the preposition *by* (Bresnan 1982a). The verb itself also undergoes modification. A form of the verb *be* is put before it and the past participle *-en* or *-ed* is attached to it. In brief, the lexicon suffix must include the information needed to determine the syntactic behaviour of a word. Much of this information will be applicable to more than one word. So it can be captured by rules like the passive rule which we have just discussed.

6.4 DOES IT RING TRUE? (PHONOLOGICAL INFORMATION)

Obviously, the lexical entry of a morpheme must include its pronunciation. The dictionary needs to say that *key* is pronounced /ki:/, as is *quay*; it needs to show that *victuals* is pronounced /vɪtlz/, and so on. But some phonological information is not specific to a particular entry. As we saw in section (2.2.1), in English certain combinations of sounds are permitted in certain positions in a word while others are not. Putative words like **tmiss*, **dnell*, **gnover* are forbidden by phonotactic rules. Any putative word must ring true. It must be a potentially well-formed phonological string. The lexicon only allows in putative words that sound right. Word-formation rules are not allowed to concoct forms that are unpronounceable.

This applies not only to the rules that create new morphemes like (**tmiss*) but also to the rules that add affixes. The rules that attach inflectional suffixes are not allowed to form a word like *twerd-s* [twɜ:d-s] which has a voiceless [s] inflectional suffix that does not agree in voicing with [d], the final consonant of the stem which is voiced. *Twerd-s* must be pronounced [twɜ:d-z]. The voice assimilation requirement would equally debar a putative noun plural form like *peeds* *[pi:ds].

The dictionary needs also to indicate any phonological peculiarities of derivational morphemes. For instance, the entry for the suffix morpheme *-al* needs to show that its *-al* allomorph is not added to bases ending in /l/. After a base ending in /l/, the right allomorph is *-ar*. If someone said something like **motoral* (instead of the correct *motorial*) meaning 'pertaining to motion' you might accept it as a possible word that you just happen not to know. But if they said **regulal* (meaning *regular*) you would raise your eyebrows.

For literate speakers, the dictionary will obviously need to contain information about the orthographic form of lexical entries, especially in cases where the written forms are idiosyncratic or unpredictable. You need to have access to lexical information such as /wɪmɪn/ is spelt *women* /baʊ/ is spelt *bough* etc. There is no way one would be able to work out these spellings unaided. (See Chapter 7 for further discussion.)

6.5 RENDEZVOUS WITH LEXICAL PHONOLOGY AND MORPHOLOGY

We have established that morphological rules are intimately coupled with phonological rules. In the rest of the chapter we will examine more closely the relationship between phonological and morphological rules in the lexicon. The theoretical framework in which the phonology–morphology interplay will be discussed is the theory of LEXICAL PHONOLOGY AND MORPHOLOGY developed by a number of generative linguists over the years (cf. Allen 1978, Siegel 1974, Kiparsky 1982a, 1982b, 1983, Halle and Mohanan 1985, Mohanan 1986, Rubach 1984, Pulleyblank 1986, Goldsmith 1990, Spencer 1991 and Katamba 1989, 1993). We will refer to it as lexical morphology for short.

6.5.1 Neutral and non-neutral affixes

The interaction of morphology and phonology is best approached from the perspective of the phonological properties of groups of affixes. As mentioned in section (4.4.1), there are two types of affixes in the English lexicon. One type is NEUTRAL in its effects on the stem to which it is attached and the other type is NON-NEUTRAL. The latter cause various changes in the vowels, consonants or stress of the bases to which they are affixed. The account presented here draws on the work of Kiparsky (1982a, 1982b).

In [6.3] I present some common neutral suffixes whose presence does not cause any phonological changes in the base to which they are attached:

[6.3]
a. -ing
   decide   /dɪˈsaɪd/   deciding   /ˈdɪsaɪdɪŋ/
   remind   /rɪˈmaɪnd/   reminding   /reˈmaɪndɪŋ/
b. -ly
   expensive /ɪkˈspensɪv/   expensively   /ɪkˈspensɪvlɪ/
   sullen   /ˈsʌlən/   sullenly   /ˈsʌlənlɪ/
c. -less
   joy   /ˈdʒɔɪ/   joyless   /ˈdʒɔɪləs/
   penny   /ˈpenɪ/   penniless   /ˈpenɪləs/
d. -er
   save   /ˈseɪv/   saver   /ˈseɪvə/
   distil   /dɪˈstɪl/   distiller   /dɪˈstɪlə/

e. *-ness*

lively	/ˈlaɪvlɪ/	liveliness	/ˈlaɪvlɪnəs/
contagious	/kənˈteɪdʒəs/	contagiousness	/kənˈteɪdʒəsnəs/
steadfast	/ˈstedfɑːst/	steadfastness	/ˈstedfɑːstnəs/

By constrast, the presence of a non-neutral affix sets off phonological fireworks. Some or all of these things may happen: stress may shift from one syllable to another (as in *Canadian* in [6.4a]), some of the vowel segments may be modified (as in *mammalian* in [6.4a]) or the consonants may change as in *electricity*. You can observe these changes in [6.4]:

[6.4] a. *Input:*   *Output:*
      Noun   [*-ian*]

Noun		[*-ian*]$_{Adj.}$	
Boston	/ˈbɒstən/	Bostonian	/bʊˈstəʊnɪən/
Cameron	/ˈkæmərən/	Cameronian	/kæməˈrʊnɪən/
Canada	/ˈkænədə/	Canadian	/kəˈneɪdɪən/
civil	/ˈsɪvl/	civilian	/sɪˈvɪlɪən/
mammal	/ˈmæml/	mammalian	/məˈmeɪlɪən/
Spenser	/ˈspensə/	Spenserian	/spenˈsɪərɪən

b. *Input:*   *Output*

Noun		[*-ic*]$_{Adj.}$	
fantasy	/ˈfæntəsɪ/	fantastic	/fənˈtæstɪk/
hieroglyph	/ˈhɪərəʊglɪf/	hieroglyphic	/hɪərəʊˈglɪfɪk/
idiosyncrasy	/ɪdɪəˈsɪnkrəsɪ/	idiosyncratic	/ɪdɪəsɪnˈkrætɪk/
metal	/ˈmetl/	metallic	/meˈtælɪk/
system	/ˈsɪstəm/	systemic	/sɪˈstiːmɪk/
electric	/ɪˈlektrɪk/	electricity	/ɪlekˈtrɪsətɪ/

c. *Input:*   *Output*

Noun		[*-ify*]$_{Verb}$	
carbon	/ˈkɑːbən/	carbonify	/kɑːˈbɒnɪfaɪ/
history	/ˈhɪstərɪ/	historify	hɪˈstɒrɪfaɪ/
object	/ˈɒbdʒekt/	objectify	/ɒbˈdʒektɪfaɪ/
person	/ˈpɜːsn/	personify	/pəˈsɒnɪfaɪ/
solid	/ˈsɒlɪd/	solidify	/səˈlɪdɪfaɪ/

Note: The suffix *-ian* (found in Canadian) can form both nouns and adjectives.

These suffixes attract stress like magnets attract iron. When any of the three suffixes is present, stress shifts from its original position and lands on the syllable immediately preceding the suffix. In this they are typical of many non-neutral affixes. As for the changes in the vowels, the broad generalisation is that vowels on which the stress falls are more prominent than they would be when they appear unstressed. For instance, a short vowel like /ɪ/ is replaced by a long vowel like /iː/ (cf. /sɪstəm/ → /sɪstiːmɪk/) or by a diphthong (cf. /ˈkæmərən/ → /kæməˈrəʊnɪən/).

For the most part neutral affixes are native, forming part of the Anglo-Saxon inheritance of English. But most non-neutral suffixes are LATINATE. They came in with words borrowed (as permanent, non-returnable loans) from Latin and its daughter, French (see Chapter 10). An example of a native non-neutral suffix is the derivational suffix -th used to form abstract nouns from adjectives. This suffix triggers a vowel change in the base, e.g. *long* → *length*; *broad* → *breadth*; *wide* → *width*.

6.5.2 The lexicon is like a layered cake

Kiparsky and the other writers on lexical morphology cited above have shown that it makes good sense to organise our lexicon in terms of HIERARCHICAL STRATA (or LEVELS) in order to characterise the differences between the effects of neutral and non-neutral affixes.

Let us assume that all the non-neutral affixes are attached at one stratum in the lexicon, which we will call STRATUM 1. Let us further assume that all the neutral affixes are attached at another stratum, which we will call STRATUM 2. Stratum 1 (non-neutral) affixes are attached before the neutral affixes found at stratum 2. So in a derivation, processes taking place at stratum 1 come before those that take place at stratum 2 (cf. 5.2.2). The distinction between strata captures very broadly the distinction between native English affixes (stratum 2) and foreign affixes of French or Latin/ Greek origin (stratum 1).

In the lexicon derivations start off with the UNDERIVED ROOT (i.e. the naked root without affixes) and work their way through relevant rules starting at stratum 1 and then progressing through stratum 2. The theory attempts to reflect the fact that at each stratum morphological rules are bonded together with phonological rules. The application of a morphological rule brings in its wake the application of a phonological rule. The reason for this is easy to see. When in the process of word-formation we put morphemes together using morphological rules, we need to know how the forms that we create are pronounced.

Look back to the tables of suffixes in [6.3] and [6.4]. See how different types of lexical information play a role in word-formation. As you can see, in order to attach an affix to a base, you need to know which kind of bases it can go with. For instance, -ian is attached to noun bases to yield adjectives. Given the noun *Canada* you can form the adjective *Canadian*. If your intention is to form a verb from a noun, then -ian is not a suitable suffix. You must try instead another suffix, e.g. -ify (as in *solidify*). Of course, in addition to knowing the grammatical characteristics of the word resulting from affixation, you need to know what it will mean. This point is obvious. We will not dwell on it.

Knowing the meanings of the words formed and their syntactic characteristics is not enough. We need to know how our words are pronounced. By associating morphological rules directly with phonological rules that account for the pronunciation, we are able to address this problem effectively. As we saw in [6.3] and [6.4] batches of affixes can be shown to have broadly similar phonological effects. Rather than state these effects separately for each affix, it is preferable to state them in more general terms. That is what we are doing here when we say, for example, that suffixes like those in [6.4] are non-neutral. They cause changes in the location of stress or in the pronunciation of vowels or consonants, or both. If a suffix is placed at stratum 1, it can be expected to have disruptive phonological effects. Conversely, if a suffix is at stratum 2, we know that it will not cause phonological disruption in the base to which it is attached.

Sample derivations of representative words listed in [6.3] and [6.4] are provided below. In [6.5] only stratum 1 rules apply while in [6.6] only stratum 2 rules apply. But in [6.7] both stratum 1 and stratum 2 rules apply.

[6.5]　*Underived root*

Canada _{Noun} /ˈkænədə/

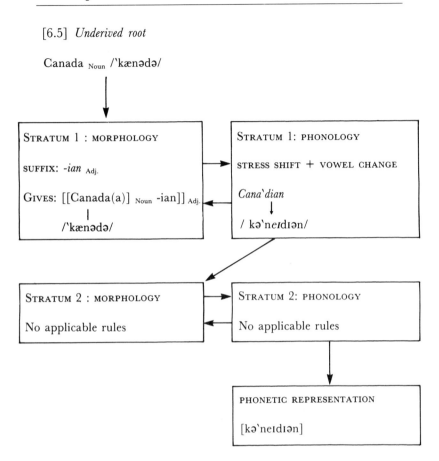

[6.6] *Underived root*

joy_{Noun} /ˈdʒɔɪ/

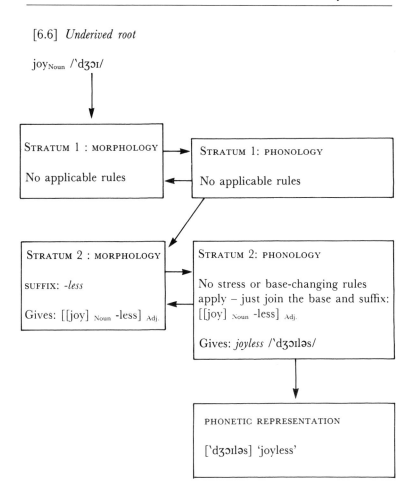

[6.7] *Underived root*

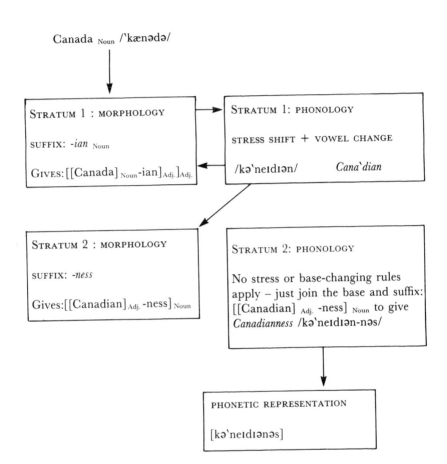

The claim that affixes are arranged on hierarchical strata has additional advantages. We will consider them briefly in turn.

First, as we saw in section (4.4.1), the order in which morphemes are arranged in words is normally rigidly fixed. Thus, *Canad-ian-ness* is the only permissible MORPHEME SEQUENCING in the word *Canadianness*. Any alternative arrangements of the same morphemes such as **ian-Canada-ness*, **Canada-ness-ian* etc. are forbidden. Clearly, in order to be able to construct words as speakers and writers and to decode their meanings as hearers and readers we need to know what the morphemes they contain mean when put together, but that in itself is not enough. If a word contains affixes we need to know where they go. We need to know if they are prefixes or suffixes. (It would not do to say **Is he ful-care?* if we want to mean *Is he care-ful?*)

Moreover, when several derivational affixes appear on the same side of a base as prefixes, or more likely in English as suffixes, there is a very general tendency for stratum 1 affixes to be closer to the root than stratum 2 ones. So, we have stratum 1 *-ian* right after the root and stratum 2 *-ness* on the outside as in *Canad(a)-ian-ness*. Further, as you will recall from section (4.4.1), derivational affixes usually go on the inside. They are nearer to the root than derivational suffixes, which are attached later and appear on the periphery of the word.

The second point concerns the way morphological rules interact in the lexicon. The organisation of strata in a hierarchical manner can be used to explain the phenomenon of BLOCKING whereby one rule makes a pre-emptive strike, robbing another rule of its potential input. I will illustrate blocking with two sets of examples, one from inflectional morphology and the other from derivational morphology.

In derivational morphology it is not uncommon to find two or more affixes with virtually identical, or at any rate closely related, meanings. In such situations, usually only one of those affixes can be attached to a particular base. You can observe this if you consider the ways of deriving from verbs AGENTIVE NOUNS (with the meaning 'someone who does X') by suffixing *-er* or *-ant*:

[6.8] a. *Agentive noun*   *Agentive noun*
          -er   -ant
          sell-er   contest-ant
          send-er   defend-ant
          gaol-er   serv-ant

There is no doubt that -er is the more productive of the two suffixes. Most verbs can be turned into agentive nouns meaning 'the doer of X' by suffixing -er. More existing and potential nouns are formed by suffixing -er than are formed by suffixing -ant.

The -ant suffix is at stratum 1. It requires stress to fall two syllables before it, if it does not do so already:

[6.9] a. *Stress-shifting*   b. *Stress already 2 syllables before*
            'applicant (< a'pply)   'accountant (<'account)
            'Protestant (pro'test)   'occupant ('occupy)

But -er is neutral and belongs to stratum 2 since it has no phonological special effects (cf. *'manage ~ 'manager; pro'duce; ~ pro'ducer* etc.).

The existence of a comparable stratum 1 affix attaching to the same class of bases and having a meaning that is very closely related to that of a stratum 2 affix usually deprives an otherwise general stratum 2 affix of its input. That is why, for example, the existence of *accountant*, formed at stratum 1, blocks the formation of **accounter*, and *applicant* blocks **applier*.

Observe, however, that blocking is only a strong tendency rather than an inviolable constraint. Sometimes closely related stratum 1 and stratum 2 affixes may be used with the same base on different occasions. Interestingly, this seldom results in synonymous words. Rather, what we tend to get is one word which has a broad meaning and another which has a narrower, specialised meaning. For instance, a *Protestant* is a member of a Reformed Christian church while a *protester* is anyone who undertakes a protest action, usually of a political nature. So even the Pope could be a 'protester' against some cause while a Protestant Pope is just not on the cards.

Thus compositionality may work only partially with some stratum 1 affixes: we may be able to work out their morphological and phonological properties but their semantic contribution to a word may be idiosyncratic. Where that is the case (cf. *Protestant*), listing in the dictionary will be needed, despite the residual element of semantic predictability.

The third point concerns PRODUCTIVITY. The relative productivity of morphemes is reflected in the hierarchical organisation of strata. It is significant that in our example -er, which is a phonologically neutral, stratum 2 suffix, is more productive than -ant, the non-neutral stratum 1 suffix. This is typical. Stratum 2 affixes are typically more productive than their stratum 1 counterparts. Thus, the stratum on which a morpheme appears in the lexicon reflects its productivity (cf. Aronoff 1976: 35–45).

Turning to inflectional morphology we can make the same points. The hierarchical organisation of strata can be used to account for the fact that in INFLECTIONAL ALLOMORPHY a particular stem does not co-occur with all the available affixes. We shall illustrate this with plural formation. In addition to the regular plural with the phonologically conditioned allomorphs [-z, -ɪz, -s] (as in *birds*, *classes* and *bricks*: cf. section (5.2)), English has several other ways of forming the plural, including the following:

[6.10] a. *Singular*   *Plural*   b. *Singular*   *Plural*
      foot   ~   feet   deer   ~   deer
      tooth   ~   teeth   sheep   ~   sheep
      goose   ~   geese   salmon   ~   salmon

[6.11] a. *Singular*   *Plural*   b. *Singular*   *Plural*
      locus   ~   loci   addendum   ~   addenda
      stimulus   ~   stimuli   curriculum ~   curricula
      fungus   ~   fungi   stratum   ~   strata

The use of internal root vowel change to signal plural as in [6.10a] is assumed to take place at stratum 1 since this is obviously a phonologically non-neutral, stem-changing process. This particular kind of plural formation, which is rare, cannot be successfully treated using normal suffixation rules. But it can be dealt with better if we assume an analysis like the 'word-and-paradigm' one for Latin in section (3.6.3). In this account there would be a rule which simply says, for example, that the lexical item *foot*, when associated with the grammatical property *plural*, is realised by the word-form *feet*.

By contrast, the zero suffix causes no problems. There are no phonological upheavals in the stem; we place it at stratum 1 in order to reflect the fact that it is a very restricted and unproductive method of pluralising nouns. Unless a noun is expressly flagged in the lexicon as taking a zero plural suffix, we assume that it does not (cf. section 5.3). The formation of the plural of the nouns in [6.10] at stratum 1 blocks regular plural formation by attaching the regular -*s* suffix at stratum 2. That way, the formation of disallowed plurals like **foots* and **gooses* or **deers* and **sheeps* is blocked.

Similarly, the plural suffixes -*i* and -*a* in the words in [6.11] which come from Latin also have to be at stratum 1. The suffixation of -*i* blocks the suffixation of -*s*. So, we get only *loci* not **locuses*. Thus, the notion of blocking enables us to explain why the formation of plural at stratum 1 hinders the formation of the plural using the regular [-z, ɪz, -s] allomorphs. By the time they reach stratum 2, the words in [6.11] are already marked as plural and so are unavailable for the suffixation of regular [-z, ɪz, -s].

However, because many speakers of English are unaware of the Latin origin of words with the -*i* plural, blocking is not any more successful in inflectional morphology than it is in derivational morphology. Commonly used words of Latin origin such as *virus* and *bonus* have been 'regularised' so that they only take the -*s* plural (i.e. *viruses*, *bonuses*). In other cases, such as *syllabuses* ~ *syllabi* and *aquariums* ~ *aquaria*, usage fluctuates between the Latin -*i* or -*a* and native -*s*. Some speakers use the stratum 2 suffix -*s*, bypassing the rule that attaches the stratum 1 Latinate one, while others use the rule that attaches the Latinate stratum 1 suffix and thereby preempt the suffixation of the regular -*s* suffix at stratum 2.

As mentioned with respect to the zero plural suffix, the placement of inflectional affixes on different strata reflects their relative productivity. The borrowed stratum 1 plural allomorphs -*i* and -*a* are not productive. If a new noun ending in -*us* or -*um* entered the language, its plural would be formed with the regular -*s* ending rather than -*i* or -*a*.

6.6 PRODUCTIVITY, THE TIME-WARP AND CRANBERRIES

Let us begin by going back to the table of suffixes in [6.3] on p. 102. You will observe that the suffixes listed there are not all equally PRODUCTIVE. They do not all have the same likelihood of forming words. Some morphemes are more productive, more alive and more active than others which may be described as moribund, dormant or, at best, relatively inactive. The active morphemes are extensively used in contemporary English to form words while the inactive ones are used infrequently, if ever, to create new words.

For examples of productive suffixes, take -*ly*, which can turn almost any adjective (e.g. *quiet*, *soft*) into an adverb (*quiet-ly*, *soft-ly*); the suffix -*er* which is used to derive agent nouns from verbs (e.g. *paint-er*, *teach-er*); and the suffix -*ing* which is used to form a gerundive noun meaning 'the act of doing X' from a verb (e.g. *wait-ing*, *sailing*). Such suffixes are attached almost exceptionlessly to virtually all eligible roots and the resulting word has a very predictable meaning. It is impossible to imagine a competent speaker of English who does not know how to construct words using these suffixes.

At the other end of the spectrum there are affixes which the erudite might be able to recognise but which have no active role in word-formation in the contemporary language. That is true of *-ery* (in *slav-ery*, *brav-ery* and *chican-ery*) which forms abstract nouns from nouns or adjectives. This suffix has the meaning 'having the property, state or behaviour indicated by the source noun or adjective'. I suspect some readers of this book may not have known that. But this is not surprising. This suffix ceased to be actively used several hundred years ago. It is not productive any more. It survives in only a few words as a fossil. At first sight, the case for isolating it as a morpheme in a purely synchronic analysis intended to reflect the knowledge of contemporary speakers of English is not altogether overwhelming. Arguably, *slavery*, *bravery*, *chicanery* and the like ought to be treated as root morphemes without affixes, whatever their history.

Treating the whole unit in the case of *chicanery* is unproblematic. But difficulties arise if we do the same with *slavery* and *bravery*. Both *slave* and *brave* are morphemes still on active service. They must be segregated from *-ery*. But doing that leaves behind a residual element whose credentials as a morpheme would be considered doubtful by many speakers. A morpheme that may have been active at some point in the past may cease to be so as time goes on. Also, the extent to which we can reliably associate meanings with some morphs that we isolate may diminish (see 4.2.1). One of the challenges that a morphologist faces is providing an analysis that distinguishes what is of purely arcane historical interest from what is relevant in an analysis of the contemporary language. The fact that linguists can see some morphological structure does not necessarily mean that Ms and Mr Average Native-Speaker are aware of it too. What in principle should be compositional for some speakers may not be for all speakers.

The classic example of this is provided by the *cranberry* words (cf. Bloomfield 1933). These words highlight the problem of treating morph-like units that do not belong to any recognisable morpheme in the language as it is used today. A *cranberry* is a kind of *berry*. So, we can identify *berry* as a morpheme in that word. But that leaves us the problem of what to do with the apparently meaningless unit *cran-* that is left behind. The only loophole available is to treat *cranberry* as a compound word made up of the free root morpheme *berry* and the bound root morpheme *cran-* which has the peculiarity of only occurring as part of the word *cranberry*. Admittedly, the word *cran* does exist, meaning 'a measure of herrings (about 750 fish)', but that word is unrelated to the *cran-* in *cranberry*.

We are in a quandry. You might be willing to accept that *cran-* is a non-recurrent morpheme with a very restricted distribution – occurring only in *cranberry*. But you may still be wondering where that leaves the definition of the morpheme as a minimal meaningful unit. It seems that definition has to be modified. It has to be weakened so that we make allowances for some morphemes which are not meaningful units on their own. All words have to mean something when they occur in isolation. However, morphemes are not absolutely required to have a clear, identifiable meaning on their own. They may be chameleon-like, with meanings that change somewhat in different words (cf. [4.2] on p. 55).

Cran- and similar words make a revision of the definition of the morpheme necessary. To overcome the problems some linguists have defined the morpheme in purely distributional terms: a linguistic entity 'uniquely identifiable in terms of phonemic elements, and occurring in stated environments of other morphemic segments (or in stated utterances)' (cf. Harris 1951: 171). This is a definition that highlights distribution. 'Cran- ' can be isolated as a morpheme on distributional grounds, like the problematic Latinate root morphemes in [4.2]. For instance, in the case of *cran-* we can use the substitution test to show that *cran-* is a morpheme. In some other *berry* words such as *blueberry* and *blackberry* we have the morphemes *blue* and *black* occurring in the same slot as *cran-*. (See also Aronoff 1976: 15.)

In all this the difficulty is the fact that between the productive morpheme used actively in the construction of words (e.g. agentive noun suffix *-er*) and dormant ones like *-ery* that are fossilised, there exists a myriad of possibilities. The difference between productive and unproductive morphemes is a gradient, not a dichotomy. There are numerous morphemes that are productive to different degrees. For instance *-aire* as in *doctrinaire* is found in only a few existing words and is unlikely to be used in the formation of new ones. Relatively few speakers recognise it as a suffix and its meaning is obscure. Nevertheless it is possible that it is moribund rather than dead. It could still be taken off the shelf and dusted down and used to form new words when the need arises. For instance, in the early 1990s those in British politics opposed to an ever closer union of the states that make up the European Community used the term *communautaire* (borrowed from French) as an insult for those firmly committed to the goal of European political unity. Although it is not likely that the average speaker of English is aware of *-aire* being a suffix in *communautaire*, it is very likely that those who use this term in political discourse, being quite erudite, are able to identify *-aire* as a suffix here.

One of the intriguing phenomena in morphology is that across-the-board productivity in word-formation is very rare. Often an otherwise general word-formation process is blocked in some circumstances. This is particularly true in derivational morphology which tends to be less predictable than inflectional morphology. Word-formation is often subject to various constraints which may be phonological, morphological or syntactic (cf. Aronoff 1976, Katamba 1993).

Here we will limit the discussion to some phonological constraints. We will see how the affixation of an otherwise productive affix may be inhibited for phonological reasons. We will illustrate this with the *-al* suffix which derives action nouns from verbs. According to Siegel (1974), for a verb base to be eligible for the suffixation of *-al*, it must meet these phonological requirements:

(i) The verb base must end in a stressed syllable.
(ii) The verb base must end phonologically in either a vowel, or a single consonant, or at most two consonants.
(iii) If the base does not end in a vowel, its final consonant must be made in the front of the mouth (i.e. it must be a labial or alveolar consonant).

These conditions are exemplified in [6.12]. (Consider the pronunciation, not the spelling):

[6.12] a. *-al* suffix after vowel-final bases
           trial denial betrayal renewal
        b. *-al* after verb bases ending in a labial consonant
           revival arrival approval removal

    c. -*al* after verb bases ending in a dental or alveolar consonant

       betrothal appraisal acquittal recital referral

    d. -*al* after verb bases ending in a (alveolar) consonant preceded by another consonant

       rehearsal dispersal reversal rental

However, if a verb ends in a palatal or velar consonant as in [6.13], suffixation of this -*al* is blocked:

[6.13] *judgeal *attackal *approachal *rebukal *encroachal

The stress on the final syllable is always a vital factor. A base that otherwise meets the conditions for -*al* suffixation will be ineligible if stress is not on the last syllable. Hence the ill-formedness of *ˋaudital, *ˋcombatal and *ˋlimital.

As Siegel's analysis predicts, a base like *aˋttemptal, which ends in a three-consonant cluster, cannot take the suffix either even though it has got stress in the right place, on the final syllable.

Even then there are inexplicable exceptions. Some seemingly well-formed potential words are disallowed although they appear to meet all the conditions. For instance, for no apparent reason, *conˋtestal, *eˋscortal and *aˋllowal are not allowed through the net.

6.7 PEEPING BEYOND THE LEXICON

After words have been formed in the lexicon, they are used in the syntax to form phrases and sentences. Even at this stage they are still subject to phonological rules. The phonological rules that affect words at this stage are called PHRASAL RULES (or POST-LEXICAL RULES: cf. section 8.3). Post-lexical phonological rules differ from the phonological rules which operate in the lexicon in that they are not sensitive to the idiosyncratic lexical properties of words. They apply mechanically whenever the right phonetic circumstances are present, regardless of any special morphological or syntactic properties that words may have. We have seen that, in the lexicon, certain phonological processes apply only if certain morphemes are present. For example, STRESS SHIFT applies only when certain stratum 1 suffixes are attached. Unlike lexical rules, post-lexical rules do not take into account any of the peculiarities of the words they affect. They are general and exceptionless. They are automatically triggered by the presence of the appropriate phonological input.

An example of a post-lexical rule is the optional assimilation of an alveolar consonant at the end of one word to the place of articulation of the consonant at the beginning of the next word in fast casual speech. Thus, the word *mad* by itself is pronounced [mæd]. But in *mad girl* and *mad man* it may be uttered with a final [g] and [b] respectively so that we get [mæg gɜ:l] and [mæb mæn] when the /d/ assimilates to the place of articulation of the following velar /g/ and labial /b/. The phrasal, place of articulation assimilation rule applies in an environment that spans two phonological words. It is not a lexical rule confined to morphemes and single words. The assimilation can affect any word with the appropriate phonetic make-up if it appears in this phrasal context. However, since our concern in this book is morphology, the study of internal structure of words, we will not explore phrasal rules any further. We will stick to processes that affect morphemes and single words.

6.8 SUMMARY

In this chapter we have explored the kinds of lexical information that need to be included in the lexicon. We have established that the lexicon needs to contain semantic, phonological, morphological, syntactic properties. Word-formation interacts strongly with processes that apply in the other modules of the grammar since they all need access to various kinds of information about morphemes and words found in the lexicon.

Most of the chapter has been given over to characterising the relationship between morphological and phonological rules found in the lexicon using the multi-layered theory of lexical morphology. (For further exploration of this model see van der Hulst and Smith 1982a, 1982b, 1982c, Katamba 1989 and Goldsmith 1990.)

We have seen that affix morphemes play a pivotal role since the division of the lexicon into strata is based on the phonological properties of affixes. Affixes are put on two strata depending on whether they are phonologically neutral or non-neutral. This enables us to handle simply several important morphological phenomena such as the sequencing of morphemes in words, the relative productivity of morphemes, and blocking.

In the course of the discussion we re-examined the role of the morpheme as the minimal unit used to signal meaning. We saw that some morphemes have very elusive meanings and we considered a distributional approach as a possible way of characterising the morpheme.

Finally, we concluded by briefly contrasting the idiosyncratic nature of lexical phonological rules with the predictable nature of phrasal rules that affect words after they have been processed through the syntax.

EXERCISES

1. a. What kinds of information must the lexicon contain?
   b. Explain why the lexicon must be much more than a long list of words that are found in a language. What kinds of generalisations should be captured in the lexicon?

2. a. In the light of the discussion in this chapter and earlier discussion in Chapter 5, show how phonological rules interact with morphological rules.
   b. Show why a theory of language that insisted on keeping morphological rules segregated from phonological rules would miss some important generalisations about English. Back up your arguments with fresh examples.

3. a. What is the meaning of *pec-* and *mut-* in the following:

pecunious impecunious	pecuniary	peculate	peculiar
commute immutable	mutant	permutation	mutate

   b. Should *pec* and *mut* be recognised as root morphemes in contemporary English? Justify your answer.

4. a. Use the data below to argue that the two distinct *-al* suffix morphemes must be recognised.

acquittal	arrival	referral	betrayal	refusal	residual
perusal	retrieval	dispersal	reversal	committal	removal
architectural	medicinal	intellectual	instrumental	ancestral	universal
habitual	conceptual	presidential	commercial	original	anecdotal

   In your analysis, pay particular attention to the following:

   (i) the meaning of the suffix;
   (ii) the word-class of the bases to which it attaches;
   (iii) the word-class of the resulting word;
   (iv) the effect, if any, that the *-al* suffix has on stress.

b. In the light of your analysis, at which lexical stratum or strata should -al be put?

5. Study the following words and answer the questions that follow:

a. bagful
   cupful
   jugful
   plateful
b. childhood
   knighthood
   parenthood
   priesthood
c. complimentary
   elementary
   evolutionary
   inflationary
   revolutionary

d. journalese
   computerese
   officialese
   telegraphese
e. friendship
   guardianship
   keepership
   membership
f. absenteeism
   colonialism
   expansionism
   fatalism
   imperialism

g. daily
   monthly
   quarterly
   weekly
h. arabesque
   grotesque
   picturesque
   Turneresque
i. decorative
   generative
   native
   productive
   speculative

a. Segment each word into morphemes.
b. List the *suffixes* together with their meanings and their historical sources. As we have seen in this chapter, the distinction between native and borrowed morphemes is important in English although most speakers are not explicitly aware of it. This task is intended to make you examine this distinction consciously. (Looking up the suffixes in an etymological dictionary is recommended.)
c. Make a phonemic transcription of the first two words in each group. Indicate the syllable that receives the most prominent stress in the word.
e. What effect on stress, if any, does each suffix you have identified have?
f. At what stratum is each one of the suffixes you have identified found? What is your evidence?
g. Is there any correlation between the stratum at which a suffix is found and its historical origin?

Chapter 7

Should English be spelt as she is spoke?

7.1 WRITING SYSTEMS

In the last couple of chapters we have examined the representation of words in speech, the way in which morphological representations interface with phonological representations of words. What is the relationship between the orthographic word and the phonological word which both represent the same lexeme? That is the question we are going to tackle in this chapter.

Writing enables people to use visual symbols to represent words. This can be done in a variety of ways (cf. Crystal 1988, Diringer 1968, Gelb 1963, Stubbs 1980, Scragg 1973, Sampson 1985, DeFrancis 1989). Some writing systems are LOGOGRAPHIC. They use visual symbols to represent entire meaningful units, which may be morphemes or words, without giving any indication whatsoever of their pronunciation. This is to some extent true of the way in which Chinese is written (DeFrancis 1989: 225–30). For example, the character (i.e. written sign) 魚 (pronounced $\hat{y}$) stands for 'fish' and the character 雨 (pronounced $\check{y}$) stands for 'rain'. In English too, there are a few comparable logographic symbols, such as the following:

[7.1] + 'plus'   & 'and'   £ 'pound sterling'
      = 'equals'   20 'twenty' $ 'dollar'

Symbols like those above, in their entirety, represent certain meanings. It would be absurd to attempt to associate any part of a symbol like $ or + with specific sounds. Arabic numerals used in English and other languages also fall into this category. That is why it would be futile to try to 'sound out' a number like *20*. The two symbols *2* and *0* do not correspond in any way to particular sounds. There is nothing about *2* or *0* that indicates its pronunciation. Indeed, different languages which use Arabic numerals will have quite different pronunciations for this number. Whereas in English *20* is *twenty* (/twentɪ/) in Urdu it is *bis*, in French *vingt*, in Swahili *ishirini* etc.

Logographic writing is rather unusual. In most writing systems there is usually a link of some kind between the orthographic and the phonological realisation of a lexeme (Gelb 1963). The symbols used in writing tend to represent, with varying degrees of accuracy, aspects of the pronunciation. However, what aspects of pronunciation are selected for representation, and the exact manner in which they are represented, may vary. In a minority of writing systems, the symbols represent syllables and hence are called SYL-LABARIES. The native American language, Cherokee (spoken in Oklahoma and North Carolina) uses a syllabary. The Cherokee syllabary is shown in [7.2].

[7.2]

a	e	i	o	u	ʌ		
D a	R e	T i	♦ o	O' u	i ʌ		
f ga	h ge	y gi	A go	J gu	E gʌ		
Oᵇ ha	? he	A hi	Ⴁ ho	Γ hu	♌ hʌ	∂	ka
W la	♪ le	Γ li	G lo	M lu	♀ lʌ	t	hna
ɣ ma	Oᴵ me	H mi	3 mo	✓ mu		G	nah
θ na	Λ ne	ɦ ni	Z no	♌ nu	Oᵛ nʌ	∂	s
I gwa	ω gwe	℘ gwi	N gwo	ω gwu	Ɛ gwʌ	W	ta
Ⴄ sa	4 se	b si	Φ so	♌ su	R sʌ	ʒ	ti
l da	f de	┙ di	Λ do	S du	♌ dʌ	L	tla
♌ dla	L dle	G dli	♌ dlo	♌ dlu	P dlʌ	ъ	
G dza	V dze	ʰ dzi	K dzo	J dzu	Cͫ dzʌ		
G wa	ω we	θ wi	℮ wo	♌ wu	6 wʌ		
ω ya	ß ye	♌ yi	ɦ yo	Gͫ yu	B yʌ		

Japanese is an even more famous example of a language that uses a syllabary. The Japanese syllabary has two sub-variants called *Katakana* and *Hiragana* which employ symbols that represent the fifty or so syllables of the language. But the situation in Japanese is complicated. There is a character-based system called *Kanji* that co-exists with the syllabary. The *Kanji* characters are borrowed from Chinese (cf. Gelb 1963, Sampson 1985, DeFrancis 1989).

Of the phonologically based systems, however, ALPHABETIC ones are by far the most common. In an ideal alphabetic system there would always be just one letter corresponding to one PHONEME (i.e. distinctive sound of the language). Probably no such system exists, but Italian and Swahili come fairly close to it. For instance, in Italian *impepare* 'to season with pepper' is pronounced /impepare/ and in Swahili *kupika* 'to cook' /kupika/. The spelling is a good indication of the pronunciation.

From your experience you know that English is not quite like this, although to begin with English spelling was no less transparent than Italian spelling: 'Once, at some remote time in the historical past, English had a "phonemic" orthography in which words were spelt as they were pronounced' (Sampson 1985: 194).

In this quotation and in the rest of this chapter the term 'phonemic' is simply meant to imply that pronunciation can be predicted by straightforward rules from spelling and vice versa. (No distinction is made between phonemes and allophones.)

7.2 IS THE ENGLISH ORTHOGRAPHY MAD?

The English orthography is still basically phonemic and reasonably regular, although it does have irregularities. I realise that the suggestion that English spelling is at all regular may come as a surprise because for almost 800 years it is the absurdly irregular aspects of English spelling that have been in the limelight in most discussions of the English orthography. Those aspects that are regular have for the most part tended to go unnoticed; the regularities are just taken for granted.

You can test for yourself the claim that English spelling is to some degree regular and phonemic by considering the relationship between the letters and sounds in words like *nap* and *pan*; *nip* and *pin*; *keel* and *leek*. It is clear that the match of sounds with letters is quite systematic. The consonant letters have the same values

that they have in the phonetic alphabet; the letter *a* corresponds
to phoneme /æ/, *i* corresponds to /ɪ/ and *ee* corresponds to /iː/.

With this in mind, examine the relationship between spelling
and pronunciation in the following extract from *The History of an
Apple Pie written by Z*:

[7.3] A Apple Pie,
       B Bit it,
       C Cried for it,
       D Danced for it,
       E Eyed it,
       F Fiddled for it,
       G Gobbled it,
       H Hid it.

(from Opie and Opie 1980: 20–1)

In this rhyme, which is not at all unrepresentative of the language as a whole, spelling is reasonably phonemic. This is inten-
tionally put in the limelight since the point of the rhyme is to
teach children the alphabet. In almost every line, the first letter
corresponds predictably to the appropriate sound. *A* is pronounced
as /æ/, *b* is pronounced as /b/ etc. Internally in words, the letter
i corresponds to the sound /ɪ/ (in *bit, it, fiddled* and *hid*) while the
DIAGRAPH (i.e. the letter combination) *ie* represents the sound
/aɪ/ (as in *pie* and *cried*).

Rumours of English spelling being absolutely chaotic are grossly
exaggerated, if not totally baseless. Nevertheless these rumours
have persisted since the beginning of the thirteenth century when
the first spelling reformer, a monk named Orm, proposed innovations intended to ensure a one-to-one correspondence between
sound and letter (Scragg 1973).

Accusations that English spelling is on the whole arbitrary are
based on quick impressionistic surveys of a relatively small number
of problem words like *through, though, enough, thigh, this, write, rite*
and *right*. Many careful, thorough studies give a totally different
picture. I will quote Crystal (1988: 69–70):

A major American study, published in the early 1970s, carried
out a computer analysis of 17,000 words and showed that no
less than 84 per cent of the words were spelt according to a
regular pattern, and that only 3 per cent were so unpredictable
that they would have to be learned by heart. Several other

projects have reported comparable results of 75 per cent regularity or more.

7.2.1 The apparent madness in the English spelling system

The English orthography is still reasonably phonemic – but not entirely so. Over the centuries, a combination of factors has undermined the phonemic nature of English spelling. Unfortunately for the person trying to become literate, although English spelling is mostly rule-governed the rules are extremely complex and riddled with exceptions. The aim of this chapter is to outline some of the principles that lie behind English spelling and to give you a flavour of how the system works. But it is not my intention to provide an exhaustive survey of the relationship between English spelling and pronunciation. For that turn to books like Scragg (1973), Sampson (1985), Stubbs (1980) and Vachek (1973).

I will start as every critic or reformer of English spelling starts – by listing (in [7.4]) some of the glaring examples of the irregularities, inconsistencies and arbitrariness of English spelling that have led some to proclaim that the relationship between spelling and pronunciation is simply mad.

[7.4] aisle	could	isle	quay
are	debt	key	rough
although	do	knight	son
aunt	does	knock	sugar
autumn	dough	laugh	trough
blood	eye	listen	two
bough	fought	move	victuals
climb	fraught	of	water
colour	friend	once	where
come	ghoul	people	who
cough	hour	psalm	you

(based on Crystal 1988: 68)

In fact, the list in [7.4] does not contain the worst examples. The pronunciation of unfamiliar place names and personal names provides even worse horrors. It is the equivalent of negotiating a verbal minefield. All too often the spelling has only a tenuous link with the pronunciation. For instance, there is a hamlet near Lancaster in Lancashire called *Quernmore* – you probably expect it to be called /kwɜ:nmɔə/, but in fact it is called /kwɔmə/; the Northumbrian town of *Alnwick* is pronounced /ænɪk/ not */ɔ:lnwɪk/; the Yorkshire town of *Keighley* is pronounced /ki:θlɪ/ not */ki:flɪ/; *Hawick* in Scotland is pronounced /hɔ:ɪk/ not */hæwɪk/; the Glasgow suburb of *Milngavie* is pronounced /mɪlgaɪ/ not */mɪlngævɪ/, and so on.

Frequently, the relationship between the spelling and pronunciation of personal names is equally unpredictable. For instance, *Beauchamp* is pronounced /bi:tʃəm/; *Cockburn* is prounced /kəʊbən/; *Maugham* is pronounced /mɔ:m/ or /mɔ:n/; *Mainwaring* is pronounced as /mænərɪŋ/, *Clowes* may be pronounced /klaʊz/ or /klu:z/, and so on.

7.2.2 There is a method in the madness: spelling rules and pronunciation

Despite the existence of a very sizeable minority of words like those we have just surveyed whose spelling is to varying degrees arbitrary, English spelling is for the most part reasonably phonemic, as hinted in section (7.2). Take your own experience as a reader. How often do you stumble when you come across an unfamiliar word? Let us imagine you are encountering for the first time the biochemical term *thiamine*: would you know how to pronounce it? I suspect you would. You would not hesitate to read it as /θaɪəmaɪn/. When you see a novel orthographic word like *bupperkinish* (which I have made up and which I invite you to assign a meaning to) you will have no trouble reading it aloud. Most of the time you have a very good idea of the pronunciation of unfamiliar words, although occasionally you will be caught out.

Part of the reason why we know how to pronounce unfamiliar words is that spelling is reasonably phonemic. Another factor that helps is that, as we saw in section (6.4), the phonological word is subject to various phonotactic constraints. Only a limited number of combinations of sounds is allowed in certain positions in the phonological word and by extension, only a limited number of letter combinations representing those sounds is permitted. Thus, for example, no word spelt as **dmell*, **tsip*, **ftalation* can be found in English because the consonant sequences *dn*, *ts* and *ft* are disallowed at the beginning of a word in English (though of course they all occur in other positions in a word as in *admire*, *cats*, and *lift*). If you saw a 'word' with any one of the impermissible word-initial consonant combinations I have just described, you would know it was not English. Furthermore, as we shall see later in this section, there are rules that predict – fairly reliably in many cases – how a given letter or diagraph is to be pronounced in different contexts. In sum, English spelling is not chaotic. There are strict restrictions on letter combinations that are allowed to represent speech sounds in different positions.

The problem is that although the system is essentially phonemic, regular correspondences between letters and speech sounds are sometimes subverted. There are about 400 very common, everyday words (in the sense of lexemes or separate vocabulary items) whose spelling is irregular. The fact that these frequently used words are irregularly spelt gives the erroneous impression that matching sound with pronunciation in a totally unsystematic fashion is the norm. The situation is made to look bleaker than it is because in discussions of spelling the distinction between words as vocabulary items and words as orthographic forms is seldom recognised. All too often each occurrence of an orthographic word-form is counted as a separate word without this being explicitly stated. As a great many of the common lexical items have irregular spelling, they skew the figures.

If, however, you distinguish between words in the sense of ortho-graphic words that have distinct written forms on the page, and distinct vocabulary items that are listable in a dictionary, the number of words with irregular spelling is considerably reduced. For example, if you count *plough*, *ploughs*, *ploughing* and *ploughed* as different words, you get five orthographic words whose spelling is irregular. By contrast, if you only recognise that the spelling *plough* which is always associated with this particular vocabulary item is always pronounced /plaʊ/, the irregularity need be noted only once, since *plough*, *ploughs*, *ploughing* and *ploughed* are all forms of the same word. If you can pronounce *plough*, the other orthographic forms present no difficulties. Similarly, while the pronunciation of *quay* as /kiː/ is arbitrary, that arbitrariness needs to be noted only once. Anyone who knows how to read or spell *quay* in the singular need not be troubled by *quays* /kiːz/ in the plural.

While emphasising the regularity, I do not wish to sweep the irregularity under the carpet. But while recognising the irregularity, I will still argue that English spelling is not simply whimsical or crazy. What I wish to do in the following paragraphs is to show that although spelling may in some instances be non-phonemic, nevertheless it follows some discernible pattern. Many of the irregularities can be accounted for. First, we will see that there are usually historical reasons for the non-phonemic spelling although unfortunately, knowing this is not of much practical use to the average speaker of English who is unacquainted with the history of the language and has spelling problems.

We will start with the spelling that represents the sound /g/. At the beginning of *get* it is spelt with the letter *g* while the same sound at the beginning of *ghost* is spelt with the diagraph *gh*. At the same time, word-initially the sound /f/ as in *fit* is spelt with the letter *f* whereas in *rough* /f/ is spelt with the diagraph *gh*. It is obvious that the same sound may be represented by different letters. On what basis is a particular spelling selected? Is the choice random?

The answer is a clear 'No'. There is a general pattern here. Although the use of the spelling *gh* is not phonemic in these examples (since only the *g* is sounded and the *h* is silent), there is a regularity which can be captured by the following pair of statements:

[7.5] Within syllables,   gh = /g/ before a vowel
    e.g.   *ghost, ghoul; ghetto, aghast*
    e.g.   gh = /f/ after a vowel
        enough, tough, rough, cough
        (based on Stubbs 1980: 51)

The complication is that these rules are not inviolable. There are certain exceptions. For instance, in a small number of words *gh* following a vowel is not pronounced at all:

[7.6] caught   taught   bought   sought
    light   right   tight   night
    plough   bough   though   through

Historical studies of English spelling hold the key to how these spelling patterns involving *gh* arose. Students of the history of English spelling have shown that the use of *gh* for *g* at the beginning of a word is the result of a historical accident (cf. Scragg 1973, Stubbs 1980). Caxton, the person who introduced printing to England in 1476, though an Englishman, had spent much of his life on the continent, in Holland in particular. He was not fully conversant with the conventions of English spelling and he brought back with him many European compositors and setters, most of whom were Dutch. Their control of English spelling was also far from perfect and their Dutch spelling habits interfered with the spelling norms of English. They used *gh*, as was the norm in Dutch, where English would have used *g*. That is how *gost* became *ghost*, and similar words came to be spelt with word-initial *gh*. In some cases this tendency was reversed. For instance, *girl* and *goose* temporarily acquired a letter *h* after the arrival of printing and were written as *gherle* and *ghoos*. But later they reverted to their original *g* spelling (Stubbs 1980: 51).

There is also a good historical explanation for the unpronounced *gh* following a vowel. English pronunciation has changed over the centuries but the spelling has not been revised to bring it up to date. At one time the letters *gh* after a vowel represented a sound like that guttural fricative /χ/ heard in the Scottish pronunciation of *och* and *loch*. Various changes in the pronunciation took place and words like *night* and *light* became pronounced as /naɪt/ and /laɪt/ but the spelling was not revised to reflect these changes. In sum, what might look like arbitrary spelling conventions may have some organising principle behind them buried deep in the history of the language. We will return to the historical dimension in more detail in the next section. Let us turn to the present. I shall now show that even where spelling is not phonemic, normally it is subject to rules. But the rules tend to be leaky.

We will use the doubling of consonants as our case study. Although the use of a single or double consonant makes no difference to the consonant itself, it is a useful clue as to whether the vowel preceding it is long or short. By spotting the single or double consonant following a vowel you can tell that the vowel in the first of the two nonsense words in each pair is short and the second is long.

[7.7] *Short*   *Long*
    ditter   deater
    hodder   hooder
    tusser   tuser

The interplay of vowel length in the pronunciation and consonant doubling in the orthography has always been important in English spelling. We will illustrate this with the example of double consonant letters in spelling monosyllabic verbs ending in a consonant when the suffix *-ing* is attached. This discussion draws on Crystal (1988).

The data in [7.8] illustrate the fact that whether the consonant following a vowel in this context is doubled as in *wetting* (*weting*), or not as in *waiting* (*waitting*), depends crucially on whether the vowel in the verb stem is short or long; for this purpose a diphthong counts as a long vowel. (See the Key to symbols used on p. xix.)

[7.8] a. *Short*   b. *Long*

hit	hitting	heat	heating
rid	ridding	read	reading
chat	chatting	chart	charting
mat	matting	mate	mating
whip	whipping	weep	weeping
wed	wedding	wade	wading
skin	skinning	scream	screaming

Should you encounter verbs like *fip* and *spleed*, which I have made up, you would instinctively know that since the former has a short vowel, its final consonant must be doubled when the suffix -*ing* is attached, to give *fipping*. But not so *spleed* which has a long vowel. It must be written as *spleeding*.

So far we have restricted our attention to monosyllabic words. But doubling is not restricted to monosyllabics where a short vowel is followed by just one consonant at the end of a word. It applies also in longer verbs. Contrast the words in A and B in [7.9]:

[7.9] A   B

cushion	cushioning	compel	compelling
permeate	permeating	expel	expelling
exhibit	exhibiting	upset	upsetting
dismember	dismembering	refer	referring
stimulate	stimulating	equip	equipping

The pattern observed here is that the last consonant is doubled if the last syllable of the unaffixed verb root is stressed, as in column B. If the last syllable is unstressed you do not double the last consonant. In a few cases there are differences between British and American English, because this rule applies less rigorously in America to words like those in [7.9]. The result is that a word like *traveling* is spelt with one *l* in American English.

A relatively small number of additional rules is needed to cover words that violate our rule. I will mention just one of them. At the end of a word, if the letter *c* preceded by a vowel needs to be doubled according to the doubling rules, it is written *ck* rather than *cc* (cf. *panic* → *panicking* not **paniccing*).

The doubling of the last consonant of a monosyllabic verb when a suffix is attached is more general than I have indicated so far. It is not simply brought into play by the presence of *-ing*. Other suffixes, e.g. *-er*, also induce consonant doubling, as seen in [7.10]:

[7.10] *Short*   *Long*

knit	~	knitter	neat	~	neater
wet	~	wetter	wait	~	waiter
sit	~	sitter	seat	~	seater
shut	~	shutter	shoot	~	shooter

Consonant doubling rules are also sensitive to how vowels are spelt. Thus, a consonant following two vowel letters, regardless of whether they represent a short or long vowel, is not doubled:

[7.11] *Short*   *Long*

spread	~	spreading	plead	~	pleading
head	~	heading	read	~	reading
sweat	~	sweating	leaf	~	leafing

Finally, doubling is used to underline the distinction between content words and function words. There is an orthographic requirement that content words (i.e. verbs, nouns, adjectives and adverbs) must be spelt with at least three letters. But there is no such minimality requirement applicable to function words: the lower limit on the number of letters in function words like articles, pronouns and prepositions is one. So, one-letter function words like *a* and *I*, as well as two-letter ones like *if*, *it*, *on* etc., are allowed but putative nouns, adjectives or verbs like *ad*, *od*, *as*, *eg*, *bo* and *se* are ruled out of court. In each case, to obtain a properly formed content word all you need to do is double the last letter. This gives you *add*, *odd*, *ass*, *egg*, *boo* and *see* (cf. Albrow 1972, Sampson 1985).

7.2.3. Is A for apple? Why vowel letters pinch like ill-fitting shoes

In this section we will continue exploring the main reasons for the inconsistencies in English spelling, paying special though not exclusive attention to vowels. The correspondence between the spelling and pronunciation of vowel sounds is much less systematic than that of consonants. We shall see the reasons why this is so.

1. The main source of the inconsistency between the spelling and pronunciation of vowels is that the Roman alphabet, with a mere five vowel letters, does not have sufficient symbols to represent all the twenty or so distinct vowel sounds of English. In many cases the representation of vowel sounds in the spelling is not phonemic: there is not a one-to-one match between letters and vowel phonemes. Often the same vowel letter represents different sounds e.g., *a* represents /æ/ in /bæd/ *bad*, /ɑ:/ in /pɑ:s/ *pass*, /eɪ/ in /leɪt/ *late*, /ɔ:/ in /fɔ:n/ *fawn* etc. (Refer to the key on p. xix.) But still certain generalisations can be made, as we will see later in this section.

2. After the Norman Conquest, Norman scribes introduced some of the spelling conventions of French into English, e.g. /kw/ which had been spelt as *cw* (as in *cwic(u)*) before the conquest was now spelt as *qu* (as in *quick*). But this was not done across the board: for example *call* (from OE *ceallian*) was not changed to **quall* nor was *come* (from OE *cuman*) changed to **quame*.

The French scribes were also unhappy with the letter *u* when next to the letters *m*, *v*, or *n* because the handwriting strokes used to form these letters were very similar and often this made them difficult to read. So they decided that the original *u* should be replaced by *o* in words like *son*, *love* and *come*. For the same reason, the earlier spelling of 'woman' as *wimman* was changed to *woman*.

3. English spelling is extremely conservative, as we saw in connection with [7.6]. While pronunciation has kept changing, spelling has remained more or less fixed since the fifteenth century. Nowhere is this more evident than in the case of vowels. As a rule, long vowels are not written phonemically. This is because in the fifteenth century the pronunciation of vowels underwent a tremendous upheaval. As you can see in [7.12] something akin to a game of musical chairs was played in the phonology of vowels, but scribes, and later on printers, took no notice of these changes and went on spelling words as they had always done. The examples on p. 133, in which the Modern English forms are written in parenthesis, illustrate how Old English vowels have evolved.

[7.12] *a* as in *habban* (have)   *i* as in *ridam* (ride)
      ɑ as in *hɑm* (home)   *o* as in *moðð̄e* (moth)
      æ as in *æt* (that)   *o* as in *foda* (food)
      æ as in *dæl* (deal)   *u* as *sundor* (sunder)
      e as in *settan* (set)   *u* as in *mus* (mouse)
      e as in *fedan* (feed)   *y* as in *fyllan* (fill)
      i as in *sittan* (sit)   *y* as in *mys* (mice)

(from Pyles and Algeo 1982: 106)

Questions, Quistions & Qhoshtions

Daddy how does an elephant feel
When he swallows a piece of steel?
Does he get drunk
And fall on his trunk
Or roll down the road like a wheel?

Daddy what would a pelican do
If he swallowed a bottle of glue?
Would his beak get stuck
Would he run out of luck
And lose his job at the zoo?

Son tell me tell me true,
If I belted you with a shoe,
Would you fall down dead?
Would you go up to bed?
– Either of those would do.

Spike Milligan

Before examining the data, a word needs to be said about the notation. In the Middle Ages there was a convention of using a macron (little line) over a vowel to indicate that the vowel was long. Later, doubling of vowel letters was used for this purpose. The vowel letters had a phonetic value similar to that they have in Italian or Spanish. The letter *y* represented a front rounded vowel – a sound similar to that found in French *tu* 'you' (sing.) or German *Güte* 'goodness'.

To illustrate the conservatism of the English orthography, let us take a closer look at the vowel in the word *mouse* which most speakers of English pronounce as /maʊs/. How did the pronunciation come to diverge so much from the spelling? This is how. In the early Middle Ages this word had the orthographic form *mus*. This spelling is reflected in the pronunciation in conservative nonstandard Scottish dialects where this word is still pronounced *mus*. Two things happened which explain the divergence of the pronunciation from the spelling.

First, 1066 and its aftermath. As already mentioned, after the Norman Conquest, French scribes came over. They did not always respect Anglo-Saxon spelling conventions for English – not an untypical attitude for a conquering power. They just spelt the /u/ sound as *ou* (as they did and still do in French in words like *vous, mousse, fou, coup* etc. If this spelling was good enough for French, it was also good enough for English.). So, /u/ of *mus* came to be spelt with the diagraph /ou/. Later, in the fifteenth century, the vowel *u* changed to /əʊ/ and so they said /məʊs/ (which sounded quite similar to the modern Canadian pronunciation of this vowel). Later still, the /əʊ/ pronunciation was changed to /aʊ/, the pronunciation that is used in most varieties of Modern English. But because the spelling had atrophied in the late Middle Ages, none of these changes in pronunciation is reflected in the spelling.

Conservatism is also to blame for the silent word-initial letters *k* and *g* before *n* as in *knee, knock, knife, knight*; and *gnaw, gnat*, etc. Neither the phoneme /k/ nor the phoneme /g/ can be combined with /n/ at the beginning of a word but at one time these consonants would have been sounded. Today, pronouncing *knock-kneed* as */knɒk kniːd/ rather than /nɒk niːd/ sounds very strange. This *k* was dropped from the pronunciation a long time ago but it lives on in the spelling.

4. Vowel pronunciation may vary depending on whether a vowel is stressed or unstressed. Cf. the pronunciation of stressed and unstressed *o* and *e* in the following:

[7.13] a. allergy   aˈllergic
            /ˈælədʒɪ/   /æˈlɜːdʒɪk/
        b. education   educative
            /edjuːˈkeɪʃn/   /ˈedjuːkətɪv/

Vowels get their full, clear value when stressed but are muffled and pronounced as /ə/ (schwa) when unstressed. There is no letter in the orthography to represent schwa. This is unfortunate since it is the commonest vowel in English speech.

5. We noted above that the same vowel letter may represent different sounds. This is not to say that it is all chaotic. Often, the vowel has predictable phonetic values if it occurs in the vicinity of certain consonants. For instance, the data in [7.14] exemplify the pronunciation of *a* in a variety of phonological contexts:

[7.14] /ɔ:/	/ɑ:/	/æ/
pawn	part	bat
spawn	calm	sat
dawn	palm	mat
walk	past	hat
swat	cast	grandiloquence

As the rules in [7.15] which reflect historical changes show, the pronunciation that is appropriate for the vowel *a* is normally predictable:

[7.15] Pronounce *a* as:
  (i) /ɔ:/ before or after *w*;
  (ii) /ɑ:/ before *r* or *l*, or before a fricative sound like /s/ or /f/;
  (iii) and usually /æ/ elsewhere.

Some of the rules interact. For example, the rule that gives /ɔ:/ if *a* is adjacent to *w* pre-empts the rule that says 'pronounce *a* as /ɑ:/ if it is followed by *r* or *l*. That is why *walk* is as pronounced /wɔ:k/ and not */wɑ:(l)k/.

6. Many words end in a silent letter *e*. This is not entirely haphazard. Although there are words like *come* whose final -*e* has no function, in many other cases word-final *e* is used as a special orthographic mark indicating that the preceding vowel is either long or a diphthong. That is the case in *nice*, *rose*, *fate* etc. where the final silent *e* indicates that the vowel letter before it stands for a diphthong and in *lute*, *rude*, *scene* etc. where it signals length.

Caveat: it would be rash to assume that a word-final -*e* is an infallible clue to the status of the preceding vowel. For instance, in *love* and *dove* the vowel is short. The *e* is there simply to ensure

that the words do not end in *v* as the presence of this letter at the
end of a word is not permitted (see p. 137).

7.3 MORPHOLOGICAL SIGNPOSTS IN THE SPELLING

In some cases, the orthographic form of a word may not attempt
to indicate pronunciation but instead may serve the function of
showing visually connections between words and allomorphs that
are related in terms of grammar or meaning. Let us take grammar
first. English spelling typically ignores alternations in the realisation of morphemes. Normally it uses the same letters to represent
allomorphs of the same morpheme even though there may be
significant differences in the pronunciation of those allomorphs.
Thus although the past tense ending is spelt *-ed*, it is pronounced
as /-t/, /-d/ or /-ɪd/ depending on the last sound in the verb to
which it is suffixed as we saw in section (5.2.2) above. The same
is true, of course, of the noun plural ending which is spelt as *-s*
but is pronounced as as /-s/, /-z/ or /-ɪz/ in different contexts. The
spelling thus fails to indicate the exact pronunciation but succeeds
in showing the grammatical identity of the ending (see Chomsky
and Halle (1968) and the discussion of allomorphs in Chapter 5,
especially section (5.2)).

The morphological signposting role of spelling can be further
illustrated by the alternation between the letters *i* and *y* at the end
of nouns with the plural suffix *-s*. If in the singular a noun ends
in a consonant followed by *y* (e.g. *berry*, *pony*), the *y* is replaced by
i in the plural (e.g. *berries*, *doggies*, *ponies*). But if in the spelling the
letter *y* is preceded by a vowel, it remains unchanged even where
it is followed by the plural suffix spelt as *-s* (as in *two donkeys*). Note,
however, that if the *-s* does not represent the plural morpheme, *y*
remains (cf. *the pony's tail*, *doggy's bone* etc. where *s* represents the
genitive).

Spelling may also do another morphological job: it may help to
distinguish native from imported words by restricting certain spelling conventions to borrowed words. Certain letters or sequences of
letters are only found in words that have come into English from
other languages and retain a degree of foreignness. For example,
native English words (excluding names and trade names) do not
end in the letters *i*, *u* or *v*. Instead of *i*, the letter *y* is used in word-
final position as in [7.16a]. Where a word would otherwise end in

u or *v*, the letter *e* is added, as in [7.16b] and [7.16c]. (Words ending in *v* like the slang word *spiv*, whose origin is uncertain, are very rare.)

[7.16] a. pity   nutty   naughty
       b. true   blue   glue
       c. shove   live   glove

No such restriction applies to words of foreign origin like those in [7.17] which are not totally assimilated:

[7.17] a. okapi   ski   yeti   kiwi
       b. tutu   gnu   guru   emu

Similarly, any word beginning with *kh* (e.g. *khaki, khalifa, khalsa* etc.) is marked as being of foreign extraction by its spelling. No native word begins with those letters. All these words come from Indian languages.

Other examples are not difficult to find. Thre are words of Greek origin which came to English second-hand from Latin whose initial consonant sound is not pronounced in English because it would give an impermissible consonant combination, for example *g* in *gnome* and *gnostic*; *p* in *psychology, psalm, pneumonia, pterosaur, pneumatic* etc.

In addition, of course, there are words which are overtly marked as foreign by the use of diacritic marks not found in English, e.g. *crèche, façade, débâcle, cliché* which come from French. We will say more about these in Chapter 10.

7.4 LEXICAL SIGNPOSTING IN THE SPELLING

Spelling may also serve the function of signposting semantic relationships between orthographic words. This is quite useful where the orthographic words in question have significantly different pronunciations:

[7.18] a. sign   /saɪn/   b. sane   /seɪn/
          signify   /sɪgnɪfaɪ/   sanity   /sænɪtɪ/
          significant   /sɪgnɪfɪkənt/   sanitise   /sænɪtaɪz/

If you were reading and came across the word *signification*, which you had not encountered before, by looking at its spelling you would probably be able to relate it to the words in [7.18a] and to work out its meaning.

Conversely, spelling may serve to distinguish homophonous word-forms which realise totally different lexemes, such as these:

[7.19]	reed	read		
	stationary	stationery		
	born	borne		
	weak	week		
	sea	see		
	site	cite	sight	
	right	rite	write	wright

Such words are like traps set to catch the unwary. They give English spelling a bad name.

But there is another way of looking at it. When the spelling does not reflect pronunciation, it is not necessarily crazy. After all, most of the time we do not read aloud. So, the lack of fit between sounds and letters need not cause problems if non-phonemic spelling conveys useful information by representing the same grammatical suffix (e.g. past tense -*ed*) consistently or by representing word-forms of related lexemes consistently, as in [7.18]. Nor is it unhelpful when by not being phonemic it distinguishes homophones, as in [7.19].

7.5 SPELLING REFORM

I have argued that English spelling is not as arbitrary and chaotic as its critics often proclaim. It is essentially phonemic with many non-phonemic quirks. But even the quirky parts are often not totally crazy. Nevertheless, I must concede that there is a *prima facie* case for some spelling reform to remove or reduce the extent to which the system is not transparent. First there is the educational argument. An ideal alphabet should consistently ensure that there is a one-to-one correspondence between letter and symbol. English does not quite live up to that ideal. If English were spelt like Italian, the pronunciation could almost always be inferred from the spelling. As a result, learning to read and write would be a piece of cake. Many a child would have a happier and less stressful life at school. Fewer people would leave school illiterate, and feeling inadequate.

Beg Parding

'Beg parding, Mrs. Harding,
Is my kitting in your garding?'
'Is *your* kitting in *my* garding?
Yes she is, and all alone,
Chewing of a mutting bone.'

ENGLISH CHILDREN'S RHYME

Second, there is the economic argument. Most people spend a lot of their time at work reading or writing. The standard orthography contains a considerable number of superfluous letters (e.g. *plough* uses six letters to represent three distinct sounds – it could be simplified to *plow* as indeed it has been in North America). This makes the process of writing slow and laborious. It costs money. Reform would save money and improve efficiency. (The discussion here draws on Stubbs 1980 and Crystal 1988.)

While in theory spelling reform to make English phonemic looks like a very sensible idea, in practice it is simply a non-starter. There are too many practical considerations that militate against it. Most of them revolve round the fact that literacy is a social phenomenon: it is not merely a matter of representing language using the medium of writing. Unless spelling reformers can persuade the users of English that the upheaval of implementing spelling reform is worth the great expense that would be involved and the attendant hassle, no movement toward reform can take place.

In the remainder of this chapter I will outline in some detail the reasons why spelling reformers have so far failed to sell the idea of producing a revised orthography.

1. English is the mother tongue of over 350 million language users and is used as a second language or lingua franca by 1,000–1,500 million people. There are many different accents and dialects. If each speaker spelt words in a way that reflected their pronunciation, the possibility of easy communication on paper by users of (standard) English would be diminished. Today, no matter how they pronounce words, speakers of standard English spell words identically in the vast majority of cases. There are only a few minor differences between British and American English, e.g. British *plough* corresponds to American *plow*, British *travelling* corresponds to American *traveling*. Otherwise, in virtually all cases, spelling is the same regardless of pronunciation. The written standard language is nearly the same in all parts of the world. This facilitates the use of written English for communication with literate speakers, regardless of where they come from.

Assuming, as most of us do, that using a common standard language is useful for communication among people whose pronunciation is significantly different, if a reformed phonemic spelling system were adopted, there would be fierce arguments about the right dialect to provide the basis for the reformed orthography. In Britain, many of the speakers of RP would no doubt insist on an orthography that reflected the pronunciation of the Queen's English. But from the English regions, Wales, Scotland and Ireland one would no doubt hear other voices arguing for other dialects and accents. Of course, the situation would become even more complex once speakers of English from other countries joined the debate. Given the fact that there are more native speakers of American English than of any other dialect, and given the prestige and power of the United States, an obvious case could and would be made for spoken American English forming the basis of the standard written language. But it is unlikely that this would appeal to speakers of other major dialects like Australian and Canadian English. Certainly most British people would not be willing to replace the Queen's English with a transatlantic standard.

But even if they were persuaded, since American English is not a monolith, the question of which variety, this time of American

English, should be represented in the new phonemic alphabet would rear its ugly head again. In brief, a single phonemic spelling system for all speakers of English is unattainable since different dialects have different phonemic systems, e.g. some dialects have an 'r' sound in *car* and *cart* and others do not. No single transcription can represent all dialects accurately.

Obviously there would be little point in introducing several competing alternative systems. That is the biggest obstacle that faces spelling reformers. This is probably the main reason why both the British Simplified Spelling Society and the Spelling Reform Association in America have made no headway, although they have been campaigning for change for almost a century.

2. Persuading those who had acquired the present orthography to give it up for the sake of making life easier for novice readers and writers would be an uphill struggle.

3. While it is difficult to learn English spelling because it is not always phonemic, once you have acquired it, some of its weaknesses turn out to be strengths. For instance, as we have seen, some grammatical forms remain invariant and hence easy to recognise on the page no matter how they are actually pronounced. For example, the plural of nouns is normally marked by the letter *-s* (or *-es*) even though it is pronounced in three different ways (as /s/ as in *cups*, as /z/ as in *mugs* and as /ɪz/ as in *glasses*). Also, the phonetically unhelpful differentiation between words like *weather* and *whether* is quite useful since these words realise different lexemes. So, there would be resistance to a transparently phonemic alphabet on the grounds that it would not be capable of conveying grammatical and lexical distinctions like these.

4. The transition from the old to the new spelling would take some time. In that period could we live tolerably with the confusion that would inevitably occur as old readers/writers learned the new system?

5. Millions of books and other materials have been produced over the last 500 or so years using the current writing system. It is inconceivable that future generations could just turn their back on the accumulated culture, scholarship and scientific knowledge that these contain. Even after the reform, many people would still need to be able to cope with the present orthography. The alternative of reprinting all existing books using the reformed orthography is just impracticable.

6. What is your attitude to the proposed revised spellings in [7.20]?

[7.20]

He pauzd for a moement and a wield feeling ov piti kaem oever him.
(New Spelling)

He pauzed for a moment and a wilde feeling ov pity came over him.
(Regularized English)

ᚾᚻ ᚱᚴ ᛃ ᚱ ᛃᛟᚱᚾᚨ ᛟ ᚱ ᛒᚱᛩ ᛃᚻᚨᛦ ᚱ ᛃᚱᛁ ᛞᚱᛃ ᛟᚱᚾ ᛃᛃᚱ.
(Shavian)

hee-pausd for a mœment and a wield feeliŋ ov pity cæm œver hiɯ
(i.t.a.)

Reformed English Spelling
(from Sampson 1985: 195)

Notes:
   (i) New Spelling was jointly proposed by the Simplified Spelling Society of Great Britain and the Simpler Spelling Society of the USA in 1956.
  (ii) Regularized English was proposed by Axel Wijk in 1959.
 (iii) Shavian was the brainchild of Bernard Shaw, who left instructions in his will that a regularised alphabet of at least 40 letters, representing systematically the distinctive sounds of English, should be produced. The winning design was by Kingsley Reed (Crystal 1988: 81).
  (iv) i.t.a. = Initial Teaching Alphabet was proposed by Pitman in 1960.

Many people are sentimentally attached to the present orthography. They would resist drastic change that made the written language they know and love look strange. Sampson points out that if New Spelling was adopted it would result in the spelling of about 90 per cent of existing words being changed. This would meet with strong resistance.

For all these reasons, the present orthography is unlikely to be drastically reformed. But this is not to say that tinkering at the margins should not take place. In the past various changes have been made and I expect that more could be profitably made without adverse side effects. For example words that came into English from Latin or French had silent consonants introduced in their spelling by scribes who wanted to be clever and reveal the etymology of words, but in fact were wrong about the etymology. Omitting such consonants should simplify matters without causing problems. A typical example of what I have in mind is the word *island* which has an *s* in it because someone imagined that it came from the same root as the word *isle* which originally had an *s* in it (because it is descended from French *île* which comes from Latin *insula*). In fact, though *isle* and *island* are related in meaning, they do not have a common ancestry. *Island* never had an *s* in it to begin with: its source was the Old English form *iegland*, where *ieg* is the earlier Old English word for 'island'.

A more general case where etymological considerations are relevant and which is ripe for reform is the spelling of the verb-forming suffix *-ise/-ize*. There are two spellings of this suffix, found in a verb such as *civilize/civilise*. Both *-ise/-ize* spellings are pronounced /aɪz/. In general Americans tend to prefer *-ize* and the British *-ise* (so, I have used *-ise* spellings in this book because that is the norm in British English), but life would be simpler if we all used *-ize*:

> but a queer conservatism, mainly on the part of printers, supported by the *OED*, forces us back on an etymological distinction which few of us are capable of making, offhand at any rate. The pundits say that words derived from those containing the Greek suffix *-izein* should be spelt with the *-ize* ending; the others *-ise*. But for ordinary people this rule conveys nothing at all.
>
> (Scragg 1973: 35)

7.6 IS SPEECH DEGENERATE WRITING?

In a literate society like this one, where the written word enjoys such prestige, it is easy to see why people sometimes regard speech as less significant than writing. Normally, if anything needs to be given legal or official status it is 'put in writing'. Some even seem to think that the spoken word in the standard language is derived from the written word, or at any rate validated by a written form. They look down with contempt on languages and dialects that are unwritten.

While it would be foolish to play down the importance of writing, it is necessary to recognise the primacy of speech both in the evolution of our species and in the life of the individual. Whereas writing has been around for only about 5–6,000 years, speech has almost certainly existed since ape-men became human over 40,000 years ago. Furthermore, whereas there are many illiterate individuals in any society, and indeed there are entire linguistic communities which are illiterate, we do not find individuals who fail to acquire the spoken language, except in isolated cases of severe physical or mental deficiency. And although illiterate linguistic communities with a language that is only spoken are commonplace, speechless but literate linguistic communities where people communicate by swapping written notes are simply unknown. Looking at language in the life of the individual, the same pattern is observed: speech is acquired before writing.

Nevertheless, the importance of writing cannot be ignored. When writing was first invented, it often involved the visible encoding (on papyrus, cave walls, tree bark etc.) of marks that represented words of the spoken language. That is why an ideal writing system is phonemic. Looking at individual English words, we can often see that the letters of the written word are meant to represent sounds of the spoken word. For instance, we can see that the orthographic word spelt *leg* is a representation of the spoken word with the three sounds represented by *l*, *e* and *g*.

However, for a highly literate society speech and writing provide two closely related, and often complementary systems. Writing and speech are parallel, partly overlapping systems that may serve different functions. The language of auctioneer speech, and what one says to start off and to end a telephone conversation, are good examples of the domain of the spoken language. It is quite likely that you have never seen either written down. Conversely, there are types of language that are unlikely to be used in speech. Examples include the language of legal contract, bibliographies at the back of books like this one, and lists in registers of births and deaths.

Once literacy becomes firmly established, it is not always the case that every written word is a record in some sense of the spoken word. Sometimes it is the written word that is primary and the spoken word that is derivative. This is most obviously true of learned words and technical terms coined using roots and affixes of Latin or Greek origin. It is quite likely that a technical word like *morphophonological* (having to do with the study of the relationship between morphology and phonology) which contains the elements *morpho-phon-olog-ic-al* was used in writing before it was used in speech. Its pronunciation would have had to be worked out from its spelling, not the other way round. This process is not marginal. As we will see in Chapter 10, many words of French origin came into the spoken language via the written language.

The upshot of this discussion is that it would be naive to assume that writing always simply attempts to mirror speech (cf. Knowles 1987: 1–23). Indeed, it is easy to think of cases of SPELLING PRONUNCIATION where pronunciation has changed in order to bring it into line with the spelling. Consider the following, for example:

(i) Names whose spelling is not closely related to the pronunciation may be changed so that pronunciation mirrors spelling. Thus, the Scottish name *Menzies* which used to be /mɪŋɪs/ or /meŋɪs/ is nowadays often pronounced /menzɪz/. When spelling and pronunciation diverge, spelling reform is not the only option available: there is always the option of 'reforming speech' to make it fit spelling.

(ii) Increasingly, the letters *t* and *d* in *often* and *Wednesday* which used to be 'silent' are sounded.

(iii) The word-initial letter *h* in many words, such as *hotel*, *humour* and *herbs* which are borrowed from French (where the *h* is normally not pronounced word-initially), is now sounded. Probably this is done because dropping aitches at the beginning of a word is stigmatised in English.

(iv) Some words with the letter *a* are pronounced with this vowel given the transparent value that it would have in, say, Italian or Spanish. Thus, for example, the older pronunciation of *trauma* as /trɔ:mə/ is being edged out by /traumə/ which reflects more clearly the spelling. Similar changes have happened to *gala* and *data*. Instead of, or alongside, /geɪlə/ and /deɪtə/ you will now often hear /gɑ:lə/ and /dɑ:tə/ (cf. Wells 1982: 108–9).

(v) Acronyms, i.e. words like *VAT* (Valued Added Tax) which are formed from the initial letters of existing words, are an obvious case of going from spelling to pronunciation (see section (9.7)).

Before we get too despondent about the fact that in English spelling does not always quite fit the pronunciation and jump on a radical spelling reform bandwagon, we should bear in mind the fact that the lack of fit between speech and writing is not necessarily an unmitigated disaster, since writing is not merely a pale visual copy of speech.

EXERCISES

1. Often a sound can be represented in writing by more than one letter or combination of letters.

   a. Show the different ways in which the sounds /ə/, /ɪ/, /k/ and /i:/ are spelt in the standard English orthography. Is the choice of letters to represent these sounds totally arbitrary?
   b. Show the different ways in which the letters *th, u, o, oo* and *ea* are pronounced in your variety of English.

2. It is often pointed out that vowel sounds vary greatly both in the ways in which they are actually pronounced in different dialects and in the ways they are spelt. By contrast, consonants show little variation in either sense. Often the outline of a word can be seen from the consonants on their own. In this exercise your task is to test out that claim by re-writing the following passage, filling in the missing vowels.

   Notes:
   (i) Although the letter *y* sometimes represents a vowel sound it has not been left out.
   (ii) The words are written with a space between them.
   (iii) All the punctuation has been retained from the original text.

   mgn lf wtht wrds! Trppst mnks pt fr t. Bt mst f s wld nt gv p wrds fr nythng. vrydy w ttr thsnds nd thsnds f wrds. Cmmnctng r jys, frs, pnns, fntss, wshs, rqsts, dmnds, flngs – nd th ccsnl thrt r nslt, s vry mprtnt spct f bng hmn. Th r s lwys thck wth r vrbl mssns. Thr r s mny thngs w wnt t tll th wrld. Sm f thm r mprtnt, sm f thm r nt. Bt w tlk nywy – vn whn w knw tht wht w r syng s ttlly nmprtnt. W lv chtcht nd fnd slnt ncntrs wkrd, r vn pprssv . . .

   Explain explicitly how you set about the task of recovering the vowels. What spelling rules did you find useful?

3. Referring to plenty of examples, work out the pattern of how the spelling of the letter *s* as single or double relates to the pronunciation in these positions:
   (i) at the beginning of a word
   (ii) before a consonant letter
   (iii) after a consonant letter

(iv) between vowel letters
(v) at the end of a word

4. a. Suggest an explanation for the use of non-standard spelling in the following advertisement:

YOU CAN'T GET BETTER THAN A KWIK-FIT FITTER

b. Find two fresh examples of similar advertisements.

5. Study the spelling of this passage.

THE TELLYFONE RINGS IN OUR HOUSE AND MY FATHER PICKS IT UP AND SAYS IN HIS VERY IMPORTANT TELLYFONE VOICE 'SIMPKINS SPEAK-ING'. THEN HIS FACE GOES WHITE AND HIS VOICE GOES ALL FUNNY AND HE SAYS '*WHAT! WHO?*' AND THEN HE SAYS 'YES SIR I UNDERSTAND SIR BUT SURELY IT IS *ME* YOU IS WISHING TO SPEKE TO SIR NOT MY LITTLE SON?' MY FATHER'S FACE IS GOING FROM WHITE TO DARK PURPEL AND HE IS GULPING LIKE HE HAS A LOBSTER STUCK IN HIS THROTE AND THEN AT LAST HE IS SAYING 'YES SIR VERY WELL SIR I WILL GET HIM SIR' AND HE TURNS TO ME AND HE SAYS IN A RATHER RESPECKFUL VOICE 'IS YOU KNOWING THE PRESIDENT OF THE UNITED STATES?' AND I SAYS 'NO BUT I EXPECT HE IS HEAR-ING ABOUT ME.' THEN I IS HAVING A LONG TALK ON THE FONE AND SAYING THINGS LIKE 'LET ME TAKE CARE OF IT, MR PRESIDENT. YOU'LL BUNGLE IT ALL UP IF YOU DO IT YOUR WAY'. AND MY FATHER'S EYES IS GOGGLING RIGHT OUT OF HIS

HEAD AND THAT IS WHEN I IS HEARING MY
FATHER'S REAL VOICE SAYING GET UP YOU LAZY
SLOB OR YOU WILL BE LATE FOR SKOOL.

(From the *The BFG* by Roald Dahl, pp. 108–9)

Suggest a plausible account for each instance of incorrect spelling in the text from *The BFG*.

Chapter 8

Word manufacture

8.1 THE PRODUCTION LINE

Morphology needs to provide an account of our ability to work out the meaning of unfamiliar words and to make up new words. Word manufacture is not a task we leave to experts. We all do it. This chapter examines some of the ways in which we do it.

Morphological theory provides the tools for analysing 'real' words like *shopkeeper* and *conversations* which are listed in dictionaries and which probably most competent, adult speakers of English know. But if it stopped at that, it would be failing in its task of characterising the nature of speakers' lexical knowledge. For our knowledge of English vocabulary goes far beyond the INSTITUTION-ALISED words listed in dictionaries. You know thousands of words listed in dictionaries. And you also know an indefinitely large number of words that have not been documented by lexicographers although they have occurred in speech or writing. Further, you have the ability to comprehend many POTENTIAL WORDS that have not yet occurred.

Obviously, a very considerable number of words must simply be memorised (see section (11.1.2)). If a word is made up of a single morpheme (e.g. *zebra*, *tree*, *saddle*), there is no way one can work out its meaning. Such words simply have to be committed to memory. However, as mentioned in our earlier discussion of compositionality in sections (4.4.3) and (6.1), if a word contains several morphemes and if you know what the morphemes mean, you are usually able to work out what the word as a whole means, even if you have never encountered it before. We made that point with the example of *Lebanonisation* in section (3.2). The same point is illustrated by the non-institutionalised word *Hollywoodisation* which

I heard in a radio discussion in which someone lamented 'the growing Hollywoodisation of the Cannes Film Festival'.

New words like these come off the production line all the time. In most cases there is no record of who first used a particular word. Only in relatively rare cases are the names of the individuals responsible for lexical creations known. But a few people who have manufactured colourful words are remembered. For example S. Foote is remembered for coining the word *panjandrum* in 1755. He intended this simply as a nonsense word; it acquired the meaning of 'mock title for a pompous dignitary' later.

However, in most cases words are manufactured anonymously. Take the word *yuppie* which was formed by adding the suffix spelled as *-y* or *-ie* to the initial letters of either 'Young Urban Professional Person' or 'Young Upwardly Mobile Professional Person'. There is some uncertainty about the correct source of this word, which originated in America in the 1980s where it was used to describe youngish people who received enormous (and possibly disproportionate) rewards for their services on the money markets. It is not known who coined it. But it caught on and for a time spawned numerous derivatives.

Imagine the year is 1987. You live in a run-down inner city Victorian neighbourhood of a British city which over a relatively short period has begun to change in character. Instead of ramshackle cars parked in the street, there have gradually appeared smart, high-powered German cars, with price tags to match. Many terraced houses that have been grimy for years have received a lick of paint and their interiors have been transformed by having fancy designer kitchens, bathrooms and stripped-pine furniture installed. Every conceivable Victorian feature has also been restored. Outside, the pigeon lofts in the back gardens have been replaced with bonsai trees, dwarf azaleas and children's swings. Many of the cloth-capped men in blue overalls and their matronly wives have been replaced by women and men in grey pinstriped suits who clutch their briefcases, filofaxes, laptop computers and mobile phones when they leave for work in the morning. You see all this and think to yourself, 'The neighbourhood is undergoing *yuppification.*' You regret the transformation and long for the good old days. You long for the day when something will happen which might cause the *deyuppification* of the neighbourhood and restore the place to its earlier state.

I expect you not to have encountered the words *yuppification* and *deyuppification* before now. They are NONCE WORDS (words expressly coined for the first time and apparently used once) that are not institutionalised. But I am confident that, nevertheless, you figured out their meaning instantly. You analysed them as containing the root *yuppie* and the suffixes *-fic* meaning 'make' and *-ation*, which derives nouns of action. Given the context (and relevant context always does help), you knew that *yuppification* of a neighbourhood means turning it into a yuppie environment. *Deyuppification* was equally easy to analyse. The prefix *de-* is a reversive verbal prefix meaning the undoing of whatever the verb means. So, you figured that if *deyuppification* happened, the yuppies (or their lifestyle) would be removed from the neighbourhood.

The moral of this story is that many complex MORPHOLOGICAL OBJECTS are compositional. They need not be listed in the lexicon since their meaning can be worked out by anyone who knows the meaning of their constituent elements. In this words such as *deyuppification* differ from simple morphological objects (morphemes or simple words e.g. *-ful*, *-ly*, *-less*, *zebra*), which must be listed in the dictionary and memorised since they contain no clues to their meanings.

The upshot of this discussion is that the listing of words in the lexicographers' dictionaries that we buy from bookshops are always partial. Even now, after *yuppification* and *deyuppification* have made their début here, they are unlikely to be institutionalised in such dictionaries. All dictionaries are selective. While no sensible lexicographer would omit obvious, commonly used, established words like *house* or *travel*, there is a considerable degree of selection when it comes to novel or unusual words (e.g. *deyuppification*) which may have been encountered by the dictionary compiler very rarely, or as a one-off in a single conversation.

Furthermore, many of the more esoteric technical terms or jargon used in various disciplines are often not included in general dictionaries. (Standard dictionaries are extremely unlikely to tell you what *morphophonemics* or *allomorph* mean, for example.)

The point that lexicographers are selective and that their dictionaries represent only a partial list of the lexical items of a language merits closer investigation. The fact that it is not in the dictionary does not mean it is not in the language. Take the word *unleaving*, in Gerard Manley Hopkins's poem 'Spring and Fall':

> Margaret, are you grieving
> Over Goldengrove unleaving?
> Leaves like the things of man, you
> With your fresh thoughts care for, can you?

Although *unleaving* is attested here in the work of a major English poet, it is not recorded in the *OED*. But that does not mean that you cannot understand its meaning. Clearly, in the context *unleaving* means a tree shedding its leaves.

This puts a fresh complexion on things. Contrary to what many of us tend to believe (and are encouraged to believe by word games like Scrabble) words are not 'proper words' by virtue of being listed in a dictionary. Rather, words are proper words if they are linguistic signs which associate arbitrary sounds with meanings in a manner that is sanctioned by the rule system of a particular language. We can distinguish three types of word, and competence in a language must include a reasonable degree of ability to handle all three of them.

First, there are the institutionalised words listed in dictionaries, e.g. *house*. Second, there are uninstitutionalised words that have been manifested in use, e.g. *unleaving* and *deyuppification*. Third, there are potential words waiting to make their début as it were when a particular meaning is matched with a particular phonological representation. Today *unreprissing* is not an English word because although it is a phonologically permissible word, it has no meaning associated with it. If you care to find a meaning for it, it will become a word – perhaps only as a nonce word.

Many of the nonce, non-institutionalised words are compounds (cf. section (2.2.1)). If a speaker wants to express an idea which would normally be expressed by a syntactic phrase in a manner that heightens its concreteness and salience, it is possible as a one-off, to make up a disposable, hyphenated compound. The newspaper columnist Melanie Phillips manufactured the word '*anything-goes-as-long-as-you-can-get-away-with-it-culture*' which is an excellent example of this phenomenon:

[8.1] Public life has fallen into disrepute and the cynicism of the people knows no bounds. It's the anything-goes-as-long-as-you-can-get-away-with-it-culture, and it is as prevalent in the corridors of Whitehall as in the joyriders' ghettos.

(Phillips 1993)

The word stockpile of an individual and of the speech community as a whole is relatively stable and restricted. So, one might suppose that in principle it should be possible to list and count the words (in the sense of lexical items) that belong to the English language. In reality such an exercise is very problematic because the inventory of words is not static. People make up new words. I have made up *yuppification*, which I do not expect to stick. According to the *OED*, someone made up the word *hydrofoil* in the 1920s and *scuba* appeared on the scene in 1956. Both innovations were successfully institutionalised.

At the other end of the spectrum old words go out of use, e.g. *wone* meaning 'home, abode' is now obsolete. If I said to you '*Where is your wone?*' you would have no idea what I was talking about. Then there is also the problem of separating the dialectal and the archaic words from obsolete ones e.g. *porret* 'young leek or onion'. While *wone* is obsolete, *porret* survives in dialectal use but it is very rare. The line between 'dialectal and very rare' and 'obsolete' is a fine one. In spite of these difficulties, it does make sense to list words. Lexicographers have not got it all wrong. We just have to bear in mind the fact that a dictionary can only be a partial list of the lexical items of a language.

To sum up, although by and large the words of a language are listable in dictionaries, it is not possible to list all of them. Speakers actively manufacture words. The lexicon is not just a vast lexical warehouse, it is also a production line where words are made in limitless quantities. For the most part, this is done by applying established rules: language users who have mastered these rules can use them to construct or unscramble words, be they old established words or new ones (cf. sections (4) and (6.1)).

8.2 KEEPING TABS ON IDIOMS

We have seen that simple words must be listed in the lexicon because their meanings are not compositional. No matter how sophisticated your analytical technique was, you would not be able to work out the meaning of a word like *tree* or *zebra* which contains just one morpheme. In this respect morphology differs from syntax. Typically, sentences produced by syntactic rules do not need to be listed since they are compositional, while many words need to be listed in the dictionary because they are not compositional (cf. Di Sciullo and Williams 1987). When we use language we do not try to re-cycle sentences that we have previously used. Normally, using general syntactic rules, we create fresh sentences to suit the communicative needs of the situation. If you know the meanings of the words in a sentence and if you can work out its structure, you can also work out its meaning even though you may never have encountered it before. Compare the sentences below:

[8-2]

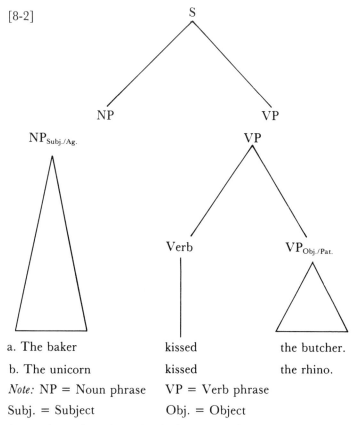

a. The baker   kissed   the butcher.

b. The unicorn   kissed   the rhino.

Note: NP = Noun phrase   VP = Verb phrase

Subj. = Subject   Obj. = Object

Ag. = Agent (i.e. the individual or entity that instigates the action)

Pat. = Patient (i.e. the individual or entity that undergoes the action)

Finally, I am using triangles to abbreviate inessential details of constituent structure.

Although you almost certainly have never seen or heard the sentence in [8.2b], you had no difficulty understanding it because you were able to work out which words form syntactic constituents, and what their semantic relationships are. Hence, since sentences are formed compositionally, they do not have to be listed.

The trouble is that it is sometimes possible to create new lexical items by converting syntactic phrases into word-like vocabulary items. A consequence of this is to upset the neat distinction that we have drawn between words, as listed lexical objects, and sentences, as unlisted syntactic objects. Syntactic phrases used as lexical items are called IDIOMS. Idioms are peculiar in that they are non-compositional syntactic phrases. This means that their meanings cannot be deduced from the meanings of the words they contain (cf. Di Sciullo and Williams 1987, Katamba 1993).

OCT. 21

The Emperor of Germany, who had been selected as Arbitrator in the dispute between Great Britain and the United States regarding the San Juan Boundary Question, gave his award to-day. It was in favour of the United States whose claims, the Emperor declared, justly accorded with the true interpretation of the Treaty of the 15th June, 1846.

HUMBLE PIE

I am still the same John Bull, who of glory once supped full,
Faced Europe with my subsidies, my soldiers, and my ships;
When I'd bites behind my barks, when I hit straight at my
   marks,
And found my foes in fisticuffs, as I found my friends in tips:
But now I'm all for a quiet life, 'jowk, and let the jaw go by';
Keep my feelings in my pockets, and put up with HUMBLE PIE.

Once foreigners looked up to me: a high head I could hold:
If my *prestige* cost me millions, those millions' worth was mine:
Strong and safe were laid my bulwarks with British blood and
   gold;
Of a grander God than Mammon my island was the shrine:

"HUMBLE PIE."

Mr. Bull. "Humble pie again, William! – You gave me that yesterday?"
Head Waiter. "Yes, Sir – no, Sir – that were GENEVA humble pie,
Sir. This is BERLIN humble pie, Sir!!"

Honour was given to honour, in those darkened days gone by;
Now honour's sold for money . . . and my dish is HUMBLE PIE.

Then, in dealing with a bully, I was game to hold my own;
And the ground once wisely taken I stood to, stiff and stout:
In smooth tongues I had little faith, but much in teeth well
    shown,
And hands as strong to use the sword as slow to take it out.
The only kind of fighting I disliked was fighting shy,
And the one dish I would *not* eat, in those days, was HUMBLE
    PIE!

'If the right cheek's smitten, turn the left,' was written then as
    now,
But the Quakers were the only sect who to that rule would
    agree:
So with so much Christian doctrine waiting practice, I allow,
I applied that text to friends, not foes, and hit them who hit
    at me:
But now it's 'Give your coat to those who to steal your
    waistcoat try,'
And the end is peace and plenty – that is, of HUMBLE PIE!

Hear Baxter and Bow Lowe prove as plain as tongue can speak,
How of all possible Governments this Government is the best,
Who cares for the foreigner's laugh in his sleeve, the foreigner's
    tongue in his cheek?
The smaller John Bull sings, 'tis clear, the warmer he lines his
    nest.
Once shame, they say, made him bilious and lean, but that is
    all my eye –
There's no meat he so thrives upon (see Baxter) as HUMBLE
    PIE!

As you can see in [8.3], the structure of idioms is similar to the
structure of ordinary syntactic phrases. The same rules that generate ordinary syntactic phrases also generate idioms:

[8.3] a.

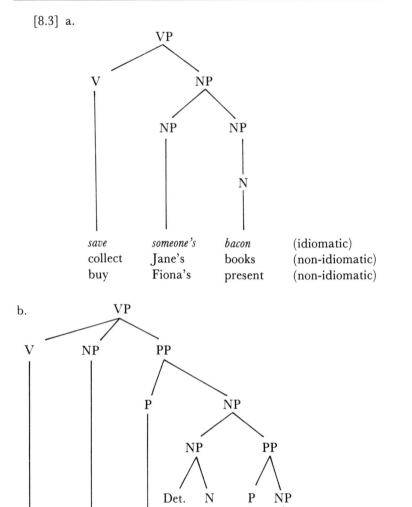

save	*someone's*	*bacon*	(idiomatic)
collect	Jane's	books	(non-idiomatic)
buy	Fiona's	present	(non-idiomatic)

b.

take	*something*	*with*	*a*	*pinch*	*of*	*salt*	(idiomatic)
drench	something	with	a	bucket	of	water	(non-idiomatic)
fill	something	with	a	gallon	of	milk	(non-idiomatic)

c.

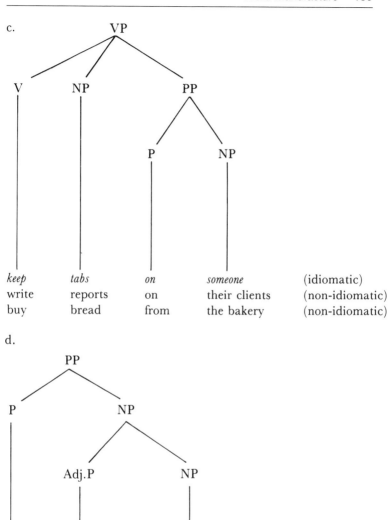

keep	*tabs*	*on*	*someone*	(idiomatic)
write	reports	on	their clients	(non-idiomatic)
buy	bread	from	the bakery	(non-idiomatic)

d.

in	*high*	*spirits*	(idiomatic)
in	dangerous	places	(non-idiomatic)
in	old	houses	(non-idiomatic)

Obviously, knowing the grammatical structure and the meaning of the words in the idiomatic expressions in [8.3] is no help in understanding what the idioms mean. The meanings of these idioms must be listed in the dictionary along the lines shown in [8.4]:

[8.4]   *Idiom*   *Example*

a. *save someone's bacon* 'save   Thanks for talking to the
   someone a lot of trouble'   police officer. You have
                                       saved my bacon.

b. *take something with a pinch*   I'd take whatever any
   of salt 'be sceptical'   politician says with a pinch
                                       of salt.

c. *keep tabs on someone* 'check   Probation officers keep tabs
   up on' ('*keep an eye on*')   on young offenders on
                                       parole.

d. *in high spirits* 'slightly   They were in high spirits
   drunk and excited'   when they got back from the
                                       party.

An indefinitely large number of syntactic phrases can be turned into idioms by assigning them idiosyncratic, lexicalised meanings. This is one of the ways in which a limitless supply of lexical items is assured, and another reason why all the lexical items of a language cannot be listed in a dictionary.

8.3 CLITICS

In this section we shall turn our attention to CLITICS. A clitic is a bound morpheme which is not an affix but which, nevertheless, occurs as part of a word (cf. (4.2.2)). We are going to see that CLITICISATION (the process of attaching clitics) takes place post-lexically after the word-formation rules of the lexicon have applied, and following the application of syntactic rules. (By contrast, affixes are attached at the lexical level: cf. sections (6.5.1) and (6.5.2).

There are two classes of clitics:

[8.5]   *Class 1 clitics*
        These always occur as appendages to words. They are totally incapable of appearing on their own as independent words. The GENITIVE 'S', (as in *a farmer's wife, the parson's nose*) is the only example of this kind of clitic in English.

Class 2 clitics

These are forms which are capable of appearing as independent words in some cases but are also used as dependent appendages to words. This is exemplified by the reduced auxiliary verbs e.g. *'ll, 've, 'd* (as in *I'll, we've, she's, they'd* which are derived from *will* or *shall, have, is, had*).

The thing that all clitics have in common is some phonological deficiency which debars them from functioning as independent phonological words. In English, it is crucial for a phonological word to have a vowel. (There are no vowelless words like **tpngs, *tvmrk, *sntd, *s, *kvpl.*) Clitics do not qualify for word status because they lack vowels. The requirement that words must contain vowels is inviolable. To become pronounceable any form like *'s* or *'d* must be annexed to a word. The word to which a clitic is appended is called a HOST.

We will now consider the two types of clitic in turn, starting with the class 1 type of clitic, i.e. the genitive *'s*:

[8.6]   a. the farmer's wife
      b. a day's work

The genitive *'s* construction in English is used to indicate that a noun (to be precise, NP) on the left which hosts the *'s* is a syntactic modifier which specifies more narrowly the meaning of the noun on the right which is the head of the entire NP. The exact semantic value of the *'s* genitive construction varies, as you can see from the following section of examples based on Quirk and Greenbaum (1973):

[8.7] GENITIVE 's   PARAPHRASE

  a. *Possessive genitive*

the farmer's cattle	the cattle belonging to the farmer
the farmer's tractor	the tractor belonging to the farmer
the farmer's wife	the wife of the farmer

  b. *Genitive of origin*

the farmer's messenger	the messenger sent by the farmer
the farmer's story	the story told by the farmer

c. *Genitive of measure*

two years' imprisonment	imprisonment lasting for two years
a day's journey	a journey lasting one whole day.

Frequently the noun on the left is the possessor of the entity that is on its right which functions as the head of the entire NP, as in [8.7a]. 'Possessor' is a misleading term for this relationship in many cases. Often the meaning of this construction is not one of 'owning'. The farmer may own the cattle and tractor, but not the wife. She is his partner, not his chattel. The genitive in this latter case indicates a relationship, not possession.

The fact that the *'s* genitive is not necessarily a marker of possession is even clearer in the rest of the examples in [8.7b] and [8.7c]. *The farmer's story* is a story told, not owned, by the farmer and *a day's journey* is a journey that lasts a whole day – not one that is owned by the day.

Thus the syntactic and semantic relationship of the genitive *'s* with its host is variable. The syntactic role of this *'s* is to mark a NP as being syntactically subordinated to another NP on its right, which it modifies. The meaning of this *'s* clitic is difficult to pin down. By contrast, affix morphemes tend to have a more readily identifiable meaning: e.g. *-s* as in *trees* has a very predictable plural meaning.

Furthermore, the relationship between a clitic and its host may show schizophrenic tendencies. It may attach to one word phonologically but relate to another syntactically and semantically. Words form cohesive units with their affixes. But CLITIC GROUPS (i.e. forms containing clitics and their hosts), do not. The morphemes belonging to a word are firmly bonded together and cannot be separated by extraneous material. Not so with a clitic group.

Often we find, especially in casual speech, clitics whose phonological host is different from their syntactic/semantic host. The phonological host of *'s* is always the word that precedes the head. From a semantic angle, we can paraphrase *the farmer's tractor* as 'the tractor that is owned by the farmer'. The genitive *'s* is appended to the noun *farmer* which is both the possessor from the semantic angle and the phonological host. However, in colloquial English the situation is more fluid. If we take a phrase like *the farmer next to our campsite's tractor*, we find that the semantic possessor and the phonological host are divorced. The *farmer* is still the owner of the *tractor*. But the genitive *'s* attaches to *campsite*, which is the phonological host.

Suffixes cannot do that. For example, if semantically a noun is plural, it receives the plural inflection itself. The plural suffix cannot turn up somewhere else in the sentence. Suppose we have a sentence like *She bought three skirts from that boutique last week* where *skirts* is the only plural noun, there is simply no way we could remove the *-s* from *skirts* and relocate it on a new site. Shifting the *-s* to another place yields ungrammatical sentences like **She bought three skirt from that boutiques last week* or **She bought three skirt from that boutique last weeks.*

Whereas genitive *'s* is the only class 1 clitic, class 2 clitics, to which we now turn, are quite numerous. As already mentioned, class 2 clitics are forms capable of appearing either as independent words or as clitics appended to a host. Many auxiliary verbs appearing in unstressed position in a sentence can be free autonomous words as in [8.8a] or they may be reduced to a consonant which is appended as a clitic to a preceding host, as in [8.8b]:

[8.8] a. *Full word*

'I am 'cold.
'He is 'cold.
'We will 'see it.
His 'wife has 'left it.
His 'wife has 'left.

b. *Clitic*

'I'm 'cold.
'He's 'cold.
'We'll 'see it.
His 'wife's 'left it.
His 'wife's 'left.

Note: ' marks secondary stress and ' marks main stress.

The cognitive meaning of the sentences in each pair is the same. Cliticisation does not affect meaning. It only affects style. Use of class 2 clitics indicates greater informality than the use of full words. In formal written English cliticised forms are usually avoided – except where the writer is portraying spoken language.

All word-formation regardless of whether it is done by inflection or derivation takes place in the dictionary. But clitic group formation does not. Clitic groups are formed later when words are put together in syntactic phrases. The behaviour of genitive *'s* described above makes this very clear. Until you know what the words that form a genitive NP are, you are not in a position to identify the word immediately preceding the head of the construction to which you attach the *'s*. Clitics are appended after syntactic rules have grouped words together in phrases.

8.4 SUMMARY

All morphemes must be listed in the dictionary since their meaning is not compositional. Many lexical items too must be listed in the dictionary because their meaning is not deducible from the elements that they are made up of. However, some lexical items are semantically compositional so they need not be listed. The lexicon is not a closed list. Normally, word-manufacture employs standard rules to produce new words that can be added to the lexicon (Bauer 1988: 57–72).

Idioms are a theoretically challenging class of lexical items for they share the characteristics of both words and phrases. Structurally, idioms are like ordinary syntactic phrases. But their meanings are unpredictable, just like the meanings of simple words. So they must be listed in the dictionary.

Finally, in addition to affixes, we need to recognise a separate class of bound morphemes appended to the hosts. These are the clitics which are attached to words to form clitic groups after words have been grouped into syntactic phrases. Some clitics are always bound morphemes but others are capable of appearing in some contexts as independent words. All clitics have a phonological deficiency which disqualifies them from appearing as independent words. Further, unlike suffixes, clitics are capable of attaching to a phonological host that is distinct from their syntactic/semantic host. Clitic groups are not lexical objects. They are not listed in the lexicon. (For further discussion see Zwicky and Pullum 1983, Zwicky 1985, Klavans 1985, Katamba 1993.)

EXERCISES

1. a. Explain why the items *n't*, *'ve*, *'s*, and *'d* in the passage below should be treated as clitics rather than suffixes.
   b. What type of clitic is each item an example of?

   '*Don't* you think *you've* got your bottom corner a bit far out?' came father*'s* voice from below. '*You'd* better be drawing in now, *hadn't* you?'

   (Lawrence 1960: 13)

2. Study the following idioms and answer the questions that follow:

stick-in-the-mud
to spill the beans
(to receive) a golden handshake
to take advantage of
to turn over a new leaf
to bury the hatchet
to feather one's nest
to be caught between a rock and a hard place
to show (someone) the cold shoulder
to throw out the baby with the bath water

a. Give a paraphrase of each idiom that clearly brings out its meaning.
b. Draw a phrase structure tree showing the syntactic structure of each idiom.
c. In the light of your answers to (a) and (b) discuss the role of compositionality in the study of lexical items of this kind.

3. a. Referring to at least two specific examples of compounds (e.g. *drawing-board*) and words containing affixes (e.g. *Hollywoodisation*), show why many morphological objects (i.e. words) need not be listed in the lexicon.
b. Should the words *environmental*, *fantastic* and *modernism* be listed in the dictionary or are they semantically transparent enough for that to be unnecessary?

4. Find texts containing examples of at least two nonce words formed by affixation or compounding. Explain how language users can work out the meanings of the words that you have chosen.

5. Why is it impossible to determine exactly how many words there are in English?

Chapter 9

Words galore

9.1 A VERBAL BONANZA

In this chapter we consider further methods of manufacturing LEXICAL ITEMS using the internal resources of the language which do not fall within the scope of affixation, compounding or conversion. The processes we will explore in this chapter generally involve some sort of recycling of existing words. We will postpone until the next chapter discussion of the alternative strategy of expanding the vocabulary through the importation of words from other languages which has been noted in passing in previous chapters.

9.2 JARGON

There are speech sub-varieties that are associated with particular occupations. These sub-varieties are primarily distinguished by their JARGON (i.e. their peculiar words and word-like expressions). The manufacture of jargon is one of the richest sources of new words.

Jargon serves a very useful purpose. It provides members of a social sub-group with the lexical items they need in order to talk about the subject matter that their field deals with. As a student beginning the study of linguistics you have had the experience of being immersed in a world of bewildering jargon. You have had to come to grips with terms like *morphemes*, *allomorphs*, *alveolar*, *gerundive*, *archiphoneme* and *phrase structure tree*. You can add to this list your own favourite bits of linguistic terminology.

Sometimes the jargon of a specialist group seeps into the common language of the wider community. This is particularly likely to happen where the activities of that subgroup are fashionable or impinge directly on the life of the wider community. So, for example, even those of us who know little, or nothing, about chemistry do talk about *catalysts* and *percolation*. Similarly, many people who are definitely not computer wizards now use words like *what-you-see-is-what-you-get* (WYSIWYG), *database, software, interface, daisychain, handshake* and *programming* for in the last few decades computer jargon has spread into the linguistic mainstream as the use of computers has spread (Green 1987). The words *daisychain* (i.e. a device that links a number of devices to a single controller) and *handshake* (i.e. communication between two parts of a system e.g., computer and printer) are particularly noteworthy for they involve metaphorical extensions of meaning. In many cases the metaphorical nature of such expressions largely goes unnoticed when they become entrenched in the general lexicon.

9.3 SLANG

SLANG is the term used to describe a variety of language with informal, often faddy, non-standard vocabulary. Slang is a major source of new words (often with a very limited life expectancy). In many cases it involves the use of standard forms in a new and non-standard way.

According to Partridge (1933), there at least fifteen good reasons for using slang. They include the desire to experiment with using language 'poetically' or creatively, for pleasure; the desire to be secretive; the desire to be expressive; the desire to use language as a badge of group membership so as to express intimacy with those inside the group and to exclude those who are not (technical jargon also does this job); to indicate that one is casual and relaxed etc. In the next few paragraphs we will consider examples of these uses of slang.

Let us start with the language of insults, which is very rich in expressive slang. An idiot may be called any one of these colourful names:

[9.1] oaf, balloon, jerk, plonker, plodger, flake (USA)
       wally, nerd, dope, goof, gwot (USA), bampot (Glasgow)

British prison life is also rich in slang which serves to create a feeling of solidarity in adverse circumstances. For instance, a prisoner may tell his mates how he was arrested by the *filth* (i.e. detectives) while doing a *job* (i.e. robbery). He may tell them how he hates being locked up in this *nick* (i.e. prison) by those horrible *screws* (i.e. gaolers). He may refer to his imprisonment variously as:

[9.2] porridge, stretch, time, bird

Visits to the toilet are as embarrassing as they are necessary. A lot of slang terms have been developed for speakers to cover up their embarrassment. Just think of your favourite term for the *lavatory*. Is it one of these?

[9.3] lav, altar, bog, john, lavvy, loo, throne, little boys' room, little girls' room, little office

If I have left out your preferred word, add it to the list.

In some working-class communities there is a well-established tradition of RHYMING SLANG which serves both the poetic function and the solidarity-with-the-in-group function.

Cockney rhyming slang is probably the best known. Here are some examples:

[9.4] *Standard word*   *Slang*
      wife   joy of my life
                          storm and strife
                          worry and strife
                          trouble and strife
                          carving-knife
                          drum and fife

(based on Franklin 1960)

Some rhyming slang words, like those listed above, are well established and can be listed in a dictionary of slang. But many others are nonce words made up on the spur of the moment and are specific to a particular context. Such words are only interpretable if one has the necessary contextual clues.

9.4 CLICHÉS AND CATCH-PHRASES

A CLICHÉ is a hackneyed expression that has become trite, insipid and banal due to over-exposure. Of course, before it became worn out by overuse, it may have had a freshness, sharpness and precision that made it memorable. As Zijderveld (1979: 11) puts it, 'clichés contain the stale wisdom of past generations – elements of the "collective consciousness" of yester-year'. This is most obviously true of proverbs and sayings like *'spare the rod and spoil the child'*, *'out of the frying pan into the fire'*, *'a storm in a teacup'*.

Memorable expressions from literary language also tend to turn into clichés. From Shakespeare we get *a rose by any other name* (*Romeo and Juliet*). The bard's *Hamlet* is also the source of *I must be cruel only to be kind* as well as *to be or not to be* (and variants thereof, some quite elaborate, like the one in the *Punch* cartoon on p. 170). *Sleeping Beauty* was awakened from her slumber by the Prince's kiss. By analogy any person rescued from death by mouth-to-mouth artificial respiration is said to receive *a kiss of life*. Even titles of books may become clichés e.g. Tolstoy's *War and Peace* and Dostoevksy's *Crime and Punishment*.

FEB. 7.

Parliament was opened by Commission. The Queen's Speech announced the projected marriage between Prince Leopold, Duke of Albany, and the Princess Helen of Waldeck and Pyrmont. It referred to the execution of the Treaty for the cession of Thessaly to the Greeks, to our joint action with France in Egypt, to the restoration of peace beyond the North-Western frontier of India, and to the ratification of the Transvaal Convention. It spoke of the continuation of negotiations with France on the subject of a new Commercial Treaty, and of improvement in the state of Ireland. it foreshadowed measures of a Local Self Government, London Municipal Reform, and some others.

It was felt, however, that the first question to be dealt with was Parliamentary Procedure. Mr. Gladstone gave notice that he would move early in the ensuing week his New Rules of Procedure, of which it was believed the Clôture in some form or other would form a chief feature.

HAMLET AND THE SITUATION.
(*Perplexed Premier ponders.*)

Clôture or no *Clôture?* That is the question:–
Whether 'tis better, on the whole, to suffer
The waste and worry of malign Obstruction,
Or to take arms against the plague of Spouters,
And, by mouth-closing, foil them? To rise – to vote –
No more; – and, by a vote, to find we end
The boredom and the thousand wanton 'blocks'
The Session's heir to. 'Tis a consummation

"CHEF SAUCE!"

Mr. P. "Very nice, William; only recollect – what's Sauce for the Goose is Sauce for the Gander!"

Devoutly to be wished. To rise – to vote –
To vote! Perchance to gag. Ay, there's the rub;
For from that Vote what tyranny may come,
When we have wriggled from Obstruction's coil,
Must give us pause. There's the consideration
That makes endurance of so long a life:
For who would bear the quips and quirks of Bartlett,
Tart Biggar's tongue, O'Donnell's contumely,
The gibes of gadfly Gorst, Warton's delay,
The cheek of callow Churchill, and the spurns
That patient Forster of rude Healy takes,
When he to them might their quietus give
With a bare majority? Who'd night-sittings bear
To yawn and faint for twenty weary hours,
But that the fear of after-hurt to Freedom, –
That glory of our Country, whose wide bourn
No Liberal would limit, clogs the will
And makes us rather bear the ills we have,
Than fly to others that we may not measure?
Thus Caution does make cowards of us all;
And thus the Statesman's native resolution,
Is hampered by the cobweb coils of doubt
And politicians of great pith and prowess,
From this reform their faces turn aside,
Dreading the name of – *Clôture!*

Like memorable titles good political slogans are effective because they are stereotyped expressions to be used over and over again. Over-exposure may eventually turn a political slogan into a cliché. That has been the fate of political slogans like *better dead than red, la lutta continua, power to the people, black is beautiful, for Queen and country, the free world, a just peace, no surrender, the new world order,* and so forth.

The same is true of religious sayings and advertising slogans. Religious sayings may become hackneyed e.g. *to fall on stony ground,* said of ideas that fail to win acceptance (an allusion to the parable of the sower in Matthew 13: 5–6) or *to turn the other cheek* (Matthew 5:39). Successful advertising campaigns can suffer the same fate, e.g. there are numerous hackneyed variations on the theme of Heineken: [*the lager that*] *refreshes the parts other beers can't reach.*

Many clichés contain words that almost invariably occur in each other's company. Although they contain several distinct words, these are often used as though they were single lexical items, e.g. *blissful ignorance, quiet confidence, a commanding lead, hawks and doves, a tower of strength, a bouncing baby, a staunch Protestant, a raving loony.*

Some clichés are called CATCH-PHRASES. Catch-phrases are popular expressions which virtually function as lexical items. Often such expressions are associated with a well-known song, film, show, book, or a famous personality. For instance, Sherlock Holmes's '*elementary, my dear Watson*' (i.e. 'obvious') is now part of the standard language. More examples are listed in [9.5]:

[9.5] a. *never had it so good*
From '*Our people have never had it so good.*'
(Harold Macmillan, British Prime Minister 1959–63)

b. *you ain't seen (or heard) nothin' yet* (i.e. it is greater, worse etc. than you think.)
(From *The Barker*, a 1927 Broadway play by Kenyon Nicholson.)

c. *good in parts, like the curate's egg*
A curate is taking breakfast in his bishop's home:
'I'm afraid you've got a bad egg, Mr Jones.'
'Oh no, my Lord, I assure you! Parts of it are excellent.'
(From an illustrated joke by Gerald du Maurier in *Punch* 1895, vol. CIX, p. 222.)

d. *anything goes!*
(= 'Anything is permissible, do exactly as you please.' *c.*1930; popularised by a Cole Porter song and musical comedy.)

e. *Never a dull moment*
Used ironically in moments of excitement or danger.
(Royal Navy, dating from 1939)
(from Beale 1985)

Sometimes the origin of even a fairly recent catch-phrase is in dispute. Take the expression *the real McCoy*, meaning 'first rate'. This catch-phrase, applied to people and things of the highest quality since the 1880s, has two possible origins. According to Partridge (1986), it originated in Scotland where it applied to an excellent brand of whisky.

However, in the USA it is said to have originated from one of the inventions of Elijah McCoy (1843–1929) an African-American mechanical engineer who patented the first 'lubricating cup' which continuously oiled the gears while the locomotive engine was running. (This was an important step in the development of engine technology. Previously engines needed to make frequent stops to be oiled, which cost their owners money in lost journeys. Lubricating caps were soon fitted on all other kinds of steam engines.) By the 1920s, the McCoy system was considered an essential part of heavy-duty engines. If you sold an engine, the buyer would ask if it was 'the real McCoy', i.e. was fitted with the McCoy system (cf. Haber 1970: 51–9).

9.5 A ROSE BY ANY OTHER NAME

The relationship between the meaning and the physical pronunciation or spelling of a word is usually ARBITRARY. (We are excluding the marginal cases of onomatopoeic words like *cuckoo* where the name of the bird imitates its song; cf. section (3.5).)

The nature of entities and individuals is in no way affected by the words used to refer to them. As Shakespeare's Juliet says:

[9.6] O! be some other name:
What's in a name? that which we call a rose
By any other name would smell as sweet;
So Romeo would, were he not Romeo call'd,
Retain that dear perfection which he owes
Without that title.

(*Romeo and Juliet*, II, ii)

This ARBITRARINESS OF THE LINGUISTIC SIGN (cf. Saussure 1916) has far-reaching implications. Any meaning can be associated with any word-form. A word form already associated with one meaning can be associated with additional meaning. This is especially clear when you consider the aspects of word meaning below:

(a) *Homonymy*, the use of the same form in speech and writing to convey different unrelated meanings is common. For example, the form *tip* represents a variety of meanings, including these based on the *OED*: (i) the slender, pointed end of a thing; (ii) the present or gratuity paid to an 'inferior' for services rendered; (iii) private information that is shared with another person; (iv) a facility where waste is dumped; (v) to fall by overbalancing. Thus, more and more meanings may be added to the language, without more word-forms being added (cf. p. 22) e.g., originally you had the *chips* that you ate. When the new word *microchips* was shortened to *chips*, the language acquired a new homonym.

(b) *Homophony*, the use of the same sounds (but not spelling) to represent different words occurs frequently, e.g. *stair* and *stare* are both pronounced as [steə]. In word-formation a new word may be given a new and distinct orthographic form but in the spoken language it might be given an old phonological word-form e.g. *bite* and *byte* are both pronounced as [baɪt].

(c) *Polysemy*, the same form can convey different but related meaning senses e.g. *stiff* [stɪf] meaning (i) not pliant and (ii) too formal (cf. p. 22). *Cool* originally meant 'become less hot'. When jazz people used it to mean 'relaxed style', the lexical item acquired a new sense.

In principle it should be easy to coin a new word-form any time the need to represent a particular lexical meaning arises. Any sound or sound combination is as arbitrary as any other that can be used in its place to represent a given meaning. In practice it is rare that completely fresh words are made up. Most of the time an existing word-form is recycled to represent a new meaning. Metaphorically speaking, a word-form is a vessel in which different measures of meaning can be poured without necessarily changing the vessel itself. There are no scientific laws that govern how this is done. None the less, as we will see in the next few subsections, there are some observable recurrent patterns in the ways in which the associations of sounds with meanings change (see also Copley 1961 and Jackson 1988).

9.5.1 Semantic widening

Semantic change often involves the WIDENING (i.e. increasing the number of lexemes with distinct meanings associated with a word-form). Widening may result either in more homonymy or in more polysemy (i.e. more distinct but related senses of a lexeme realised by a pre-existing word-form; see section (2.2)). Examples of widening are listed in [9.7]:

[9.7] a. *Manage* (originally spelt *menage*) means 'to handle anything successfully' but originally it meant 'handle a
horse'.

b. *Manufacture* 'the process of making products'. Manufacture comes from Latin *manu factum* 'make by hand'. In
early modern times its meaning was extended so as to
include 'to make by hand or by machinery'. Subsequently,
in the industrial and post-industrial age it came to mean
to make by machinery rather than by hand. The original
link with manual work was eventually lost.

Personal names often undergo widening. Many commercial products are named after the principal people who were instrumental
in bringing them to the market-place. We vacuum floors with
Hoovers and drive *Ford* cars on *macadamised* roads. In so doing we
are (unknowingly) paying tribute to Hoover, Henry Ford and John
Loudon McAdam.

Many scientific principles and instruments are also named after
their inventors. Thus the instrument for measuring radiation is
called the Geiger-(Müller) counter after its inventor. In the centi-
grade system, temperatures are measured in degrees *Celsius*. Anders
Celsius was an eighteenth-century Swedish astronomer. Mathemat-
ical concepts deriving from the work of the nineteenth-century
British mathematician George Boole are described as *Boolean*. The
ratio of the speed of an aircraft in a fluid to that of the speed of
sound at the same point is referred to as *mach one, mach two* etc.
after the Austrian physicist E. Mach who died in 1916.

9.5.2 Semantic narrowing

The converse of widening is narrowing. The range of meanings
associated with word-forms may become more restricted. This is
called SEMANTIC NARROWING. The discussion and exemplification of
narrowing draws on the *OED* and Room (1986).

[9.8] *Accident* means an unintended injurious or disastrous event.
Its original meaning was just any event, especially
one that was unforeseen. Thus, in the final act of
The Tempest Prospero speaks of what has happened
to him since his arrival on the island as:

> . . . the particular accidents gone by
> Since I came to this isle.

Adder   in Old English meant any serpent. Later the meaning of this word was restricted to vipers.

Deer   originally referred to any four-legged beast. Later the meaning of *deer* was narrowed to a family of ruminant mammals with deciduous antlers that includes the reindeer, red deer etc. The imported French word *animal*, meaning beast, supplanted deer around the middle of the sixteenth century.

Fowl   in Old English referred to any bird. Subsequently, the meaning of this word was narrowed to a bird raised for food, or a wild bird hunted for 'sport'.

Ledger   was originally a word that referred to any book, e.g. a register, or large bible that lay permanently in the same place, but by the seventeenth century its meaning had narrowed to an accounts book.

9.5.3 Going up and down in the world

The associations and connotations of a word may change. If a word acquires a more positive meaning, we speak of AMELIORATION; if it acquires a more negative meaning we speak of PEJORATION.

Take the meaning of the word *villain* (originally spelt *villein*). It has gone downhill. In the age of fuedalism a villein was just a type of humble serf who cultivated the lord's land. (The feudal *vill* was a farm). Today a *villain* is not a peasant, but a person of doubtful virtue, a scoundrel. Note also how *peasant* has acquired negative connotations. I think you would be insulted if someone called you a peasant. When it was first adopted from French, this word simply meant a country person who worked the land. Current French *paysan* comes from Old French *païsant*. Old French *païs* became Modern French *pays* 'country'. The *-ant* suffix indicated origin in Old French. So, a *peasant* was someone from a country district. That meaning is not lost in modern English *peasant*. But the word has acquired the additional negative connotations of 'boorish, very low-status person'.

While the words *villain* and *peasant* have gone down the scale, the opposite has happened to *knight*. Originally it meant 'servant'.

(In modern German the related word *Knecht* still means 'servant'.) But in the age of chivalry the *knight* went up in public esteem. Being knighted is still considered a great honour.

Amelioration and pejoration of meaning have a lot to do with social values. Nowhere is this clearer than in the attitude to different occupations. For instance, at one time the *surgeon* enjoyed no more prestige than the butcher. Both were seen as tradesmen very skilled in cutting and chopping flesh and bones with sharp knives. However, with the professionalisation of surgery and the establishment of the Royal College of Surgeons, practitioners of surgery enjoyed ever increasing public esteem. Today nobody would contemplate lumping them with butchers. (Would butchers too have enjoyed improved status had they established a Royal College of Butchers?)

9.5.4 Loss account

Words get lost. This may happen for a number of reasons. For instance, a new word may come into the language and supplant the old. The new word may be created using the internal resources of the language, or it may be imported from another language. For instance, in the late Middle Ages the adjectives *wæstmbærce* and *wynnfæst* that had been handed down from Old English became obsolete. They were replaced by 'fertile' and 'pleasant', which came from French. The Old English nouns *greed* 'voice' and *læcedom* 'medicine' suffered the same fate.

These were not isolated changes. The replacement of Old English words by French ones was particularly widespread in the language of religion and government (cf. Chapter 10). You can see this if you compare the two columns in [9.9] below:

[9.9]   *Obsolete Old English word*   *Current word*
    a. hǣlend or nergend   saviour
       scyppend   creator
       gesceaft   creation
    b. healdend   chief
       rǣdend   ruler
       æðeling   prince
       dēmend   judge

Loss does not always occur across the board. Words that have become obsolete in standard English may survive in some dialects.

Thus, according to the *OED*, late Middle English *tonguey*, meaning 'loquacious', is still used in some dialects in America, but is lost elsewhere. The word *gigot*, meaning 'a leg of veal, mutton etc.' was borrowed from French in the sixteenth century. It is now generally obsolete – except in Scotland where a butcher will still sell you a *gigot*.

Change, be it in fashion, cultural, social or political institutions, values, science or technology, is a factor in the loss of words. For example, because hardly any men (except a tiny minority of monks who are out of the public eye) shave their heads to create a bald patch as part of a religious rite, the word *tonsure* which describes such a bald patch is no longer in current everyday use. In medieval times when the practice of shaving such bald patches was common, *tonsure* was a useful word to have.

Similarly, *breeches*, a word of Norse origin, gradually fell into disuse when fashion changed and *trousers* replaced *breeches* in the seventeenth century as the garment that covers the loins and legs. But *breeches* was retained for a longer time in the dialects of the North of England and in Scotland (where in some dialects it survives as *breeks*, meaning 'trousers').

The same points can be made about changes in social institutions. With the end of feudalism, a great many words associated with it disappeared from common use and remain only in historical textbooks. Outside books on medieval history, you are not going to find words like *bondsman*, *serf*, *steelbow* and *vassal*. These words are defined by the *OED* as follows:

bondsman 'one who becomes surety by bond'.
serf 'a slave, bondman'.
steelbow (Scottish Law) 'a quantity of farming stock, which a tenant received from his landlord on entering, and which he was bound to render up undiminished at the close of his tenancy'.
vassal 'in the feudal system, one holding lands from a superior on conditions of homage and allegiance'.

Scientific and technological terms too may become archaic when the technology to which they refer is superseded. With the demise of alchemy and the rise of chemistry, the need for the term *alkahest* ('the universal solvent' used in experiments seeking to transmute base metals into gold) disappeared. In technology similar cases also abound. For instance, in the 1780s the *spinning-jenny* was state-of-the-art technology. Now it is a museum piece. We only encounter the word 'spinning-jenny' in books on the history of the Industrial Revolution.

The discussion here has concentrated on the loss of words. In fact, it is not just words that can be lost. Languages also lose morphemes. For instance, in Old English, from the verb *dēman* 'judge' one could form the noun *dēmend* 'judge'; from the verb *hǣlan* 'save' one could form the noun *hǣlend* 'saviour', and so on. Today, we cannot form a noun like **kepend* meaning *keeper* from the verb *keep*. The suffix *-end* which was used in English to derive masculine, agentive nouns is now extinct.

9.5.5 Lexical revivals

The reverse can also happen. Sometimes a word that had become a museum piece is dusted down and put back in circulation, albeit with a changed meaning. Barber (1964) cites *frigate, corvette* and *armour* as examples of LEXICAL REVIVALS. *Frigate* and *corvette* had become moribund words only used technically in historical books to describe types of obsolete, small, fast sixteenth- and seventeenth-century fighting ships. The word *armour* had also become obsolete after the end of the age of chivalry and the disappearance of medieval knights in shining armour.

All three words were revived early in the twentieth century and came back into general use – with new meanings. The two naval terms were pressed back into service to refer to modern fighting ships which were very different from the *frigates* and *corvettes* of early modern times. Similarly, when the word *armour* was revived, it referred to tanks and other mechanised fighting vehicles rather than to knights' suits of mail.

9.5.6 Metaphors

Figurative language is yet another source of lexical terms. Worn-out figures of speech often end up becoming conventional lexical items. We speak of 'the *legs* of tables and chairs' because *leg*, meaning 'limb', was metaphorically extended to furniture. We speak of 'the *tongue* of a shoe' by analogy to the tongue of an animal. For the same reason we speak of 'the *eye* of a needle' and 'an *ear* of corn', 'the *foot* of a mountain' and 'the *brow* of a hill'.

As seen, many DEAD METAPHORS are based on body parts.

However, metaphors and metaphorical extensions of meaning from other sources are not difficult to find. In recent years, British political pundits have talked about *banana skin* meaning 'a political misadventure that causes a politician to metaphorically skid and suffer a humiliating fall'. Continuing in the fruity vein, a concoction of narcotics is colloquially referred to as a *fruit salad*. The comparison with the legal and innocuous fruit salad served as a dessert is obvious.

In the late 1980s, in popular speech, if a person received shocking news that left them totally devastated, they could say that they were *gutted* or *kippered* or *filleted*. The analogy between the effect of the shock that goes to the very core and what a fishmonger does to fish is plain to see.

The metaphorical dimension of such expressions is obvious if you stand back and think about their structure and likely source. But normally people use such expressions without thinking about their metaphorical basis. They simply treat them as plain, ordinary lexical terms.

9.6 CLIPPING

CLIPPING is the term for the formation of a new word-form, with the same meaning as the original lexical term, by lopping off a portion and reducing it to a monosyllabic or disyllabic rump. This phenomenon has been around for a long time. Eighteenth-century purists like Swift and Campbell fought a determined, but in the end unsuccessful, campaign against it. George Campbell, writing in 1776, objected to what he saw as the barbarism of shortening polysyllabic words and retaining just the first syllable or just the first and second syllables, as in:

[9.10] *hyp* for *hypochondriac*   *rep* for *reputation*
        ult for *ultimate*   *penult* for *penultimate*
        incog for *incognito*   *hyper* for *hypercritic*
        extra for *extraordinary*   *mob* for *mobile crowd*
                          (from Baugh and Cable 1978: 256–9)

Despite eloquent protests against it, clipping did survive as a fairly productive word-formation process. In contemporary English, very occasionally, the middle of a word is dropped. That is how *vegan* was formed from *veg(etari)an*. More commonly we have FORE-CLIPPING, where the front of the word is trimmed, as in [9.11].

[9.11] *Fore-clipping*

plane	aeroplane
bus	omnibus
van	caravan
brolly	umbrella

However, BACK-CLIPPING, where the end of the word is trimmed, is by far the commonest:

[9.12] *Back-clipping*

ammo	ammunition
amp	ampere
info	information
rep	representative
homo	homosexual
guv	guvnor (< governor) 'boss'
disco	discotheque
micro	microcomputer/microwave oven
mike	microphone
limo	limousine
bike	bicycle
lab	laboratory
navvy	navigator
stereo	stereophonic

In colloquial speech, clippings tend to end in a familiar suffix pronounced [ɪ] (and spelled *-ie* or *-y*) as in [9.13]:

[9.13]

Gerry	<	Gerald
Monty	<	Montgomery
Lizzie	<	Elizabeth
Aussie	<	Australian
loony	<	lunatic
telly	<	television
poly	<	polytechnic

Clipping accompanied by [ɪ] (*-ie/-y*) suffixation is especially common in nicknames and familiar versions of names. It is not easy to predict what part of a name is going to be retained because the principles that determine the version of the clipping process that applies in a particular instance are not clear. Back-clipping may take place, as in *Gerald > Gerry*, *Montgomery > Monty* etc. Or it can be fore-clipping, as in *Antoinette > Netty*, *Patricia > Trish* and

Alexander > *Sandy*. Or again, occasionally, it may be a combination of the two as in *Lizzie* from *(E)liz(abeth)*.

9.7 ACRONYMS AND ABBREVIATIONS

The shortening of words is taken to its logical conclusion in ACRO-NYMS. Words forming a complex expression referring to the name of an organisation, company or a scientific concept may be reduced to their initial letters alone which together represent sounds that form perfectly acceptable syllables and hence can be pronounced as words. Words formed in this way are called ACRONYMS.

[9.14]   SALT   Strategic Arms Limitation Talks
         HALO   High Altitude Large Optics
         NASA   National Aeronautics and Space Administration
         RAM   Random access memory

As mentioned in section (7.6), this type of word-formation is an interesting example of a role reversal: spoken word-forms are derived from words in the written language.

Usually, to begin with acronyms are spelt with capital letters as shown in [9.14], when people are conscious of their special status. But with the passage of time, some commonly used acronyms end up being transmogrified into simple root morphemes and are treated as common or garden words. Then they tend to be spelt like any other word. This is happening to *NATO* (North Atlantic Treaty Organisation) which is now sometimes spelt as *Nato*. Farther down the road is AIDS, which is very frequently written as *Aids*. Indeed, many people do not know that *Aids* is an abbreviation of 'acquired immune deficiency syndrome'.

In the twentieth century an increasingly large number of acronyms have become established, institutionalised words. Few people have the slightest inkling that these are acronyms:

[9.15]   Anzac   Australian and New Zealand Army Corps
         basic   Beginner's All-purpose Symbolic Instruction Code
         derv   diesel-engined road vehicle
         midi   musical instrument digital interface
         radar   radio detection and ranging
         sonar   sound navigation and ranging
         scuba   self-contained underwater breathing apparatus
         naffy   The Navy, Army, and Airforce Institutes (naafi/
                   NAAFI)

Sometimes shortened forms are created using the initial letters of words which do not give permissible syllables. They fail the phonological test. In such cases, each letter is sounded separately. We call such forms ABBREVIATIONS rather than acronyms. The term acronym is restricted to forms that are pronounceable as normal words.

In the last few decades there has been an explosion in the growth of abbreviations. A short list is given in [9.16]. I am sure you can think of dozens more.

[9.16] EC   European Community
       UN   United Nations
       IBM   International Business Machines
       ITN   Independent Television News
       BMA   British Medical Association
       BR   British Rail
       LAGB   Linguistics Association of Great Britain
       CIA   Central Intelligence Agency
       LA   Los Angeles
       TLC   tender loving care

9.8 FADS AND COPYCAT FORMATIONS

Word-formation is subject to fashion. A word in vogue often gives rise to copycat formations which are fashionable for a time, and then quickly become dated. Let us take the 1980s in-word *yuppie* (see p. 150). It spawned a number of words formed by analogy, such as:

[9.17] woppies   Wealthy Older Professional Persons
       yummies   Young Upwardly Mobile Marxists
       dinkies   Double-Income-No-Kids
       nilkies   No-Income-Lots-of-Kids

Yuppie will probably survive. But it is unlikely that the other faddy words will still be in use in another ten years. They already sound dated.

9.9 BACK-FORMATION

Normally words are formed by adding affixes. Less commonly the reverse happens and a word is formed by removing affixes from a base. This is called BACK-FORMATION. Typically this happens when there is an apparent gap in the lexicon, i.e. there 'ought to be' a word from which an apparently affixed word is derived, but there is not.

According to Marchand (1969), on whose work this account of back-formation is based, the verb *peddle* was formed from the noun *pedlar*, and the verb *juggle* was formed from the noun *juggler* by a series of deductive steps. If a noun meaning 'someone who does X' ends in [ə] (spelled variously as *-er/-or/-ar*), there exists a corresponding verb which is minus the suffix, e.g. keep ~ keeper, ride ~ rider etc. But in fact, the verbs did not exist in the case of *pedlar* and *juggler*. So speakers formed them by dropping the suffixes from the nouns.

Likewise, *typewrite*$_{Verb}$ was formed from *typewriter*$_{Noun}$ at the end of the nineteenth century by analogy to *write*$_{Verb}$ → *writer*$_{Noun}$ and the verb *edit* was derived in the eighteenth century from the noun *editor* using the same analogical formation. And when the age of television dawned in the early twentieth century, the language got the noun *television* first. There was a perceived need for a verb. So, the verb *televise* was created from the noun *television* following the pattern of *revise*$_{Verb}$ → *revision*$_{Noun}$.

Back-formation applies equally to compounds. The verb *stage-manage* is a back-formation from the noun *stage-manager*. So is the computer-age verb *word-process* which comes from the noun *word-processor*.

9.10 BLENDS

BLENDS are hybrid words. They are compounds made in an unorthodox way by joining chunks of word-forms belonging to two distinct lexemes. This word-formation method has grown in popularity in recent decades. Many ordinary words are blends. Like acronyms, some of them are so well installed in the lexicon that most speakers are unaware of the fact that they are hybrid words rather than simple roots. Which of the following words did you know were hybrids?

[9.18] smog   smoke + fog
        spam   spiced + ham
        brunch   breakfast + lunch
        privateer   private + volunteer

stagflation	stagnation + inflation
chunnel	channel + tunnel
Oxbridge	Oxford + Cambridge
pornotopia	pornography + utopia
napalm	naphthenic + palmitic
guestimate	guess + estimate
Reaganomics	Reagan + economics
telethon	telephone + marathon
Fortran	formula + translation
selectric	select + electric
quasar	quasi + stellar
heliport	helicopter + airport
Franglais	Français + Anglais

9.11 EUPHEMISM

People normally try to avoid topics or words that they or their interlocuter might find distasteful, unpleasant or embarrassing. So they use EUPHEMISMS to replace an unpleasant word with a more pleasant one (cf. Holder 1987, Green 1987). Euphemisms motivated by the need to be sensitive to other people's feelings came into the foreground in the late 1980s and early 1990s in a lively debate about 'political correctness'. The issue was the extent to which language that might be offensive to any of the less powerful groups in society should be avoided – or even banned. For instance, a vigorous discussion was conducted in the media about attempts to replace the term *disabled* with the more positive term *differently abled*, and even more recently, *physically challenged*. Interestingly, what many people do not know is that the term *disabled* was itself a euphemism for *crippled*, which was abandoned because of its pejorative connotations.

Similar examples from earlier periods in history are numerous. *Imbecile* originally meant 'weak' and *idiot* meant 'non-expert, layperson'. When these words had their meanings extended to soften the blow of saying that someone had very limited intellectual powers, the original meanings were obscured and eventually got lost. Unfortunately, when we use euphemisms, the unpleasant associations eventually catch up with the new word. Then it is time to find another one. Surely, a more effective solution to the problem of reducing the hurt caused by using pejorative language is to change the attitudes of people who consciously or unconsciously use such language.

Euphemisms are often motivated by TABOO rather than the desire not to hurt people's feelings. Every culture has its forbidden subjects which are normally not referred to directly because of decency or respect or fear. Let us take respect first. At one time *God* could not be referred to by name – for using his name in vain was blasphemous. So, instead of saying God, people spoke of *the Lord, the Lord of Lords, the King of Kings, the King of Glory, the Omnipotent, the All-Powerful* and so on.

There are many euphemisms for the *devil* too, but these are motivated by fear rather than respect. As the saying goes 'Speak of the devil . . .'. So, euphemisms were used in more superstitious times. Many of these are immortalised in the poem 'Address to the De'il' (devil) by Robert Burns (in Beattie and Meikle (1972) which opens with the lines:

[9.19] ADDRESS TO THE DE'IL

> O thou! whatever title suit thee,
> Auld Hornie, Satan, Nick or Clootie,
> Wha in yon cavern grim an' sootie,
>> Clos'd under hatches
> Spairges about the brunstane cootie,
>> To scaud poor wretches!
>
> Hear me, auld Hangie, for a wee,
> An' let poor damnèd bodies be;
> I'm sure sma' pleasure it can gie,
>> E'en to a de'il,
> To skelp an' scaud poor dogs like me,
>> An' hear us squeel!

Taboo may also be due to decency. Sexually explicit language is often avoided. Thus, the Victorians spoke of a lady's *limb*, not her *leg* because that was deemed too suggestive. (This was even extended to pianos. They would refer to a piano's limbs rather than its legs.) And today in North America a *rooster* is called a *rooster* in order to avoid saying the embarrassing *c . . .* word.

There is a particular kind of euphemism that involves using language in a perverse way to conceal thought. This is called DOUBLESPEAK. It is an indispensable weapon in the armoury of totalitarian regimes. It endeavours to make acts of unspeakable brutality look tolerable, or even humane and civilised. When political opponents are incarcerated without even a semblance of a trial, they are said to be in *preventive detention*. Extra-judicial killings are referred to as mere *disappearances*. Torture colonies are called *protected villages* or *re-education centres*. The state agency responsible for the assassination of political opponents during the apartheid regime in the Republic of South Africa was called the *Civil Co-operation Bureau*. Population purges, pogroms and forced migrations are referred to as *ethnic cleansing* in Bosnia and Zaïre. Hitler called the genocide of the Jewish people in death factories the *final solution*.

A perverse use can be found for almost any word in doublespeak. Let us illustrate this with the word *friendly*. In the carve-up of Europe at Yalta, Stalin insisted on the governments of Eastern Europe being 'friendly'. A reasonable demand? We all know what he meant. He wanted Eastern Europe to be part of the Soviet empire which he ruled with an iron fist.

Doublespeak is very common in the language of the military of all colours – even the good guys. Many a militaristic regime which regularly terrorises its neighbours will refer to its war machine as a *defence force*. An unprovoked attack is often referred to as a *preventive war*. If a campaign goes badly wrong and the troops are forced by enemy fire to retreat, the official report that goes out describes the disaster as a *strategic withdrawal*. If things go disastrously wrong and you kill soldiers who are on your own side, you tell the world that they were killed by *friendly fire*.

Killing people is something that shocks even the hardened professional soldier or the executioner. The shock is usually dampened by using euphemisms like:

[9.20] neutralise   kill
       take out   kill
       stretch the hemp   to kill by hanging
       the (electric) chair   electrocution
       neck-tie party   lynching

Thus language is used not to reveal thought or represent reality, but to obscure both. The false images created using doublespeak replace the inconvenient reality one would rather not confront.

APPELLATION CONTROLEE

FUSIL DE·GUERRE

FUSIL DE PACIFICATION

SOUSTELLE

LACOSTE

– TOUTE LA DIFFERENCE EST LA . . .

(1956 – Robert Lacoste (S.F.I.O.) replaces Jacques Soustelle as Governor-General of Algeria.)

9.12 SUMMARY

This chapter has dealt with ways of changing and enriching the vocabulary. We have seen that jargon created for a specialised linguistic field may seep into the mainstream vocabulary. We have also seen that the vocabulary may be enlarged by associating new meanings with existing word-forms. This may involve metaphorical extensions of meaning, widening, narrowing, amelioration or pejoration. Slang too is an important source of lexical innovation: non-standard meanings may come to be associated with word-forms of the mainstream language.

Conversely, the same meaning may be kept but the word-form representing it may be changed, usually by shortening. This takes a variety of forms such as clipping whereby a word-form is shortened, back-formation whereby new lexical terms are created by removing affixes, and blends produced by joining the rumps of two word-forms.

The words of a language are used by speakers to convey meanings in a social context. So, inevitably social factors impinge on the lexicon. Sayings and slogans encapsulating a shared value system are turned into clichés which trigger socially conditioned reflexes. Euphemisms are used to smooth over reality where its jagged edges as expressed by the normal non-euphemistic terms are too disconcerting. This may be done for the best of reasons or for sinister purposes.

EXERCISES

1. With the help of a good dictionary, find out the methods by which the following words were formed.

   laze, con, temp, deli, porn, pram, nappy, disco, cobol, leotard, wasp (of the human variety in America), *laser, VATman, GI, Frisco* (San Francisco) and *Philly* (Philadelphia).

   Find one more word formed using each of these methods.

2. If you call someone 'a queer' you are not only referring to their sexual orientation, but also doing so in a denigrating manner because the word *queer* has very negative connotations. Find two other words which you know to be offensive to other people. Is there a way of communicating effectively without using these offensive words?

3. Like words, affixes can have both referential and cognitive meaning.

   a. Find at least six words with the suffix *-ess* as in *baroness, manageress, priestess* and *mistress*.
   b. Comment on both the cognitive and connotative meaning of words formed with this suffix. Bear in mind the fact that the connotations of a morpheme can change over time as social values change.

4. Look up in a good etymological dictionary the entries for the words below and comment on the semantic changes which they have undergone:

    a. *villa, village, villain* and *-ville* (as in Hopkinsville, Madison-ville, Louisville in Kentucky; Nashville in Tennessee and Jacksonville in Florida).

    b. *ace, boor* (Boer), *meat, garbage, lad, kill* and *lavatory*.

5. a. Provide one example of semantic narrowing and one of semantic widening.

    b. Give one fresh example of a lexical item whose use is motivated by taboo. What kind of taboo is involved?

    c. If possible, find out from a person from another culture the kinds of taboo that influence lexical choices in their culture.

6. a. Study the following text and comment on the word-formation method used in the jargon.

> The Greenfreeze fridge, as it will be known, is unlike just about every other fridge made commercially in the last generation. It uses a mixture of propane and butane to cool it and not chlorofluorocarbons (CFCs), those great destroyers of the ozone layer, or their second generation replacements, the hydrofluorocarbons (HFCs) which are even more dangerous in the short run.

(John Vidal 'The Big Chill', *The Guardian*, 19 November 1992)

    b. Find another short, jargon-ridden passage exemplifying lexical innovation. Comment on the method of word-formation used in the passage you have chosen.

7. What do the following catch-phrases mean? What kinds of connotation do they have? In what circumstances are they used?

    a. *I am not just a pretty face*
    b. *Public enemy number one*
    c. *I am down, but not out*
    d. *His master's voice*

Chapter 10

A lexical mosaic: sources of English vocabulary

10.1 THE NATURE OF BORROWING

In the last chapter we saw the ways in which a language may use its internal resources to create new words. This chapter explores how, instead of building words and other vocabulary items using its own resources, a language can add to the number of words in its lexicon by BORROWING vocabulary from other languages. English has borrowed so extensively from other languages that the English lexicon is like a large mosaic.

10.1.1 Direct and indirect borrowing

It is useful to distinguish between direct borrowing and indirect borrowing. If a language takes a word directly from another, as English got *omelette* from French, we call what happens DIRECT BORROWING. But in other cases a word may be passed indirectly like a relay baton from one language to another, and to another, e.g. *kahveh* (Turkish) > *kahva* (Arabic) > *koffie* > (Dutch) > *coffee* (English). This is called INDIRECT BORROWING. If a word is directly borrowed the chances of its undergoing drastic phonological modification are considerably less than those of a word that is indirectly borrowed. Anyone can see that French *omelette* and English *omelette* are evidently related. But I suspect many Turkish speakers would not recognise English *coffee* as a word originating from *kahveh*. For by the time *kahveh* had gone through Arabic and Dutch to reach English it had undergone considerable phonological changes, which are partly reflected in the spelling. Each time a word passes from one language to another, its pronunciation is adjusted to make it fit into the phonological system of the recipient language.

An even better example of phonological distortions arising in the course of indirect borrowing is *avocado*. The pear-shaped fruit produced by the Caribbean and Central American tree whose botanical name is *Persea gratissima* was called *ahuacatl* in Aztec. At the end of the seventeenth century the Spaniards borrowed this word as *aguacate*, which was a reasonably close approximation to the Aztec pronunciation. But in popular speech it was changed to *avigato* and then to *avocado* (like the Spanish word for *advocate*), from which we get English *avocado*. It was modified even more drastically in popular speech giving *alligator pear* from *avigato* in the eighteenth century.

This illustrates how often FALSE ETYMOLOGY plays a role in the phonological changes that take place when foreign words are nativised. People tend to rationalise; they want a reason for the imported word sounding the way it does. So they link it with a plausible real word in their language. Thus, they might have thought that since the *ahuacatl* (avigato) fruit came from the Americas, the land of alligators, it 'made sense' to call it the *alligator pear*. Presumably because this fruit was exotic and expensive, it was something that only rich people, like advocates, would be able to afford. Hence the name *avocado* pear must also have seemed reasonable.

As an aside, note that in fact false etymology is not all that rare. There are quite a few words formed by joining psuedo-bases to affixes e.g. *trimaran* 'a vessel with three hulls' is formed from the *catamaran* 'a twin-hulled sailing boat' as though *-maran* were a base meaning 'hull'. Conversely, a form may be re-analysed as a pseudo-affix which is attached to bases. A famous example of this is *-holic*. By analogy to *alcoholic*, we get *work-a-holic*, *ice-cream-holic* etc. The form *-holic* is treated as a suffix meaning 'someone who overindulges in something' although that was not its original meaning.

As you would expect, meaning alterations may also occur as a word is handed from language to language. The more indirect the borrowing, the greater the alterations are likely to be. For instance, Luganda borrowed *pakitimane* from Swahili which in turn borrowed it from English *pocket money*. *Pakitimane* means 'wallet' rather than 'pocket money'. This is due to a misunderstanding of what the word denotes in English. The contents of a wallet may be someone's 'pocket money' but the wallet itself is not 'pocket money'. When borrowing words, there is always a danger of misunderstanding what exactly words denote, what aspect of an object they specifically pick out. A degree of drift is almost inevitable when a game of Chinese whispers is played. So it is with borrowing when meaning is handed on through several intermediaries. Thus, English *howitzer* 'light gun' comes from Dutch *houwitzer* which was itself borrowed from Czech *houfnice* 'catapult'.

10.1.2 Loanwords and loanshifts

We will recognise two kinds of borrowing: LOANWORDS and LOANSHIFTS (cf. Haugen 1950). A loanword is a word belonging to one language which is IMPORTED or ADOPTED by another, e.g. *catamaran* was imported into English from Tamil and *shopping* was imported into French as *(le) shopping*.

By contrast, a loanshift involves taking on board the meaning represented by a word in a foreign language, but not the word-form itself. Loanshifts are also called LOAN TRANSLATIONS or CALQUES. (The 'calque' metaphor comes from fine art where a calque is a tracing.) In a loanshift the borrowing is done by translating the meaning of the vocabulary item. Let us start with the English word *loanword* itself which is a loan translation from German *Lehnwort*. Similarly, the name of *Superman*, that great popular culture hero made famous by Hollywood, is a loan translation of the German *Übermensch*. There are also a number of loan translations of Latin origin, especially in religious language, which is not surprising since for centuries Latin was the language of western Christendom. From *omnipotens* (*omni-* 'all' + *potens* 'power') have come the loan translations *almighty* and *all powerful*. Latin *Spiritus Sanctus* (*spiritus* 'spirit', *sanctus* 'holy') was rendered in English by the translation *Holy Spirit* or *Holy Ghost*.

However, it is from French that English gets most of its loan translations. Many English sayings are translations of the French:

[10.1] | *French* | *English* |
|---|---|
| ça va sans dire | it goes without saying |
| d'un certain age | of a certain age (i.e. getting on in years) |
| sans cérémonie | without ceremony |
| dialogue de sourds | dialogue of the deaf |
| en principe | in principle |
| le commencement de la fin | the beginning of the end |
| plus royaliste que le roi | more royalist than the king (by analogy we get 'more English than the English', 'more Catholic than the Pope' etc.) |

Note in passing that the loan translation traffic is not all one way. English loans are also translated into other languages. Thus, *skyscraper* is translated and rendered as *le gratte-ciel* (*gratter* = 'to scratch' + *ciel* 'sky') in French. It is not simply borrowed as (*le*) *skyscraper*. (Italian too translates skyscraper as *gratta-cielo*.)

French is the most important source of imported vocabulary items by a very clear margin, so we will devote most of the space in this chapter to the discussion of borrowings from this language. Further, since loanwords are the dominant type of borrowed words, we concentrate on these rather than on loan translations.

10.1.3 Likely loans

In principle anything in language can be borrowed. In practice most of the words that are borrowed belong to the open lexical classes (i.e. nouns, verbs, adjectives and adverbs). And of these, nouns top the list, followed by verbs and adjectives. The reason why nouns are the commonest loanwords is not difficult to see. Normally, borrowing takes place because a word is needed to give a name to an unfamiliar animal, thing or cultural phenomenon.

It is rare (but not impossible) for a language to borrow words in the closed classes. In Old English, for example, the third person plural pronoun was *hie* (I am only considering the nominative and accusative cases for simplicity's sake). In the twelfth century Old English borrowed from Old Norse the third person plural pronoun *þeir* /θei/ from which *they* is descended.

For borrowing to take place, some degree of bilingualism or bi-dialectalism (knowledge of two dialects of the same language) is a prerequisite. Speakers need to know – or think they know – what the words that they import mean. (See the discussion of *pakitimane* above.)

10.1.4 Why borrow?

As mentioned in previous chapters, in principle there is no limit to the number of words that can be formed in a language. There is no reason why a particular meaning should not be associated with any given form. So, there is really no purely linguistic reason for borrowing. Whenever the need for a word arises following contact with another culture, people could just make one up. But in most cases they do not. It is relatively rare for speakers to create completely new words. When a suitable word exists in another language, the easiest thing in the world to do is to adopt that word rather than to make up an original one from nothing. This is a reason for borrowing. But it is not the only one.

There is a number of other good reasons for importing words. One of them is IDENTITY. Language is much more than simply a means of communication. It is also a badge that we wear to assert our identity. By using a particular language, bilingual speakers may be saying something about how they perceive themselves and how they wish to relate to their interlocutor. For instance, if a patient initiates an exchange with a doctor in the doctor's surgery in Yiddish, that may be a signal of solidarity, saying: you and I are members of the same subgroup. Alternatively, rather than choosing between languages, these two people may prefer CODE-SWITCHING. They may produce sentences which are partly in English and partly in Yiddish. If foreign words are used habitually in code-switching, they may pass from one language into another and eventually become fully integrated and cease being regarded as foreign. That is probably how words like *schlemiel* (a very clumsy, bungling idiot who is always a victim), *schmaltz* 'cloying, banal sentimentality' and *goyim* 'gentile' passed from Yiddish into (American) English. The fact that there is no elegant English equivalent to these Yiddish words was no doubt also a factor in their adoption. (See p. 197 below for further discussion.)

Sometimes the reason for code-switching is PRESTIGE, i.e. one-upmanship. People have always liked showing off. By using fashionable words from a fashionable foreign culture one shows that one is with it, one is modern, one is part of the *crème de la crème*, and so on. Shakespeare's Mercutio is his parody of the *pardonnez-moi* brigade puts this point across succinctly:

[10.2] Why, is not this a lamentable thing, grandsire, that we should be thus afflicted with these strange flies, these fashion-mongers, these *pardonnez-mois*, who stand so much on the new form that they cannot sit at ease on the old bench? O, their *bons*, their *bons*!

(*Romeo and Juliet*, II, iv)

Another obvious reason for borrowing is to provide a word that meets a need for a word where no suitable English one exists. When new concepts, creatures, artefacts, institutions, religions etc. are encountered or introduced through contact with speakers of another language, the words for them from the source language tend to be retained. At various periods in history different civilisations have been pre-eminent in one field or another. Normally, the language of the people who excel in a particular field of human endeavour becomes the international lingua franca of that field. Words belonging to the SEMANTIC FIELD (i.e. area of meaning) of a domain of experience, such as music, dance, religion, government and politics, architecture, science, clothes and fashion, are imported from the language of the pre-eminent civilisation during that period. Thus, the concentration of borrowed words in certain semantic fields reflects the nature of the contact between speech communities. It reflects the areas where new words had to be acquired in order to fill a perceived gap. I will illustrate this in a preliminary manner now and return to it later in this chapter.

During the Middle Ages, when scientific knowledge was more advanced in the Arab world than in the west, a number of Arabic scientific terms were indirectly borrowed by English from French, which had acquired them from Spanish, a very important conduit of Arab science and culture to western Europe because Spain was occupied by the Moors in the Middle Ages. Examples of such terms include the following in [10.3a] (many of which begin with *al* – the Arabic definite article):

[10.3] a. alchemy, alcohol, alembic, algebra, alkali, zenith, zero
      b. Koran, imam, caliph, muezzin, mullah, Ramadan etc.

Besides being the language of science in the Middle Ages, Arabic was, and still remains, the language of Islam. Virtually all the words used in English connected with Islam are borrowed from Arabic.

For centuries, French was the language of government, politics, the military, diplomacy and protocol. Hence a large number of words in this semantic area are from French:

[10.4] a. *Military*
      cordon sanitaire, barrage, hors de combat, matériel, RV
      (rendez-vous), reveille (in English pronounced /rɪvælɪ/)
    b. *Diplomacy and protocol*
      corps diplomatique, chargé d'affaires, communiqué
    c. *Government and politics*
      ancien régime, dirigiste, coup d'état, laissez-faire, l'état
      c'est moi, agent provocateur

We will return to this in more detail in section (10.3).

Names of animals, birds and plants from around the world have entered English from all kinds of languages spoken in different parts of the world, for example:

[10.5] chimpanzee (Angola)   panda (Nepalese)
       koala (Australia)   tsetse (fly) (Tswana)
       kookaburra (Australia)   zebra (Congo)
       kudu (Xhosa, South Africa)

Names of diseases found in foreign lands have also been imported. *Beriberi* came from Sinhalese in the last century. *Kwashi-orkor*, a children's disease caused by protein deficiency, came from a Ghanaian language in the 1930s. *Malaria* came from Italian *mal aria* 'bad air' in the mid-eighteenth century when it was believed to be caused by the 'bad' steamy air exuded by the marsh-lands. It was only later that it was discovered that this disease is caused by a mosquito-transmitted parasite.

Numerous words referring to food have been imported as the range of foreign foods eaten here has increased. Think of:

[10.6] goulash (Hungarian)   enchiladas (Mexican Spanish)
       moussaka (Greek)   tacos (Mexican Spanish)

The same point can be further illustrated with examples of words referring to dress. We could in principle coin a fresh word or just use a roundabout description of a *sarong* (Malay), *kimono* (Japanese), *parka* (Aleutian), *anorak* (Greenlandic Eskimo) and *shawl* (Persian). But it is simpler to import the object together with the name for it.

Sometimes borrowing occurs for a different reason – the need to acquire the *mot juste* which is available in another language. For instance, English does not have a native word or expression with the precise meaning conveyed by the French loanwords *chic*, *flair*, *esprit de corps*, *naïve*, *elegant* or *blasé*. Try to think of how you would convey these ideas without using the French imports. I suspect that almost any alternative you come up with would appear somewhat clumsy. Or, think of a *ménage à trois*. You could use the loan translation 'a household with three partners', but it does not quite roll off the tongue.

In section (9.11) above, we saw how euphemism is used to avoid causing annoyance or embarrassment. The same motivation may also lie behind borrowing a word from another language. It seems that less embarrassment is caused when awkward things are said using words from a foreign language. So English borrowed *faeces* and *defecate* from Latin. Using them enables one to avoid distasteful four-letter words. Latin *faeces* meant 'dregs' and to *defecate* meant 'to clear from dregs or impurities'. This was metaphorically extended as a euphemism for 'to empty the bowels'. Propriety also lies behind the euphemistic use of the borrowed Latin words *genitalia* and *pudenda* as well as the importation of several words used to talk discreetly about shady sexual activities and participants therein, e.g. *maison de rendezvous*, *gigolo* and *madame* from French, and *bordello* from Italian.

10.1.5 The grass is ever greener on the other side

English has an extremely rich and varied vocabulary because it has enthusiastically borrowed foreign words in very large numbers. Each century the number of words adopted from foreign languages has increased. As we saw earlier, the main source of imports over the centuries has been French. This can be seen in the following tables from Bliss (1966: 26) which show the number of foreign words in use at various points in the history of English (c is short for 'century' in these tables):

[10.7]

	Medi-eval	16c	17c	18c	19c	20c
French	19	42	166	316	736	1103
Classical	89	237	371	173	328	250
Italian	–	26	48	100	90	153
German	–	2	2	4	58	240
Spanish	–	13	14	14	47	32
Other European	4	10	13	22	49	53
Non-European	2	12	56	35	97	55
TOTAL	114	342	670	664	1405	1886

In another table on page 27 of the same book (see [10.8]), Bliss presents figures showing the percentage of the total borrowing during each period which is made up of words from each of these different languages:

[10.8]	Medieval	16c	17c	18c	19c	20c
French	16.7	12.2	24.8	47.7	52.3	58.6
Classical	78	69.4	55.3	25.9	23.4	13.2
Italian		7.6	7.2	15.1	6.4	8.1
German		0.6	0.3	0.6	4.1	12.7
Spanish		3.8	2.1	2.1	3.4	1.7
Other European	3.5	2.9	1.9	3.3	3.5	2.8
Non-European	1.8	3.5	8.4	5.3	6.9	2.9

The preponderance of French loans becomes even clearer when they are seen as a percentage of the total number of words from other languages.

Although the classical languages, Greek and Latin, are major sources of roots and affixes we will not deal with them separately here, for two reasons. First, there was extensive borrowing by Latin from Greek and this sometimes makes it difficult to tell which words are Latin and which Greek. Second, French, the most important source of English loanwords, is descended from Latin. This muddies waters. It is not always clear whether a word is a direct Latin import or one that came in indirectly, via French. This does not mean that loans from the classical languages are ignored. We have dealt with them already in other contexts: see the earlier discussion in sections (4.2.1) and (6.5.1).

10.1.6 Nativisation of loanwords

Many foreign words that are borrowed become fully NATIVISED. In the case of English, nativisation means ANGLICISATION. The words become assimilated and undistinguishable from indigenous English words, which raises the question: how do we distinguish between code-switching, the use of a foreign word as part of an English sentence, and borrowing, the use of a word that was once foreign but has become Anglicised? Evidently, there is no real problem in cases where the foreign import has been fully adopted and integrated into the English lexicon for so long that anyone who is not especially knowledgeable about etymology would be unable to sniff out its foreignness. Some, like *parent*, even take native English suffixes (e.g. *-hood* as in *parenthood*). Contrast this with the less well assimilated word *paternity*, which takes the Romance suffix *-ity* which has roughly the same meaning: 'the state of being X'. I suspect that very few readers of this book would have been aware before now that everyday words like these:

[10.9] animal   aunt   chair   change colour   cost
       dinner escape flower poor   table   uncle

and dozens more, are adopted French words. We cannot do without French loanwords in English. It would be extremely difficult to talk for even a few minutes without using any word of French origin (see Phythian 1982).

Equally unproblematic when considering nativisation are words and expressions that are very clearly French like those in [10.10a] which are typically used to add local colour, say in a tourist brochure, or those in [10.10b] which are mostly used to impress the interlocutor, saying to them 'See me, I am sophisticated':

[10.10] a. auberge   maître d'hôtel   château
           autoroute   la défense   concierge
                            (district in Paris)
           gendarme   mistral   midi
        b. deraciné   façon de parler   soi-disant
           mauvais quatre   mauvais sujet   longueur
           d'heure

We would probably recognise this as code-switching.

The problem is that many words in the category of [10.10] are not totally foreign, although they are not fully Anglicised either. Words may resist nativisation to a greater or lesser degree. Even after a long period of use in English some words fail to become fully adopted. Instead, they remain on the fringes, as tolerated aliens with one foot in and the other foot out of the English lexicon. For the rest of this section we will consider in some detail 'les mots français' in English which, to different degrees, resist assimilation. Archetypical examples of such marginal entries in the English lexicon are the expressions *billet doux* and *esprit de corps* which still feel foreign despite having been in use in English since the seventeenth and eighteenth centuries respectively.

A complicating factor in all this is that English speakers' judgements are not uniform. Some people may regard a word as foreign which others consider nativised. We will use a few rules of thumb to determine whether a foreign word is Anglicised or not. But always bear in mind that they are very crude rules. There is no set of exact, scientific principles that can enable us to infallibly separate foreign words used in code-switching from nativised borrowed words.

(i) Foreign grammatical properties may be ignored when a borrowed word is assimilated into the grammatical system of English. Thus grammatical gender inflection gets ironed out since it is not relevant in English. Contrasts like *naïf* (masculine) as opposed to *naïve* (feminine) disappear. In English both men and women can be simply *naïve*. I have heard people say either in English. My impression is that conservative, older, highly educated speakers who are aware of the origin of this word are the most likely to treat this word in this fashion.

(ii) If a word is not perceived as foreign any more, writers stop giving it special treatment. Any foreign marks and diacritics used in its spelling disappear. They stop italicising it or putting it in inverted commas, or offering a gloss, or doing anything to draw attention to it any more than they would an indigenous word. Contrast the spelling of the fully Anglicised words in [10.11] with the spelling of those in [10.12]; the latter are not yet fully Anglicised, so normally retain their French spelling.

[10.11]

French	*English*	*French*	*English*
théâtre	theatre	détour	detour
bâton	baton	débris	debris
bric à brac	bric-a-brac	dépôt	depot
café	cafe	élite	elite
châlet	chalet	rôle	role
décor	decor	simplicité	simplicity
détente	detente	naïve	naive

[10.12]

French	*English*
à la rigueur	à la rigueur
appliqué	appliqué
démodé	démodé
déshabillé	déshabillé
engagé	engagé
glacé	glacé, glace (cherries)
grandes écoles	grands écoles

(iii) In the spoken language, the more nativised a borrowed word is, the more it is made to fit in with the standard rules that govern the pronunciation of words in the host language. If a

French word containing sounds not found in English is Anglicised, such sounds are modified or replaced. If it contains sounds which do also occur in English, but has them in awkward combinations, changes are made to make the word conform to the phonotactic requirements of English. Stress is changed, if necessary, to fit in with the stress patterns of English. Thus, even the most pedantic person would not try to pronounce a French borrowing like *parent* [peərənt] in the French way as [paRɑ̃], with the rolled guttural Parisian 'r' and nasalised vowel. *Parent* has been fully assimilated. It does not smell of any Frenchness at all.

However, when words are only partially assimilated there is considerable scope for variation. Rarely is there unanimity in the way such words are treated. Compare the English pronunciations of the words in [10.13] with the French pronunciation. It is likely that you will disagree with what I say:

[10.13]   *French*   *English*
   a. buffet   [by'fɛ]   [by'fɛ]   ~[bʊ'feɪ]
   b. garage   [ga'Raʒ]   [gə'rɑ:ʒ]   ~['gærɑ:dʒ] ~
                                                             ['gærɑ:ʒ] ~
                                                            ['gærɪdʒ]
   c. impasse   [ɛ̃'pas]   [æm'pɑ:s]   ~['ɪmpɑ:s]
   d. ensemble [ɑ̃sɑ̃bl]   [ɑ̃:n'sɑ̃:mbl] ~[ɔ̃:n'sɔ:mbl] ~
                                                           [ɑ:n'sɑ:mbl]
   e. débâcle   [de'bɑkl] [de'bɑ:kl]   ~[deɪ'bɑ:kl] ~
                                                            [dɪ'bɑ:kl]

Do you have any strong feelings about the 'correctness' of these pronunciations? Do you believe that remaining as close as possible to the original French pronunciation is highly desirable? Personally, I am agnostic. My opinion is that whereas such questions might provide useful topics for the chattering classes to occupy themselves with on a dull day, they are not particularly important for most language users. As foreign words become fully integrated in a language, the pressure to make them conform to the standard rules is often irresistible. But until they are fully assimilated, it is to be expected that speakers will treat them differently.

10.1.7 Effects of borrowing

Language is a system where all the pieces fit together (Saussure 1916). Borrowing has repercussions for the entire system. The introduction of words from other languages may affect the structure of the recipient language at the level of meaning, grammar (morphology and syntax) or pronunciation.

First, let us consider the PHONOLOGICAL EFFECTS OF BORROWING, which have not been drastic, using the history of *sk* as our illustration. Very early in its history, Old English underwent a phonological change which resulted in the consonant combination [sk] being pronounced as [ʃ]. Old English *scip* [skip] had become [ʃɪp] ('ship'), *sceap* [skæəp] had become [ʃæəp] ('sheep'), *scruncen* [skrunken] had become [ʃrunken] ('shrunken') etc. As a consonant cluster, [sk] became extinct although [s] and [k] continued to occur in other combinations.

After the arrival of the Norsemen on the scene at the end of the ninth century, who raided, and later settled in many parts of the British isles, English borrowed many Scandinavian words that contained [sk], e.g. *scatter, sky, skin, skill* and *skirt*. (The original Old English *scyrte*, the garment covering the upper part of the body, had become *shirt*.) As a consequence of borrowing, the [sk] cluster was re-introduced by the eleventh century.

Later on, borrowing from French during the Middle Ages also had some consequences for English phonology. It resulted in a PHONEME SPLIT. This is what happened. In Old English the fricatives [f v] and [s z] were not distinct phonemes. They were allophones of the phonemes /f/ and /s/ respectively. The voiced allophones occurred in heavily voiced environments. So they were found where these phonemes intervened between a stressed vowel and (i) another vowel (e.g. *lēofost* (with *f* pronounced [v]) 'dearest'; or (ii) a nasal or a liquid that was followed by a vowel (e.g. *lēofra* (with *f* pronounced [v]) 'dearer'. The voiceless fricative [f] occurred elsewhere: word-initially as in *feorr* 'far'; word-finally as in *lēof* 'dear'; when followed by a voiceless consonant as in *lufsum* 'amiable'. The same pattern of distribution was also shown by [s] and [z].

By contrast, Old French contrasted voiced and voiceless fricatives. So, as a consequence of borrowing French words like *vain, value, variable, veal, veil, zeal, zodiac* etc. it now became possible to contrast voiced fricatives with voiceless ones in the same environment as in *zeal* and *seal* (both borrowed from Old French). Hence these fricatives split into separate phonemes.

Borrowing may also have GRAMMATICAL EFFECTS, although these too have been quite modest in English. Adopting foreign nouns with their inflectional morphemes has resulted in the acquisition of a considerable number of allomorphs of the plural morpheme. In addition to the regular, native -*s* plural, English has other plural suffixes. Many Latin loans ending in -*um* (e.g. datum) take -*a* as their plural suffix (*data*); those ending in -*us* in the singular (e.g. *fungus*) take -*i* in the plural (*fungi*); those ending in -*a* in the singular (e.g. *larva*) take -*ae* in the plural (*larvae*).

Some Greek loans also bring with them their plural endings. Nouns ending in -*is* in the singular take *es* in the plural e.g. *thesis* ~ *theses*. Those ending in -*on* in the singular take -*a* as their plural suffix as in *ganglion* ~ *ganglia*.

Nouns borrowed from French which end in -*e(a)u* take -*x* in the plural, e.g. *bureau* ~ *bureaux* and *adieu* ~ *adieux*. And nouns borrowed from Hebrew take the plural -*im* as in *kibbutzim*.

Lastly, the introduction of new borrowed items may have SEMANTIC EFFECTS. These are the most obvious and most important. Here I want to show that borrowing can affect the *structure* of the lexicon when the meanings of imported words are put side by side with the meanings of words which are already in the lexicon.

This is because the lexicon is not just an unstructured list. Adding a new word may disturb the equilibrium of the words already in the language, causing semantic narrowing, for example. The new, borrowed word may take over part or most – but not all – of the meaning of the original word, and the original word may survive with a restricted meaning. An often cited example is the Old English noun *dēor*. This word originally meant any beast; but when the French word *animal* was borrowed, the original word *dēor* (which eventually became 'deer') was restricted to denoting the class of ruminant mammals with deciduous antlers. Similarly, the acquisition of the Norsemen's verb *cut* squeezed into a corner the original meaning of Old English *ceorfn* 'carve'. The meaning of *ceorfn* 'carve' was narrowed down to a special type of cutting.

The converse is also possible. Semantic narrowing may affect the borrowed word itself and not the words already found in the language. A word borrowed from a foreign language may have a more restricted meaning in the recipient language than it does in the source language. For instance, in Swahili *safari* means 'journey', any kind of journey. However, when it is used in English, it normally has the meaning of a touristic, game-viewing African trip.

This concludes our survey of general issues in borrowing. In the remainder of this chapter we will look more closely at examples of loanwords that have come into English from various major sources.

10.2 SCANDINAVIAN LOANWORDS

Very often language contact is through trade or colonial occupation. As a result of raids that started in the ninth century, which eventually led to the settlement of the Norsemen in Britain in the tenth and early eleventh centuries, English acquired Scandinavian loanwords, many of which are everyday words, such as the following:

[10.14]	*aloft*	ME<ON: *á* = on + *lopt* = air
	anger	ME<ON: *angr* = grief, sorrow. Whence adj. angry
	bag	ME: *bagge* < ON: *baggi*
	bang	(to beat violently) ON: *banga*
	club	ME: *clubbe, clobbe* = ON: *klubba*
	die	ME: *deghen* < ON: *deyja*
	flat	ME: *flat* = ON: *flatr*
	gift	ME: *geten* < ON: *geta*
	husband	Late OE: *hūsbōnda* < *húsbóndi* = householder
	ill	ME: *ille* < ON: *illr*
	ken	ON: *kenna* (= know, discern as in 'beyond one's ken' obsolete except in Scotland)
	knife	ME: *knif* < ON: *knifr*
	leg	ME: *legge* < ON: *leggr*
	outlaw	Late OE: *utlag* < ON: *útlagi* = one who is outside the law
	sky	ME: *skie* = cloud < ON: *ský*

(based on Geipel 1971)

Note: ON = Old Norse, OE = Old English, ME = Middle English

10.3 THE FRENCH INFLUENCE

We have already emphasised the point that the most far-reaching language contact that English has had through the ages has been

with French. In this section we will consider the French influence
in the English lexicon in two parts. First, we will deal with contact
with Norman French in the Middle Ages. The account of the effect
of medieval French on English draws on standard histories of the
language by Baugh and Cable (1978), Strang (1970), Lass (1987),
Pyles and Algeo (1982) as well as Trevelyan (1949) for a social
history of medieval England. In the second part of the section we
will turn to borrowing that has taken place in modern times.

10.3.1 The Norman French legacy

Following the Norman Conquest, England was taken over by the
French, who now controlled the church, the government and adminis-
tration. Initially, the new masters did not take too much trouble
learning the language of their subjects and continued to speak
French. As time went on society came to be divided roughly between
those who spoke French, who might at a generous estimate have
numbered about 20 per cent of the population, and the rest who
spoke English, the ordinary people, who formed the overwhelming
majority (Lass 1987). At least 80 per cent of the population were
peasants, who never learned French. Outside the elite circle of the
court, nobility, higher clergy and assorted hangers on, English was
never totally eclipsed. It always remained a vibrant, albeit low-status
language. As Chaucer put it in *The Canterbury Tales*:

[10.15] Some can French and no Latin
         That have used courts and dwelled therein:
         And some of Latin a party
         That can French fully febelly:
         And some understandeth English
         That neither can Latin nor French:
         But lerid and lewid, old and young
         All understanden English tongue.

Medieval England was a multilingual society. Chaucer could
have added that in addition to all those languages, in provincial
Cornwall they spoke the now extinct Celtic language, Cornish. The
most urbane and erudite members of the intelligentsia, especially
clergymen, used Latin (at least in official writings). The lower-
level officials of both church and state needed to speak to the
people in order to try to save their souls, to exact taxes from them,
to administer justice to them, to make them work in the fields of

the monastery or in the lord of the manor's household, and so on. This relatively small group of people had to be bilingual. The people who only used French in their daily lives were the exclusive and self contained upper classes. The top echelons of the nobility and bishops could get by without knowing the language of the common people.

An example of the very routine use of Norman French is this extract from a contract in which Johan Lewyn undertook to build a wall round the keep of a castle:

[10.16] Ceste endent'e faite a Baumburgh le xxv iour doctobre lan &c. quart parentre Johan Roy de Castille &c. dune part et Johan Lewyn mason dautre part tesmoigne les couenances fatite parentre le dit Johan Roy et Duc par lauys de son conseil et le dit Johan Lewyn. Cestassauoir q'le dit Johan Lewyn ad empris p^r faire de nouell bien et couenablement un mantelett de freeston en certein lieu a lui diuise par le dit Johan Roy et Duc et son Conseil ento^r le grant tourre etc.

(Salzman 1952: 460)

Many of the nobles had estates in both Normandy and England and had split loyalties. In many cases they were more French than English. The Norman kings remained dukes of Normandy and some of them spent most of their time in France. This is understandable. Through marriage and conquest their French possessions had expanded to such an extent that by the late twelfth century, Henry II (1154–89) was not only king of England but also ruler of almost two-thirds of France. But gradually, through intermarriage and ever-closer contact, the Normans were integrated into English society. By the mid-twelfth century the integration was virtually complete.

For the small, but influential social group who were at the apex of society English was a second-class language in terms of status. And their competence in it was rather limited. They practised some code-switching, which contributed in a relatively small way to borrowing. But you should not get from this the impression that the use of French and code-switching between English and French was widespread throughout the population. The eclipsing of English only affected the upper classes.

Most of the borrowing took place after the middle of the thirteenth century after French had been knocked off its perch as the most prestigious language in everyday use in high places and had increasingly become a written language.

According to some estimates, about 10,000 French words entered English during the Middle Ages. Most of them came into the language after the mid-thirteenth century when the marginalisation of English in high places had been reversed and most came into English via the written language: many French (and Latin) words originally used only in writing eventually found their way into the spoken language (cf. Lass 1987).

In the period 1200–1500 a number of historical factors conspired to revive the fortunes of English. Not least among them was King John's loss of Normandy in 1204. Disaster on the battlefield saved the English language from obscurity. The bitter, protracted Hundred Years War with France which began in 1337 put an end to French linguistic hegemony. Now the ruling classes had to put their mind to the task of becoming fully English and learning how to use the English language properly. The ties between the nobility in England and France were loosened. Understandably, the English aristocracy no longer had such warm feelings towards the French. And, in any event, those nobles who had estates in both countries were forced to make a choice: those who chose to be English had to renounce their French interests and learn to be truly English.

The following is the text of a letter written in 1440 by Robert Repps to John Paston, a member of one of the leading families of gentry in Norfolk. Although this letter was written a long time after English had been re-established, it is richly spiced with French. You can see how French loanwords used in writing eventually became part of spoken English as well.

1440 Nov. 1

Sir, I pray you, wyth all myn hert, hold me excusyd that I wryte thus homly and briefly on to you, for truly convenable space suffycyd me nowt.

No more atte this tyme, butte the Trynyte have you in proteccion, &c.; and qwan your leysyr is, resorte ageyn on to your college, the Inner Temple, for ther ben many qwych sor desyr your presence, Welles and othyr, &c.

Wretyn in le fest de touts Seynts, entre Messe et Mateyns, *calamo festinante*, &c.   Yours,   ROB REPPES.

So what is the balance sheet of the linguistic effects of the Norman Conquest?

(i) The Norman Conquest had a very far-reaching effect on the English lexicon. It started the habit of borrowing French words in large numbers which English has never been able to kick (cf. [10.7] and [10.8]).

(ii) Generally, the influx of French words into English had very little effect on the structure of English except in phonology where it led to [f] ~ [v] and [s] ~ [z], which had been allophones of the same phoneme, splitting into separate phonemes, as we saw in section (10.1.7).

During the period of the French ascendancy following the Norman Conquest, a very large number of words were adopted from Norman French into English. Most of the vocabulary to do with the court and nobility, government and the law, war and diplomacy was borrowed from French:

[10.17] a. *Government*:
president, government, minister, territory, counsellor, council, people, power

b. *Nobility*:
sovereign, royal, monarch, duke, prince, count, princess, principality, baron, baroness, noble

c. *Law*:
assizes, judge, jurisdiction, puisne judge, advocate, jury, court, law, prison, crime, accuse

d. *War*:
peace, battle, admiral, admiralty, captain, lieutenant

The adoption of French words that followed in the wake of the Norman Conquest has continued unabated.

10.3.2 French words in modern English

The discussion and examples in this section are based on Laure Chirol's (1973) book *Les 'mots français' et le mythe de la France en anglais contemporain*, which is an extensive survey of French words in contemporary English. We have already shown that English is hooked on French words. The number of French imports has risen steadily over the centuries. Chirol speculates on the reasons for this. She suggests that the use of French words in English serves to project the stereotyped, positive image of France on to the speakers themselves or the objects they speak about. And what is that image? It is an image of the French way of life, of high culture, sophistication in dress, food and social relations. This is reflected in the words and phrases habitually employed when an English speaker wraps herself or himself in the tricolour. (The fact that the real France and real French people might not live up to this idealised mythical image seems to be of no consequence.)

The French, who are not at all coy in these matters, would say that the appeal of the French language is probably due to the English-speakers' admiration of the French contribution to civilisation, which is well known. And, of course, the French never tire of reminding the world of it. France is perceived as the land of the arts in the broadest sense – encompassing literature, music, architecture, ballet, painting and sculpture. So, Chirol asks, what is more natural than that the nation which has given the world many of its greatest artists and artistic movements should be the leading supplier of critical terms for talking about the arts? Many English-speakers would concur. It is not that long since a sojourn in Paris by an American writer and a spell in Dieppe by an English painter were very useful ingredients of a successful career.

Many essential technical terms used in the arts are French. We will take literature and painting first. Examples are given below, together with the century when they appeared in English:

[10.18] LITERATURE

17th century	18th century	19th century	20th century
ballade,	comédie noire,	enjambement,	engagé,
chef d'œuvre,	brochure,	genre,	nouveau
précis	dénouement,	nom de plume,	roman,
(résumé),	troubadour	pastiche	dada,
mémoir(e)			faux amis,
			mot-clé (key word),
			monologue,
			intérieur,
			œuvre

[10.19] PAINTING

17th century	18th century	19th century	20th century
critique,	artiste,	avant garde,	art
chef-d'œuvre	baroque,	expertise,	nouveau,
	embarras de	genre,	calque,
	richesse	motif,	collage,
		renaissance	salon,

Turning to music, we observe that Italian (as we will shortly see) is the language which provides most musical terms. But here too French loans are by no means insignificant.

[10.20] MUSIC

17th century	18th century	19th century	20th century
aubade, rêverie	ensemble, pot-pourri	bâton, conservatoire, suite, timbre	musique concrète

French is the international language of ballet. Virtually all ballet terms used in English are from French.

[10.21] BALLET

17th century	18th century	19th century	20th century	
ballet, gavotte	pirouette, terre à terre	pas de deux, chassé, danseur, danseuse	échappé, plié, tutu, fouetté	jeté, coupé, plié, tutu

Society, refinement and fashionable living are also believed to be areas where the French excel. Hence the borrowing of words and expressions such as those below in order to enable English-speakers to bask in the reflected elegance of the French:

[10.22] SOCIETY

17th century	18th century	19th century	20th century
doyen, finesse, bizarre, brusque, tête-à-tête, rendez-vous, par excellence	coterie, élite, clique, protégé(e), esprit de corps, gauche, savoire-vivre, tout court, en route, nuance	bête noire, camaraderie, débutante, divorcée, fiancé(e), milieu, prestige, rentier, personnel, nouveau riche, élan, blasé, aplomb, risqué, volte-face, chez nous, bon voyage	chauffeur, échelon, éminence grise, haut mode, drôle, facile, gaffe, folie de grandeur, R.S.V.P., c'est la vie, touché, mot juste

Victorian values encourage the hypocritical 'No-sex-please-we're-British!' mentality. Figures in public life in Britain are hounded out of office and governments may collapse because of sexual peccadilloes. It seems to be thought to be more important that public figures have impeccable private lives – no extra-marital sex, and certainly no lesbian or homosexual tendencies – than that they are up to the job.

Probably this is why there is a secret admiration for the French who do not have such hang-ups about sex. The British admire the sexual prowess of the French – or more precisely, the French attitude to sex. That may well be the reason for the large number of words to do with love and sexuality that have been adopted from French:

[10.23]   LOVE AND SEXUALITY

17th century	18th century	19th century	20th century
amour, belle, beau, billet doux	chaperon	liaison, affaire de cœur	cri du cœur, madame, ménage à trois, gigolo, mal d'amour, crime passionnel

The French have always been renowned for their cuisine. So, naturally, French words to do with food and cooking have been borrowed in substantial numbers down the ages (some French words have been fully Anglicised, and are therefore presented in English spellings). A few fancy French phrases on the menu always add to the quality of the gastronomic experience and are deemed to be worth an extra pound or two on the bill.

[10.24]   CUISINE

14th–15th centuries
mustard, vinegar, beef, sauce, salad
16th–18th centuries
sirloin, gigot, carrot, cuisine, pastry, dessert, omelette, meringue, haricot, cognac, crème caramel, sage, pâtisserie, liqueur

19th–20th centuries

bombe, éclair, flan, gâteau, nougat, petit mousse, mille-feuilles, flambé, garni, en casserole, glacé, sauté, au gratin, brasserie, café, restaurant, à la carte, haute cuisine, rôtis-serie, hors-d'œuvre, entrée

French fashion has also been held in high esteem for centuries. Hence the extensive list of borrowing in the area of clothes, hair, cosmetics etc. (See the advertisement for Yves St Laurent perfume on p. 214.)

[10.25] FASHION

17th century	*18th century*	*19th century*	*20th century*
coiffure,	lingerie,	béret, chic,	après-ski,
blonde,	bouquet	boutique,	culottes,
brunette		haute couture,	brassière,
		eau de	rouge
		cologne,	
		crêpe,	
		appliqué,	
		velours,	
		massage	

Even fashionable car transport gets its terms from French, e.g. *marque, coupé, cabriolet.*

As we saw in section (10.1.2) at the beginning of this chapter when we discussed loan-translation, borrowing from French is not restricted to individual words. Whole phrases and sayings are also borrowed, for example:

[10.26] à la rigueur   à propos
         à la carte   au gratin
         à la mode   au contraire

10.4 WORDS FROM OTHER MODERN EUROPEAN LANGUAGES

English has acquired many words from a number of other modern European languages in addition to French. We will focus on Italian and German and mention other languages very briefly.

Italian loan words, though much fewer than the French ones,

are nevertheless numerous. They are concentrated in the areas of the arts (in particular music) and food. Italian is the international language of classical music in the same way that French is the international language of ballet. So, the majority of musical terms are from Italian:

[10.27] adagio   allegro   allegretto   alto   andante
         arpeggio   bravura   cantata   concerto   lento
         finale   mezzo forte   noblimente   piano   pizzicato
         rondo   scherzo   sonata   tempo   vivace

In the nineteenth and early twentieth centuries, Italians emigrated in large numbers to America. Many of the Italian immigrants went into the food business and popularised Italian food. Consequently many Italian food words entered American English and then spread to other dialects:

[10.28] pizza   pasta   spaghetti   macaroni
         cannelloni   lasagne   zucchini (= courgette) tagliatelle

German has also been an important source of adopted words (see [10.7] and [10.8] above). In the arts, the Bauhaus design school (1919–33) gave us the loanword *Bauhaus*. The musical term *leitmotif* was borrowed from German as well, and a few German words referring to food (e.g. *sauerkraut, schnitzel*) have found their way into English.

The rate of borrowing from a given language is rarely constant. Loans from a language may come flooding in during one period and trickle in during another. For reasons that are not difficult to surmise, during the 1930s and 1940s English assimilated many words from German which are associated with the Nazis and World War II:

[10.29] *swastika* (= Nazi symbol)
         Nazi (< National socialist) (German *Nationalsozialist*)
         Gestapo acronym formed from *Geheime Staats-Polizei* (Secret State-Police)
         Blitzkrieg (shortened to *Blitz*)
         panzer (i.e. armoured) as in *Panzer division*
         Luftwaffe (= airforce)

10.5 LOANWORDS FROM NON-EUROPEAN LANGUAGES

Though less numerous than loans from European languages, words adopted from non-European languages are not insignificant in number. Following increasing contact with peoples from outside Europe from the sixteenth century onwards, growing numbers of words were borrowed from their languages. Naturally, some of these words had to do with people, e.g. *pakeha* (Maori) white person; *Sherpa*, the name of a Tibetan people living on the slopes of the Himalayas; and *Gurka*, people of Nepal. Others are in the semantic field of culture (music, dance, art etc.), e.g. *samba* (Brazil), *rhumba* (Cuba), *tango* (Argentina), *didgeridoo* (Australia) and *batik* (Javanese).

The languages of the Indian subcontinent in what is now India, Pakistan and Bangladesh, have been an especially important source of verbal imports. India has been in contact with Britain since the seventeenth century, and these centuries of contact have left their mark on English. There are many words borrowed from Indian languages in various areas of the English lexicon. The account below of Indian loanwords in English is based on Rao (1954).

Rao points out that the nature of the borrowed words changed as time went on, reflecting developments outside language. There are a few loanwords for trade goods which pre-date the Raj, e.g. *copra, coir, pepper, sugar, indigo, ginger* and *sandal*. These were indirect borrowings which came into English via Latin, Greek, French, and so on.

In the early years of the British colonisation of India, loans reflected the commerce between India and Britain – not surprisingly, since that is what colonising India was all about. Words for various kinds of Indian textiles, e.g. *calico, chintz, dungaree* (extended in the nineteenth century to trousers made from this material) came into English with the goods.

With the passage of time, the range of Indian loanwords widened. As they became more involved with the Indians, the British realised that the subcontinent had more to it than *calico* and *chintz*. Words for mundane trade goods still figured in the verbal imports, but they were joined by words in diverse areas of meaning such as religion, philology, food and cooking and so on. The table in [10.30] (from Rao 1954) gives some idea of the wealth and diversity of the Indian borrowings.

[10.30] a. *Hinduism*:
Buddha, Brahmin, karma, pundit, yoga, yogi, mantra, nirvana, sutra
b. *Food*:
chutney, chapati, curry, poppadom
c. *Clothing*:
cashmere, pyjamas, khaki (= brown), mufti, saree (sari)
d. *Philology (19th century)*:
sandhi, bahuvrihi (compounds), dvandva (compounds)
e. *People and society*
Aryan (Sanskrit), pariah, mem-sahib, sahib, coolie
f. *Animals and plants*
mongoose, zebu, bhang, paddy, teak
g. *Buildings and domestic*
bungalow, pagoda, cot
h. *Assorted*
catamaran, cash (= small coin), chit, lilac, tattoo, loot, polo, swastika (Sanskrit), cushy, juggernaut, tom-tom

A smaller number of loanwords have come from farther east, from languages such as Japanese and Chinese. The stereotype of the warlike, militaristic Japanese addicted to martial arts may have both encouraged and been encouraged by loanwords like *samurai*, *karate*, *hara-kari* and *kamikaze*. Fortunately, the image of Japan as reflected through borrowings is not all negative. The militaristic words are balanced by the artistic *origami*, the elegant *kimono*, the poetic *haiku*, and in popular entertainment the *kabuki* and *karaoke*.

10.6 THE GERMANIC INHERITANCE

Borrowing is the main external cause of LANGUAGE CHANGE. As we have seen, borrowing has had a big impact on the English lexicon: a high proportion of English words and affix morphemes are of foreign origin. Does that make English a hybrid language? In this section we will see that in spite of the very large number of foreign acquisitions, much has remained of the original language.

English belongs to the GERMANIC branch of the INDO-EUROPEAN FAMILY of languages, which includes these languages:

[10.31] HELLENIC the mother of Ancient Greek,
    GERMANIC languages (e.g. German, English, Dutch, Flem-
      ish, Afrikaans, Danish, Norwegian, Swedish, Icelandic),
    ROMANCE languages (e.g. French, Italian, Spanish), which
      are descendants of Latin, itself a daughter of Italic,
    CELTIC languages (e.g. Breton, Welsh, Scottish and Irish
      Gaelic),
    SLAVIC languages (e.g. Russian, Ukrainian, Serbo-Croat,
      Czech),
    INDO-IRANIAN languages (e.g. Sanskrit, Hindi, Punjabi,
      Kurdish, Persian).

Historical linguists have shown that much of the core vocabulary
of Indo-European languages is COGNATE, i.e. it developed from the
same historical source. You can verify this for yourself by examining the table below:

[10.32] Indo-European cognates

	heart	lung	night	sun
Old English	heorte	lungen	niht	sunne
German	Herz	Lungen	Nacht	Sonne
Old Norse	hjarta	lunga	nátt	sól, sunna
Gothic	hairto	leihts 'light'	nahts	sauil, sunno
Latin	cordis	levis 'light'	noctis	sōl
Greek	kardia	elachus 'little'	nuktos	hēlios
Russian	serdtse	legkoe	noch'	solntse
Lithuanian	ʃirdis	lengvas 'light'	naktis	saule
Irish	cridhe	laigiu 'less'	nocht	heol (Breton)
Sanskrit	hrd-	laghus 'light'	naktam	surya
Proto-Indo-European	*kerd-	*le(n)gwh-	*nokwt-	sāwel-/sun-

Source: based on Algeo (1972: 90–1)

Languages belonging to the same family inherit from the parent
language many structural features (of phonology, morphology and
syntax) as well as CORE VOCABULARY items (i.e. basic words, such
as words for parts of the body, kinship terms, numbers, basic
bodily functions like eating and sleeping). The more closely related
languages are, the more shared vocabulary items they have.
    Borrowing does not alter the genetic inheritance of a language.
The acquisition of foreign words has led to diversification in the
English lexicon, but it has not destroyed the Germanic and Old

English inheritance. Words of Anglo-Saxon origin are still the words people use most frequently in everyday conversation (e.g. *I, the, am, a, are, on, child, see, sun* etc.).

However, extensive borrowing has had very important stylistic consequences. Often there are near synonyms, one of which is an everyday word of Anglo-Saxon origin and the other a foreign (usually Latinate) word which is used in formal situations – or just by people 'talking posh':

[10.33]	*Old or Middle English*	*Latinate*
	house, home	habitation, domicile
	limb	member
	walk	promenade
	food	victuals
	dying	expiring
	leave	depart
	get	obtain
	give	donate
	sweat	perspiration
	gushy	sentimental
	put out (a fire)	extinguish (a fire)

10.7 SUMMARY

Over the centuries, English has expanded its vocabulary by extensively borrowing lexical items from other languages. Of all sources of loanwords French is by far the most important. But there is a significant number of words borrowed from other languages, which reflects the contacts English-speaking people have had with other peoples and their cultures.

Normally, a loanword (i.e. a word-form plus meaning) is imported, but sometimes loan translation takes place – the meaning of a foreign lexical item is simply translated into English. For borrowing to take place it is obviously necessary to have some bilingual speakers who regularly code-switch or use foreign words in English. This may result in words seeping into English from another language.

Foreign words are borrowed for a number of reasons, e.g. to meet the need for a way of expressing a particular meaning, to court admiration etc. Borrowed words from a particular language tend to reflect the nature of the contact, e.g. cultural contact, colonisation, religion, trade and so on.

The likelihood of being borrowed is not the same for all words. Content words are more likely to be borrowed than function words. And among content words nouns are the most likely candidates for borrowing, but words in other word-classes are not exempt. Once borrowed, words may get Anglicised to different degrees. Borrowing words from foreign languages may affect the phonological, grammatical and semantic structure of the recipient language.

Borrowing has enriched the English lexicon. But at the core English remains a Germanic language. Most of the commonest and most basic words used today are descended from Anglo-Saxon. Often there are near synonyms, one of which is native and the other borrowed, which differ stylistically.

EXERCISES

1. Why do languages borrow words?

2. Explain how different types of borrowing can be classified.

3. What is meant by the 'nativisation of loanwords'? Give two examples of foreign words that have become nativised in English.

4. a. Give two fresh examples of affixes and bound roots borrowed from Latin.
   b. With the help of a good dictionary, explain the meanings of each of the morphemes that you have selected.

5. A large number of Latin words, phrases and abbreviations are used in English such as:

AD	de jure	homo sapiens	moratorium
ad hoc	e.g.	honorarium	non sequitur
ad infinitum	ego	i.e.	prima facie
ad nauseam	et al.	in loco parentis	primus inter pares
alma mater	etcetera (etc.)	magnum opus	referendum
bona fide	exeunt	malefactor	sine die
caveat	exit	modus operandi	status quo
de facto	ex gratia	modus vivendi	subpoena

   a. State in plain English what each of these abbreviations, words and phrases means. Where appropriate, indicate whether there is a standard loan translation of the Latin phrase.

b. In what area of the vocabulary (i.e. semantic field) is each phrase found? Is there any reason for this? Can any generalisation(s) be made?

6. Many words in the scientific, technical and learned vocabulary are borrowed from Greek. Study the words below and, using a good etymological dictionary, find out the meanings of the morphemes in each word:

chemotherapy	laryngoscope	physiology	stethoscope
econometrics	microbiology	physiotherapy	telescope
economics	microscope	psychology	theology
kilometre	morphology	psychotherapy	thermometer

7. Look up the words below in a good etymological dictionary and answer the questions that follow:

banana	female	mosquito	serve
bandit	fjord	moussaka	shampoo
banquet	flamenco	ombudsman	shinto
beauty	fruit	opossum	ski
biology	Führer	orange	skunk
bog	goulash	paper	sugar
boil	honour	pecan	sumo
booze	igloo	philharmonic	Talmud
boss	inhabitant	piano	tea
buffalo	judo	plaza	theory
caftan/kaftan	jungle	pleasure	thermometer
chihuahua	junta	pneumonia	tobacco
chop suey	kangaroo	poach	tomato
church	kirk	potato	tulip
clan	landscape	pound	virgin
coffee	maize	pray	virtue
cosher/kosher	mardi-gras	propaganda	wigwam
cotton	mayonnaise	ptarmigan	wildebeest
courage	mazurka	regal	wine
crag	menu	religion	yoga
culture	mercy	roast	yoghurt
deck	military	robot	zany
delicatessen	model	scene	zen
falcon	moose	school	zenith

a. Find out when and from which language the above words came into English.
b. Where appropriate, attempt to make generalisations about the observed patterns of borrowing (e.g. are words from certain languages concentrated in certain semantic fields? If the answer is yes, is there a plausible reason for this?).

Chapter 11

The mental lexicon

11.1 A MIND FULL OF WORDS

We shall now conclude the book by bringing together the different issues that have been raised about words. Seemingly abstract points considered in preceding chapters that may have looked purely theoretical will be used now in our exploration of the nature of the MENTAL LEXICON – the representation of words in the mind. There are some obvious similarities between the contents of the mental lexicon and the more familiar lexicographer's dictionaries sold in bookstores. Both must contain information about the meaning, grammatical properties, pronunciation (and orthographic representation) of an enormous number of words (cf. Chapter 6).

The focus in this chapter is on how that information is handled in the mental lexicon. How do we store thousands and thousands of words in the mind? How do we manage to retrieve them correctly and so effortlessly, most of the time in speech, both as speakers and as hearers? How do we manage to correctly associate sound with meaning? (We will restrict ourselves to speech and exclude a detailed discussion of written language so as to keep this chapter within manageable proportions.) This is an achievement that makes finding a needle in the proverbial haystack look like child's play.

In speech, the matching of sound with meaning is essential for communication to happen. There would be very little successful communication if the speaker chose a word to express a certain meaning but had no idea of its pronunciation. Conversely, comprehension would not take place if the listener decoded the sounds of a word correctly but had no idea what they meant. But, by itself, a successful match of sound with meaning is not enough. It is equally important for the speaker to be able to associate the word chosen with the right set of morpho-syntactic properties (e.g. noun, feminine, singular, present tense, past tense, definite, indefinite, etc.) and for the hearer to be able to recognise information about those grammatical properties on hearing the words. It is important, for instance, to know whether the speaker said '*He feared the dog*' or '*He fears dogs*'. The tense, definiteness and number differences between the two sentences are important. We cannot arrive at the right interpretation if they are not grasped.

11.1.1 Types of lexical information

In this section we will elaborate on the points raised in the introduction. In so doing we will outline an answer to the question: what must a person know about words in order to be able to use them both as a speaker and as a listener?

Phonological information

The mental lexicon must indicate how words and morphemes are pronounced, e.g. *quay* is pronounced /ki:/ (cf. section (6.4)). Further, lexical entries for affixes need to indicate the stratum at which they appear, since that reflects some of their properties. So, for instance, the lexicon needs to indicate that *-esque* and *-ian* are non-neutral suffixes. The former attracts stress to itself, as in *pictu'resque*, and the latter puts stress on the immediately preceding syllable, as in *Ca'nadian*. They contrast with a neutral suffix like *-ful*, as in *con'tainerful*, which has no effect on stress.

Further, for literate speakers the grammar also needs to link orthographic with phonological representations. This is especially important in a language like English where the spelling of a word is not always a totally reliable guide to its pronunciation, as we saw in Chapter 7. Consider these examples:

[11.1] a. Orthographic
representation: $read_{(Verb.\ Pres.)}$ $read_{(Verb,\ Past)}$ $red_{(Adj.)}$
Phonological
representation: /ri:d/   /red/   /red/
b. Orthographic
representation: $quay_{(Noun)}$ $key_{(Noun)}$
Phonological
representation: /ki:/   /ki:/

The same sequence of letters can be pronounced in different ways. Interpretative rules are needed to link orthographic words to phonological words. Here, the rules need to say that the letters *ea* in *read* represent either the sound /i:/ or /e/, depending on whether the verb is in the present tense or past tense. Conversely, the same sound can be represented by different letters as in [11.1b] where all the letters except for final *y* are different and yet the words have exactly the same pronunciation. Likewise, in [11.1a], the letter *e* in the adjective *red* is sounded the same way as the diagraph *ea* in the past tense form of the verb *read*.

Grammatical information

Grammatical information must also form part of entries in the mental lexicon. At first blush, it might seem reasonable to expect words with certain meanings to naturally belong to certain word-classes, in which case their word-class membership would not need to be listed in the mental lexicon. It may seem natural that *tree* and *house* are nouns because they are words which denote entities. It may seem natural that *chase* and *fall* are verbs because they denote actions and events. It may seem natural that *bitter* and *delicious* are adjectives because they attribute qualities or predicate states of entities. However, comparative scrutiny of languages leads us to a different conclusion. In English *bitter* and *delicious* are adjectives but in Luganda *kukaawa* and *kuwoooma*, the words which express corresponding meanings, are verbs. The word-class that a word belongs to is not necessarily determined by its meaning. It is fixed by the conventions of a particular language. So, it must be listed in the lexicon.

The lexicon must also list any idiosyncratic grammatical properties of a word. In section (6.3) we emphasised regularities in the grammatical behaviour of words which can be captured by general rules. This should not overshadow the fact that there are some grammatical aspects of word behaviour which are peculiar to a word and defy any systematic, general rules. For instance, there is no way of predicting from their meanings why some verbs allows a complement clause that begins with either the infinitive marker *to* or the conjunction *that* while other verbs only allow *to*. Contrast [11.2] with [11.3]:

[11.2] a. She expected that John would play another match.
        b. She expected John to play another match.

[11.3] a. She persuaded John to play another match.
        b. *She persuaded that John would play another match.

So, our lexical entry for a verb will have to specify the kind of complements that a verb is allowed (Chomsky 1965, 1986).

Some of the grammatical information that needs to be specified has to do with morphological features. For instance, there are cases where we need to know if a word is native or foreign before we can attach an affix to it. Usually foreign affixes have to be used with foreign loans and native affixes with native stems, which is why the plural of Greek loan *phenomenon* is *phenomena* not **phenomenons*. In derivational morphology too, foreign affixes tend to occur with foreign roots and native affixes with native roots. Thus, the native suffix *-ness* tends to co-occur with native roots and bases and the Romance suffix *-ity*, which is very closely related in meaning, occurs with Romance roots and bases. That is why the abstract noun formed from the *light* which comes from Old English is *lightness* not **lightity*. By contrast, the French borrowing *futile* takes *-ity* to give *futility* (**futileness*). This is the essential insight which the theory of lexical phonology captures (cf. section (6.5.2)).

Also, if a word is an exception to a general rule which would otherwise affect it, we need to flag it with an exception feature in the lexicon. For instance, nouns like *furniture* and *equipment* have to be expressly marked as not being eligible for the plural inflection.

Meaning

Obviously, the lexicon would be of little use if it contained phonological and grammatical information but said nothing about meaning. The whole point of having words is to be able to mean. We look up in lexicographers' dictionaries the meanings of words we do not know, and many of us have an unshakeable trust in dictionary definitions. Yet, interestingly, even the best standard dictionaries provide only a very bare and selective statement of meaning. They are a very pale reflection of the meanings contained in the mental lexicon. (Cf. Fodor (1981), Hudson (1984) and Aitchison (1987) for more detailed discussion.)

I will illustrate what I mean with the word *dog*. *Webster's* dictionary says that a *dog* is 'any of a large group of domesticated animals belonging to the same family as the fox, wolf, jackal, etc.', but your mental representation of 'dog' is much more elaborate. It includes all sorts of information – that the prototypical dog is like a Labrador rather than a Great Dane or Chihuahua; that it barks; that it is carnivorous; that it can be a good companion or a fierce guard; that it leaves a terrible mess on the pavement etc.

The specification of the meaning of a word in a lexicographer's dictionary tends to convey the most salient aspects of its cognitive meaning and to omit important aspects like other words to which it is related, its semantic associations and connotations. Your dictionary might say, for example, that the *Commonwealth* is the free association of nations formed by Britain and her former dominions and colonies. Given this definition, you might expect the expression 'New Commonwealth' to refer to states that have recently joined the Commonwealth. But this kind of standard definition is of little value in understanding the euphemism *New Commonwealth* as it is used in the press. The unconventional definition from Holder (1987: 221) is more like the definition people have in their mental lexicons:

[11.4] 'New Commonwealth' non-white
    After WW II 'Empire' had too many over-tones of conquest and superiority and the Br. adopted 'Commonwealth' as a collective noun of those former colonies which wished to stay in the club. Whatever the relative length of your associ- ation with Britain, you remain in the 'New Commonwealth' if your citizens are Black.

So that is why a country like India or Jamaica, whose association with Britain goes back more than 300 years, is part of the 'New Commonwealth'. Interestingly, there is no 'Old Commonwealth'.

Connotations and associations are important even when talking about issues that are less emotionally charged. Words may be 'synonymous' at the cognitive level but differ greatly in the associ- ations they bring with them. Compare these words, which might be listed together in a dictionary of synonyms:

[11.5] stoned plastered drunk inebriated intoxicated

In order to choose the situations in which it would be appropriate to use each one of these words, we need to consider the level of formality, the relationship between the interlocutors and the nature of the communication situation. *Drunk* is neutral. *Intoxicated* and *inebriated* are more formal, so are used in more formal situations. *Stoned* and *plastered* are informal. Part of our lexical knowledge involves knowing what is appropriate to a given situation.

In sum, both the mental lexicon and the lexicographer's dictionary must contain orthographic, phonological, grammatical and semantic information. The various kinds of information outlined here must be instantaneously retrievable by both speakers and hearers from their mental lexicon.

11.1.2 The organisation of the mental lexicon

The similarities between the mental lexicon and the lexicographer's lexicon are important. But so are the differences. The mental lexicon differs in at least two important ways: in structure and in content.

Whereas lexicographers' dictionaries list words alphabetically, we do not keep words in an alphabetical list in the mind. That is why it is extremely unlikely that a speech error would involve mistakenly retrieving a word with a letter near that of the word that you intended to use. We do not have slips of the tongue where we confuse words that end in letters that are near each other in the lexicographer's dictionary such as *cornet* and *corner*. We do not find slips of the tongue like **The teashop is just round the cornet* (meaning *The teashop is just round the corner*). We do not find people confusing *tip* with *tiny* although they are next to each other in the *OED*. So, you will probably never hear *I saw a tiny rabbit in the garden* being erroneously uttered as **I saw a tip rabbit in the garden*.

The mind is crammed all the way up to the rafters with words. Soon after the age of two, the average infant has a vocabulary of more than 200 words. By age 7, the figure has risen to over 1,300 words. Oldfield (1963) estimated that the average Oxford undergraduate has a vocabulary of about 75,000 words. Other studies (cf. Seashore and Eckerson (1940), Diller (1978)), claim that a college-educated adult's mental lexicon may range from a conservative but still very substantial 50,000 to 250,000 words. The estimates vary widely in part due to a number of methodological difficulties. There are problems in agreeing on what units count as distinct words. There are also problems in determining what 'knowing a word' means, and so on.

Everyone agrees that the mental lexicon is vast. So how does the mind store all those words? Our starting assumption is that words are stored in a very orderly manner in the mind. Without your mental lexicon being very systematically organised you would have a better chance of finding the proverbial needle in a haystack than of finding the word you wanted. We have thousands and thousands of words in our minds and yet we are able to find them in a flash. If they were all piled in the mind like old clothes on a jumble sale table, it would take hours, if not days, to find the right word.

Human memory works most efficiently when it deals with structured information rather than a pot-pourri of facts and information. You can verify this by reading and trying to remember the same telephone number presented in two ways, in [11.6a] and in [11.6b]:

[11.6] a. (254) 326–4121
        b. 2543264121

Although the same digits are presented to you in both cases, they are not equally easy to remember. It is much easier to recall [11.6a] where the area code (254) is bracketed off, and the district code 326 is separated from the specific account number (4121) (cf. Gregg (1986)). It is reasonable to assume that the speed of lexical retrieval is possible only because lexical information is highly structured in the mind.

The same point can be made about speech production. We all marvel at the fluency of speech of the auctioneer, or of the radio commentator covering a horse race. No less remarkable is Mr Average Twitter-Machine's rate of delivery when chatting with his friends. In normal conversation, speakers produce words at a very brisk rate – 100–200 words per minute. So, just finding the correct word time after time (never mind making sense, which we manage to do as well a good bit of the time) is a great accomplishment. Hence the vital importance of having a well organised mental lexicon and a super-efficient retrieval system.

11.1.3 To parse or not to parse

In psycholinguistic literature, one of the topics that has attracted a lot of interest in recent years is the mental storage and retrieval of morphologically complex words. The literature on this subject is quite extensive. I have drawn on the survey of the main issues by Hankamer (1989).

One model of the way in which words are stored in the mind is that of Taft and Foster (1975) which was refined by Taft (1979, 1981). In this model roots (including bound ones) and prefixes are stored separately in the mind: complex words are not stored in a pre-assembled state. Word recognition crucially involves MORPHO-LOGICAL PARSING. According to Taft and Foster, the dictionary in the mind engages in PREFIX STRIPPING, a process where a word is parsed and all the prefixes are identified. This is followed by looking up the root in the dictionary. Stanners *et al.* (1979) took the logical step of extending the same model to inflectional suffixes. This is the model that has been loosely assumed and implicitly used throughout this book.

An alternative model, and one that has won the approval of most psycholinguists, is that of Butterworth (1983). It is called the Full Listing Hypothesis (FLH). Advocates of FLH assume that familiar words are entered in the lexicon already fully assembled, but if confronted with unfamiliar words, one might resort to pars-ing. Routinely, speech recognition need not entail any morphologi-cal parsing. In other words, normally there is no affix stripping.

There are two versions of FLH. Version 1 assumes full listing, with information of morphologically complex entries spelt out. A complex word like *recovering* is listed, complete with its morphologi-cal analysis. So it would appear in the lexicon as (re(cover)ing). Version 2 of FLH assumes that every word has a separate entry in the dictionary. But the entries of related complex words are linked as SATELLITES forming part of a constellation whose nucleus is a simple un-affixed bound root or word (cf. Bradley (1978, 1980), Bybee (1987)). For example, the dictionary would indicate that there is the word *cover* which functions as the nucleus of the constel-lation containing the satellites listed in [11.7]

[11.7]
cover	covers	covering	coverings
covered	uncover	uncovers	uncovered
recovered	recovering	coverable	recoverable
recovery	uncovering	recoverability	

As already mentioned, parsing is not entirely ruled out in this model. Butterworth (1983) suggests that it is resorted to, *in extremis*, when a hearer needs to cope with a novel or unfamiliar word such as *Lebanonisation* or *deprofessionalisation*.

A theme that has run through this book is that listing of totally unpredictable lexical items is essential. But many lexical items are compositional and hence not unpredictable. Such items need not be listed in the lexicon. FLH takes the opposite view and assumes that the morphological parser is used sparingly: listing of pre-assembled words is the norm. I am inclined to disagree. In the remainder of this section, following Hankamer (1989), I will argue that FLH is not a plausible model of how to produce or recognise words.

Hankamer examines the morphological complexity of Turkish, a typical agglutinating language. He shows that the number of word-forms corresponding to a single lexeme is so large that even assuming that a speaker has a very modest word-hoard, it is simply impossible that they would have the storage space to store the billions of word-forms they know. This is how Hankamer puts it:

> It seems that agglutinative morphology is even more productive than has been thought. Given a lexicon containing 20,000 noun roots and 10,000 verb roots, which does not seem unreasonable for an educated speaker of Turkish, the FLH would require over 200 billion entries. Furthermore, most of the entries would necessarily be complex, and thus would take up significant storage space in the human brain.
>
> (Hankamer 1989: 403)

Hankamer shows that this is what the word-cluster containing some of the satellites of the nucleus *ev* 'house' would look like:

[11.8]
ev	'house'
evler	'houses'
evlerimiz	'our houses'
evlerimizde	'in our houses'
evlerimizdeki	'the one in our houses'
evlerimizdekiler	'the ones in our houses'
evlerimizdekilerin	'of the ones in our houses'
evlerimizdekilerinki	'the one of (belonging to) the ones in our houses'

We have here already eight forms, some of them quite complex, without going through all the grammatical cases and without listing the various persons (*my, your, her* etc.) Since house is pretty much an everyday word presumably it would have to reside permanently in the mental lexicon, all pre-assembled. That would require a lot of storage space. Now, if you look at the data in Chapter 3 from Latin, a typical inflecting language (cf. [3.17]), and those from Eskimo, a typical incorporating language (cf. [3.20]) you will see that the idea of listing pre-assembled words would be no less implausible in those languages.

The storage implications make the FLH untenable. The human brain is estimated by Sagan (1985) to have a storage capacity of 12,500,000,000,000 (12.5 billion) bytes. This estimate is based on the number of neurons in the brain. If the storage of a fairly simple word takes, say 10 bytes (and that of complex words like *evlerimizdekilerinki* requires considerably more), it would be possible to store a maximum of 125 billion word-forms. And that would only be possible if the brain was exclusively dedicated to storing words. Since at a conservative estimate educated speakers of Turkish would need to store 200 billion word-forms, the FLH model fails to account for how these speakers manage to list the words they know. But, of course, a bigger problem is the fact that even to cope with the lower figure of 125 billion words, the FLH would need to make the absurd assumption that our Turkish speaker uses the brain exclusively as a word-store.

While conceding that the FLH cannot work for Turkish, one might say that as English is not an agglutinating language like Turkish (we established in Chapter 3 that English is essentially an isolating language), there is no reason to be pessimistic about the chances of the FLH accounting for the storage of English words in the mind. The problem is that English does have a sizeable number of words, many of them not rare by any means, which contain several affixes. When we listed the satellites of the nucleus *cover* in [11.7], we stopped at 14 word-forms. We could have gone on. In this respect *cover* is not particularly unusual. Clearly, even in English there is quite a big number of agglutinative words. If we take the vocabulary of an educated speaker, any attempt to apply the FLH would mean listing millions of word-forms, many of them quite complex, in the mental lexicon. Again the pressure this would exert on storage space would be intolerable.

If the human mind is equipped with a morphological parsing device to cope with extensive agglutinating languages like Turkish, there is no reason to assume that it cannot be turned on whenever the need arises to deal with morphologically complex words in a language like English. Given the existence of words like those in [11.7] it is reasonable to assume that morphological parsing is needed fairly often in English.

11.2 MODELLING THE MENTAL LEXICON

Models of the mental lexicon fall into two broad types: those that have attempted to characterise words in the mind from the speaker's perspective and those that have done so from the hearer's perspective. The former have attempted to represent speech production and the latter speech comprehension. We will explore the speech comprehension models first before treating speech production models.

11.2.1 Understanding speech

What part is played by the mental lexicon in speech comprehension? Marslen-Wilson (1989b: 3) gives this answer:

> The role of the mental lexicon in human speech comprehension is to mediate between two fundamentally distinct representational and computational domains: the acoustic-phonetic analysis of the incoming speech signal, and the syntactic and semantic interpretation of the message being communicated.

Marslen-Wilson observes that the central problem in speech perception is that the hearer is simultaneously faced with two tasks. One task is decoding the acoustic signal that hits the ear-drums; the other task is untangling the higher levels of word meaning, grammatical structure, sentence meaning and the meaning that the speaker intended to convey. In other words, the task is one of deciphering noises and attaching meanings to them. As we noted above, just the ability to do this is in itself remarkable. What is even more amazing is the speed with which it is done. Normally we understand speech instantaneously. When someone says something to us, we do not go away for half an hour and do all the necessary acoustic–phonetic computations, followed afterwards by the syntactic–semantic analysis before coming up with an interpretation. Native speakers of English have been shown to be able to recognise a word within about one fifth of a second from the moment the speaker begins uttering it. If all goes well, in normal conversation you literally figure out the words and their meaning before they are out of your interlocutor's mouth. On average, words are recognised in context 200 milliseconds from the moment the speaker utters the first sound of the word, even though at that point there are insufficient auditory clues to identify the word

(Marslen-Wilson 1987, 1989b). Clearly, sensory input plays a role in identifying the words heard, but it is not the only factor. The listener must be able to use other means. A lot of intelligent guessing goes on. A particular auditory cue is tested for goodness of fit in the linguistic and non-linguistic context. With the minimal phonetic clues obtained in the first 200 milliseconds, which word is most likely to make sense? We will return to this later in subsections (11.2.1) and (11.2.2).

Let us take a closer look at the acoustic decoding task first. To recognise a word it helps if one can identify the individual sounds which represent that word. So, the hearer goes through a PHONETIC STAGE. This involves the identification of noises. To this end, the hearer looks out for the acoustic clues which help to identify segments. For instance, to identify the first two sounds in the word *spin* the hearer, among other things, detects the turbulence of the fricative [s] and the fact that it is followed by a stop. It is quite likely that initially it will be impossible to determine whether the stop is [p] or [b] because acoustically it will be very unclear which it is. The next stage in sound perception is the PHONOLOGICAL STAGE. It is at this stage that it will become clear that the sound in question is /p/, not /b/. If you are a speaker of English, you know how sounds in your language function. You know the phonotactic constraints on the positions where sounds can appear.

(i) You know that if a word-initial fricative is followed by a stop, that fricative must be /s/. Only /s/ is allowed to occur at the beginning of a word if the second sound of the word is a consonant. No English word can begin with /zk/, /fm/, /ʃk/ etc.

(ii) You also know that if the word begins with /s/ and the sound following /s/ is a stop, that stop must be voiceless. There are words like *spin, spoon, stick, skin* etc. where /s/ is followed by a voiceless stop. But there are no words like **sbin, *sboon, *sdick,* or **sgin* where /s/ is followed by a voiced stop. This is a phonotactic constraint on the combination of fricatives with stops in English phonology. It is not something simply determined by their acoustic properties. If the /s/ of *spin* is electronically spliced, you would probably hear the word left behind as [bɪn], not [pɪn]. Why is this? It is because the main cue for distinguishing between [p] and [b] occurring initially in a stressed syllable is aspiration. If you detect aspiration, you assume it is [pʰ]; if you do not you assume it is [b]. As the sound in *spin* was preceded by /s/ before splicing off the [s], it was not initial and so it was unaspirated. So it is perceived as [b]. Obviously, linguistic knowledge of this kind, this COMPETENCE, lies hidden deep in the mind and you are unlikely to be conscious of it without taking a course in linguistics.

We have established that there is no one-to-one match between acoustic phonetic cues and the phonological interpretation we give them. What is perceived as the 'same' sound is not physically the same sound in all contexts. Very much depends on the context in which the cues are perceived and on what we know to be permissible in that context in the language.

One model that has been proposed to account for the way people perceive speech is ANALYSIS BY SYNTHESIS (cf. Halle and Stevens (1962), Studdert-Kennedy (1974, 1976), Stevens and House (1972)). Its proponents claim that hearers recognise speech sounds uttered by speakers by matching them with speech sounds that are synthesised in their heads. Specifically, the synthesising is said to involve modelling the articulatory gestures that the speaker makes to produce those sounds. In the light of what was said above concerning the incredible speed of word recognition, it is implausible to expect hearers to perform the analysis by synthesis routine. So, many reject this model.

Clearly, the perception of individual speech sounds is far from straightforward. But the perception of running speech presents an even greater challenge. A major problem (which people are most acutely aware of when listening to a language in which they have little competence) is that, in fluent speech, words come out in a gushing stream. In purely physical terms, it is normally impossible to hear where one word ends and the next one begins. Looking up each word in the mental lexicon as it is heard is not a credible strategy.

But even if it were possible to separate out words, which clearly it is not, there would be the additional problem of NOISE, in a very broad sense. In many real life situations, there is not a perfect hush around us as we speak. There is noise. Lots of noise. In a pub, at a party, at work, in a railway station, in the home, there are often other people talking, banging, operating noisy machines, playing loud music etc. So we hear some of the words only partially

– if at all. Yet we manage to work out what the other person is saying. How do we do it? Knowing what is relevant in the context helps. We can make intelligent guesses.

In cases where we communicate using almost fixed formulas, GUESSING is relatively easy. Imagine you drop in at a friend's house at 11 a.m. and shortly after welcoming you, your host says:

[11.9] Would you like *** or ***?

You do not hear the bits marked by asterisks because a loud heavy goods lorry goes past the open window as she says ***. I expect you would have no problem guessing that the words you did not hear were *tea* and *coffee*. Experience tells you that in this situation they are the most likely words to be used.

Sometimes you are luckier. You manage to hear part of a word properly. In this situation again it is usually possible to make out the entire word. Suppose the hearer identifies a bit of speech three syllables long, beginning with [r] and ending in [tə] as in [11.10a]:

[11.10] a. If you're cold, get closer to the r***[tə].
     b. If you're cold, get closer to the *radiator*.
      If you're cold, get closer to the *red heater*.

The hearer can then guess which word or group of words with the phonological outline that has been perceived seems to make sense in the context. Either a *radiator* or a *red heater* could provide warmth. A quick inspection to see whether there was a *radiator* or a *red heater* in the room would help to settle it.

If we are in a particular situation, and know what is RELEVANT in that situation, we can discard some of the possible words we might think we hear; we can also reject homophonous words which are inappropriate in the circumstances, and select the more plaus-ible, relevant word:

[11.11] [vɪkəz ər ən straɪk]

If you live in the English shipbuilding town of Barrow where most of the working population are employed in Vicker's shipbuilding yard and you have seen hundreds of women and men staging a protest outside the gate of the shipyard, you would probably recog-nise the word as referring to workers at *Vicker's* and not the *vicars* with dog collars from all the town's churches. Knowledge that priests do not strike is also helpful, of course. So you would use your world knowledge to eliminate *vicars*. Context and relevance are vitally important in speech recognition when for some reason the meaning of the words perceived is to some extent unclear.

11.2.2 Selective listening

Listening is an active, not a passive activity. The perception of continuous speech is not a simple matter of deciphering raw noises that impinge on the eardrums. The classic example of SELECTIVE LISTENING is the so-called 'cocktail party phenomenon' where the listener's role in creating meaning is vital. You can choose to home in on a specific conversation when a dozen loud conversations are going on in the room. This shows the importance of selection. The listener constructs meaning from a specific set of auditory signals – and ignores the rest.

Psychologists have performed experiments to explore the nature of selective listening. They have done this by designing SHADOWING experiments where subjects repeat instantaneously a taped utterance, word for word, as they listen to it. Meanwhile, the subjects listen simultaneously, in one ear, to another message which they are told to ignore. The experiment is set up in such a way that the two messages that are listened to are equally clear and have the same tempo and volume.

In these experiments people easily manage to focus on the utterance that they are shadowing and to ignore the utterance that they are not shadowing. They might not even notice that the utterance which they are not shadowing is in a foreign language, or whether the speaker was a man or a woman (Cherry 1953).

11.2.3 Exploiting syntactic and semantic clues

Do you have a friend or acquaintance who has that most infuriating habit of finishing your sentences for you? Both the syntactic and semantic aspects of the utterance may be so predictable that the listener knows what you are going to say even before the words come out:

[11.12] *A.* Do you know what? She has threatened to . . .
     B. . . . sue the police.

The syntactic semantic context plays a role in speech comprehension. Listeners use frames provided by the syntax to retrieve a word with the appropriate meaning from the mental lexicon. This is easily seen in the handling of ANAPHORIC EXPRESSIONS (i.e. grammatical elements that refer back to something already mentioned) which are only interpretable in a specific syntactic context. To interpret anaphoric expressions the hearer must be able to identify the element that has already been mentioned which is being referred back to. Imagine reading the following sentence in a recipe book:

[11.13]   Add cream to the meat casserole and leave *it* in the oven for 10 minutes.

How do you work out what *it* refers to? In this sentence *it* could conceivably refer to the *meat* or the *cream*. But you do not even consider the *cream*. This sentence is not ambiguous. Our knowledge of the world rules out the *cream*. It would be crazy to leave the cream cooking in the oven. But it is reasonable to leave *meat* cooking in a casserole in the oven.

A similar point can be made with regard to STRUCTURAL AMBIGUITY (i.e. situations where a string of words has different interpretations depending on how we group together the words). Take this example:

[11.14]   I bought some new shirts and jumpers.

The sentence can be paraphrased as 'I bought some shirts and jumpers all of which were new', in which case words are bracketed as in [11.15a] or, 'I bought some new shirts and some jumpers which may not be new'. This latter interpretation is reflected in the parsing:

[11.15]   a. [some new shirts and jumpers]$_{NP}$
          b. [some new shirts]$_{NP}$ and [jumpers]$_{NP}$

Understanding speech is impossible without the listener working out which words go together. Correct parsing is a prerequisite to comprehension.

Sometimes, parsing is complicated. The listener makes a provisional analysis which has to be revised immediately as more information becomes available. A key feature of the speech comprehension process is the way in which listeners constantly update and revise their putative analyses. Nowhere is this clearer than in the analysis of so-called GARDEN PATH SENTENCES. These sentences metaphorically lead you down the garden path. You start doing a parse that looks plausible, but it turns out to be flawed when you get more information:

[11.16] a. After taking the *right* turn at the lights, we rejoined the highway.

   b. After taking the *right* turn at the lights, we rejoined the highway, but soon we realised that it was the wrong turn.

The sentence in [11.16a] is ambiguous. *Right turn* may mean 'right-hand turn' or 'correct turn'. You need more information to resolve the ambiguity. If the sentence continued as in [11.16b], you would realise that *right* is to be interpreted as 'right-hand' rather than 'correct'.

How much of a sentence does a listener need to hear in order to be able to make intelligent guesses? Not a lot. I suspect that as soon as you hear '*but*' you immediately suspect that *right* does not mean 'correct' here. Everything that comes after that confirms your guess.

The point is driven home by this famous example of a garden path:

[11.17] The horse raced past the barn fell.

This sentence is as clumsy as it is bizarre. Working out its meaning requires a number of attempts at syntactic analysis and semantic interpretation. *The horse raced past the barn* would be a problem-free sentence. This is the interpretation that initially springs to mind. But the verb *fell* at the end jolts us. It looks as if it should go with *the barn fell*. But that would make a nonsense of the whole sentence. So, we go back to the drawing board. This time we interpret *The horse raced past the barn* as a reduced relative clause which we paraphrase as *The horse that was raced past the barn fell*. And it works – which goes to show that syntactic parsing is done and updated continually by the listener in the light of inferences that make sense. Speech comprehension is not simply a matter of associating sounds with the meanings of words.

These speech comprehension findings are not easy to reconcile with the position adopted in (11.1.3), which otherwise seems justified, that we wheel out the morphological parser quite frequently to deal with complex words and that they are usually not stored as pre-packaged units for the simple reason that there is insufficient space in the mind to store all the word-forms we know. But the speed of processing argues for listing in the mind pre-packaged units which are retrieved as soon as clues to their identity are obtained. Although my inclination is to go for morphological parsing rather than listing, it not absolutely clear that it is the solution. More research is needed to resolve the issue fully. The jury is still out on this one.

11.3 THE ARTICULATORY PROGRAMME

Let us now consider the other side of the coin: SPEECH PRODUCTION. Using evidence from speech errors, Fromkin (1971, 1973, 1980) has proposed a model of how speakers go about the task of finding and using words when they produce speech. The production of speech involves five stages which take place in the order in which they are listed in [11.18] (cf. Clark and Clark 1977):

[11.18] a. *Meaning selection*
The first task is to decide what meaning the constituent being constructed will have.

b. *Selection of the syntactic outline*
The second task is to decide in broad terms what the structure of the syntactic constituents will be (e.g. NP, PP). At this stage the speaker also determines where stress will fall.

c. *Content word selection*
The speaker selects the words that will fill the slots for content words (nouns, verbs, adjectives and adverbs) in the syntactic frame (e.g. having got the syntactic frame Det N, the speaker may decide on the words *a book, the girl* etc.)

d. *Affix and function word selection*
The speaker selects function words (e.g. prepositions, pronouns and conjunctions) and inflectional affixes (e.g. plural -*s*, past tense -*ed*).

e. *Specification of phonetic segments*
Syllable by syllable, phoneme by phoneme and distinctive feature by distinctive feature (e.g. voiced, high, nasal etc.), the speaker goes through the words fully specifying how they are to be pronounced.

Monitoring goes on concurrently as the speaker implements any of the five stages. A change of mind or the detection of an error may result in production being aborted. Errors can and do creep in at any one of these stages.

11.3.1 Speech errors as evidence in favour of the articulatory programme

There is a considerable variety in the range of errors found in speech. The various types of error give us a window on the production process. Some errors result from the simultaneous selection of two words. These errors are called BLENDS (cf. section (9.10)).

[11.19] a. didn't bother me in the *sleast*.
           (from *slightest* + *least*) (Boomer and Laver 1968).
        b. Don't *frowl* (*frown* + *scowl*) like that! (Aitchison 1987)
        c. *dreeze* (*draft* + *breeze*) (Fromkin 1973)

The confusion resulting in blends stems from the fact that words are retrieved from the mental lexicon on the basis of their phonological and semantic properties. Usually blends involve two words that are phonologically and semantically similar.

However, as Fromkin (1971) points out, many errors have no basis in phonology. They involve words that only share *semantic properties*. For instance, the relationship may be one of antonymy (oppositeness), as in [11.20a]:

[11.20] Utterance: This room is too damn *hot – cold*.
        Target: This room is too damn *cold*.

or it may involve some other semantic property:

[11.21] a. Utterance: I'd better give you a *calendar*.
           Target: I'd better give you a *map*.
        b. Utterance: He has to pay her *rent*, I mean alimony.
           Target: He has to pay her *alimony*.
        c. Utterance: They're doing some experiments with the
                      four *blind* – deaf children.
           Target: They're doing some experiments with the
                      four *deaf* children.

Fromkin (1971) has argued that in this type of error the speaker gets the semantic wires crossed, as it were. This results in the selection of the wrong word, which has a meaning that is related to the intended meaning but which is different in pronunciation. Consider the further examples of semantic substitution from

Fromkin (1971). In [11.22a] the oppositeness in meaning of *hate* and *love* is the important property and in [11.22b] *oral* and *written* belong to the same semantic field and are complementary:

[11.22] a. I *like* to – *hate* to get up in the morning.
         b. The *oral* – *written* part of the exam.

The reason for the confusion of meaning in [11.23] is also equally easy to see:

[11.23] a. Utterance: I'm going to *April* in *May*.
             Target: I'm going to *England* in *May*.
         b. Utterance: Are my *legs*, I mean tires, touching the kerb?
             Target: Are my *tires* touching the kerb?

(from Fromkin 1973)

To sum up, all these errors show that meaning plays a very important role in the retrieval system of the mental lexicon. Blends and semantic substitutions occur because in normal speech speakers tend to line up several words in the target semantic area before homing in on the one that they finally select.

11.3.2 Two-stage models of lexical access in speech production

It has been proposed by a number of scholars that access to words stored in the mental lexicon takes place in two distinct temporal stages. At stage one, the speaker looks up words in the SEMANTIC LEXICON where meanings are stored. The second stage involves looking up the PHONOLOGICAL LEXICON for pronunciation of the words accessed (Fromkin (1971, 1973); Butterworth (1983, 1989)).

As mentioned earlier, words are not stored alphabetically in the mental lexicon. Rather, it would seem, they are stored in a manner more akin to that of a thesaurus. Groups of words with related meanings cluster together. The relationship may be, for example, close semantic similarity (near synonymy) or, antonymy (oppositeness) or some other kind of semantic relatedness unaccompanied by phonological similarity (cf. [11.21], [11.22] and [11.23] above).

By contrast, in the second type of error a word with a *similar pronunciation* and belonging to the same word-class but having an unrelated meaning is substituted for the right word. Many things can go wrong with the phonological retrieval process without the semantic dimension of words being affected. Fromkin (1971) cities many examples of phonological muddles caused by phonetic similarity, e.g.:

[11.24] a. Utterance: bottle of page five
          Target: bottom of page five
       b. Utterance: while the present – pressure indicates
          Target: while the pressure indicates.
       c. Utterance: it spread like wild flower
          Target: it spread like wild fire

Fromkin recognises a number of different phonological errors:

[11.25] a. *Phonological anticipations*
          Utterance: bake my bike
          Target: take my bike
       b. *Phonological preservations*
          Utterance: pulled a pantrum
          Target: pulled a tantrum

In [11.25a] we see the replacement of the initial consonant of the first content word with that of the second. But in [11.25b] the opposite happens. The initial consonant of the second word is replaced with that of the first.

It is not always entire sounds that are substituted. Sometimes it is the DISTINCTIVE FEATURES of which phonemes are made up that are exchanged or confused:

[11.26] a. Utterance: Cedars of Lemadon
          Target: Cedars of Lebanon
       b. Utterance: flesh queer water
          Target: fresh clear water
       c. Utterance: blake fluid
          Target: brake fluid

(cf. Fromkin 1971)

What is involved in [11.26a] is the changing of oral [b] into nasal [m] and nasal [n] into oral [d]. The phonetic feature [± nasal] is present in the word, but appears as part of the wrong segment in each case. In [11.26b] and [11.26c] it is the feature [± lateral] that is swapped round and appears in the wrong word.

The phonological behaviour displayed in SPOONERISMS lends further support to the two-stage model of lexical retrieval. In a spoonerism, a content word is moved from its intended position and turns up elsewhere. The result is often an (un)intentional comic effect:

[11.27] a. Utterance: I told them to open their *desks* and leave
                      them on the *books.*
           Target: I told them to open their *books* and leave
                      them on the *desks.*
        b. Utterance: *queer* old *dean*
           Target: *dear* old *queen*
        c. Utterance: You *hissed* my *mystery* lectures.
           Target: you *missed* my *history* lectures

> (The last two slips are attributed to the Revd William A. Spooner (1844–1930), Warden of New College, Oxford, and the first to a schoolteacher friend of mine.)

In spoonerisms content words swap places without affecting the pattern of sentence stress as in [11.27a] and [11.27b]. Or, words are substituted with others that have similar sounds and stress patterns, as in [11.27c]. This shows that assigning stress to a sentence is done separately from inserting content words.

By contrast, when function words are shunted round by mistake, the word that is moved normally takes with it its stress:

[11.28] a. Utterance: Can I turn *off* this.
           Target: Can I turn this *off.*
        b. Utterance: Well I *much* would have preferred the owl.
           Target: Well I would have *much* preferred the owl.

> (from Cutler and Isard (1980), cited in
> Butterworth (1980))

Clearly, content words differ from function words in the way in which they are processed in the mind.

Speech processing errors also give us a window on the storage and retrieval of grammatical elements. Some errors show that grammatical function morphemes are stored in a very abstract manner. This can be clearly seen in errors involving NEG TRANSPORTATION. A disembodied notion of negation is stored separately from the specific morphemes that represent it (e.g. *in-*, *un-*, *non-*, *dis-*, *any-*). Neg transportation is a process whereby some negative prefix (e.g. *in-*, *un-*, *non-*, *dis-*, *any-*) is moved from its normal, intended position and appears incorrectly in a different position where a different negative prefix may be substituted for it. Fromkin (1973) gives these examples:

[11.29] Utterance: I *dis*regard this as precise.
        Target: I regard this as *im*precise.

Sometimes the negative morpheme is not transported to a new position in the sentence, but a different, incorrect negative morpheme is used instead of the target one. Thus, in the sentence in [11.30], the clitic -*n't* attached to *was* replaces the correct negative prefix, *un-*, that should appear before *plugged*:

[11.30] Utterance: I was unplugged in . . .
        Target: I wasn't plugged in for a second.

Negative transportation lends further support to the assumption that content words are stored separately from affixes. That is why you may succeed in retrieving the correct content word (*plug*) and produce an incorrect sentence in the end if the wires get crossed so that the affix with the meaning you want (*neg*) appears on a different site in the sentence (after *was*) from the one intended (as a prefix (*un-*) attached to *plugged*).

The claim that grammatical, functional morphemes are stored and retrieved separately from content morphemes is further buttressed by additional instances of the uncoupling of affixes from stems and bases. An interesting morphological error results in the root morphemes in different words exchanging places leaving behind affixes that should have been attached to them. This phenomenon is called AFFIX STRANDING. It can be seen in the following examples from Garrett (1980) (where the stranded suffixes appear in upper case letters):

[11.31] a. Utterance: You have to *square* it *face*LY.
      b. Target: You have to face it squarely.

[11.32] a. Utterance: I've got a load of *cook*EN *chick*ED.
      b. Target: I've got a load of cooked chicken.

Garrett claims that affix stranding shows that affixes are not stored with stems as integrated wholes, but that they are stored in separate places. The insertion of stems in syntactic 'positional frames' by syntactic rules is distinct from morphological operations that attach affixes to stems. When all goes well these two processes are fully synchronised. But a slight hitch may cause a mismatch between stems and affixes.

But, as Butterworth (1989) points out, there are problems with Garrett's account. In irregular morphology there are examples of a word being placed in the wrong position with its correct irregular inflected form, as in the following:

[11.33] a. Utterance: I don't know that I'd *hear* one if I *knew* it.
       b. Target: I don't know that I'd *know* one if I *heard* it.

The expected form according to Garrett's theory is:

[11.34] Utterance: I don't know that I'd *hear* one if I *knowed* it.

In this case the stranding predicted by Garrett does not materialise. Instead whole-word movement takes place. Butterworth (1989) argues that the evidence for a separation of roots from affixes in the manner proposed by Garrett is not so strong. In [11.34] the inflectional affix is integrated with the stem and moves with it.

Arguably, Garrett's position can be defended. If we assume a lexical morphology model with a distinction between essentially irregular stratum 1 affixes and the regular stratum 2 affixes, we can hazard the prediction that stranding only applies at stratum 2. Irregular inflection in verbs like *knew*, *sang*, *rode* and nouns like *feet*, and *mice*, is integrated so early and so firmly into the stem that there is no chance of the affixes being left stranded on the beach when the stem is moved elsewhere.

11.3.3 It's just on the tip of my tongue

We have all been there. You know the name of the boy who sat next to you in the maths class in your first year at secondary school. It begins with a *B* and ends in an *-n*; you know it has three syllables; you know its main stress is on the first syllable. Yet, no matter how hard you try, you cannot recall it. You can come up with several other names that sound like it – with similar sounds and a similar stress pattern. But as soon as you access these words you know that none of them is the right word. Some time later you remember he was called *Benjamin*. How annoying!

That is a typical tip-of-the-tongue experience. It can happen with any content word, not just names. For instance, you may go bird-watching and spot a bird. You recognise its plumage is black above, and white below. Its legs are bright orange. And so is its bizarre-shaped bill. You do know what that bird is called – but the name just eludes you. You come up with the words *penguin* and *pigeon* but dismiss them immediately. It certainly is not one of those. Half an hour later you remember. It is called a *puffin*.

When everything works like clockwork, we manage to recall the meaning and pronunciation with perfect synchronisation. However, tip-of-the-tongue experiences like the ones described above confirm what I have said already about semantic representations being stored in the mind separately from phonological representations. The fact that meaning can be recalled separately from pronunciation is even clearer in certain speech disorders, as we will see in section (11.4.2).

11.3.4 Malapropisms

Some tip-of-the-tongue experiences do not end up in frustrated silence, but in uttering the wrong word. We might say 'oops!'. But it is too late. We have confused two words. We have uttered a word which is phonologically, and perhaps also semantically, similar to the word we intended to use. Such a slip is called a MALAPROPISM, after Mrs Malaprop, a character in Sheridan's play *The Rivals*.

In *The Rivals*, the contrast between supercilious Mrs Malaprop's vanity and her verbal ineptitude is hilarious. Her haughtiness is constantly punctured by her verbal gaffes. She is not nearly as literate and sophisticated as she believes herself to be. We laugh at her expense when she says:

> 'But the point we would request of you is, that you will promise to forget this fellow – to illiterate him, I say, quite from your memory.'

> (*The Rivals*, I, ii)

Of course, she meant to say *obliterate* him from your memory.

Malapropisms occur in real life. In the second half of the twentieth century perhaps the most famous public figure with an unfortunate reputation for the ludicrous misuse of words has been the late Mayor Daley of Chicago, whose famous blunders include 'harassing the atom' (meaning 'harnessing the atom') and 'rising to higher platitudes of achievement' (cited in Bolinger 1968: 103).

In Britain, several famous TV sports commentators are notorious for their malapropisms. The publishers of the satirical magazine *Private Eye* were quick to see the commercial potential of these gaffes and produced a series of anthologies called *Colemanballs* (named after David Coleman, the doyen of TV sports commentators). The selection in the 1984 volume of *Private Eye's Colemanballs 2*, edited by Fantoni, includes this one in the football section:

Again Mariner and the Butcher are trying to work the oracle on the near post.

MARTIN TYLER

Tyler probably intended to say *miracle*. Elsewhere in the same volume we read this insight into the game of cricket:

No captain with all the *hindsight* in the world can predict how the wicket is going to play.

(Trevor Bailey)

For *hindsight* I suspect you should read *foresight*.

Some of the erroneous associations of phonological representations with meanings may become widespread. In time, a malapropism may become the established usage. This seems to be happening to the word *mitigate*, which has become confused with *militate*. Many people will use [11.35a] instead of [11.35b]:

[11.35] a. The bad weather *mitigated* against the rescue operation.
       b. The bad weather *militated* against the rescue operation.

Malapropisms are an important source of evidence of how we store and retrieve words from the mind with the meaning separate from the phonological representation. When retrieval goes wrong, a mismatch of meanings with phonological representations may result.

In sum, slips of the tongue occurring in normal speech are one important source of evidence concerning words in the mind. As Fromkin has shown in the various publications cited above, anomalous utterances are a window through which we can glimpse how normal language storage, retrieval and processing work.

11.4 APHASIA

Another window on language in the mind is what happens in APHASIA. By aphasia is meant severe damage to a specific part of the brain which plays a role in producing or understanding spoken or written language. The brain damage is usually due to a stroke or, less frequently, to a horrific head injury caused by an accident or a vicious blow to the head. Aphasia does not wipe out language totally. Rather, a speaker's language faculty is partially impaired: aphasics (sufferers from aphasia) have some language facility left (see Caplan (1987), Lecours and Lhermitte (1983)).

The left hemisphere of the brain performs most of the linguistic functions. Different types of aphasia are distinguished on the basis of the part of the brain that is damaged, as shown in the illustration on pp. 250–1, *Language and the Brain* (from Crystal 1987: 261).

11.4.1 Broca's aphasia

BROCA'S APHASIA (or MOTOR APHASIA) results from damage to Broca's area of the brain. Its symptoms are inability to produce fluent speech.

(i) Speech is slow, laboured and minimalist.
(ii) The patient has reasonably easy access to the content words in the mental lexicon, but finds it very difficult to locate function words and grammatical affixes.

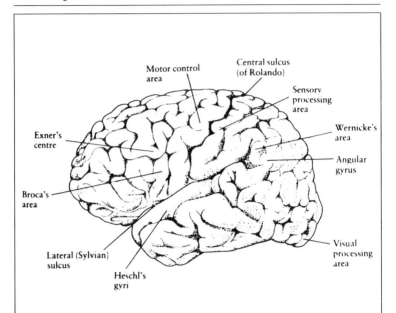

Language areas

The areas which have been proposed for the processing of speaking, listening, reading, writing, and signing are mainly located at or around the Sylvian and Rolandic fissures (p. 250). Several specific areas have been identified.

• The front part of the parietal lobe, along the fissure of Rolando, is primarily involved in the processing of sensation, and may be connected with the speech and auditory areas at a deeper level.

• The area in front of the fissure of Rolando is mainly involved in motor functioning, and is thus relevant to the study of speaking and writing.

• An area in the upper back part of the temporal lobe, extending upwards into the parietal lobe, plays a major part in the comprehension of speech. This is 'Wernicke's area'.

• In the upper part of the temporal lobe is the main area involved in auditory reception, known as 'Heschl's gyri', after the Austrian pathologist R. L. Heschl (1824–81).

• The lower back part of the frontal lobe is primarily involved in the encoding of speech. This is 'Broca's area'.

- Another area towards the back of the frontal lobe may be involved in the motor control of writing. It is known as 'Exner's centre', after the German neurologist Sigmund Exner (1846–1926).
- Part of the left parietal region, close to Wernick's area, is involved with the control of manual signing.
- The area at the back of the occipital lobe is used mainly for the processing of visual input.

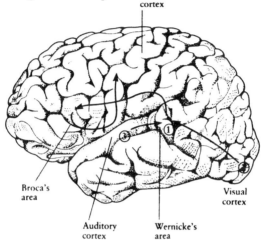

Motor cortex

Broca's area

Visual cortex

Auditory cortex   Wernicke's area

Neurolinguistic processing

Some of the neural pathways that are considered to be involved in the processing of spoken language.

1. *Speech production*   The basic structure of the utterance is thought to be generated in Wernicke's area and is sent to Broca's area for encoding. The motor programme is then passed on to the adjacent motor area, which governs the articulatory organs.

2. *Reading aloud*   The written form is first received by the visual cortex, then transmitted via the angular gyrus to Wernicke's area, where it is thought to be associated with an auditory representation. The utterance structure is then sent on to Broca's area, as in (1).

3. *Speech comprehension*   The signals arrive in the auditory cortex from the ear (§25), and are transferred to the adjacent Wernicke's area, where they are interpreted.

Consequently, this kind of aphasic produces ungrammatical, minimalist (or telegraphic) speech, with content words correctly used, but with few or no inflectional affixes or function words. Hence the label AGRAMMATIC APHASIA is also used for this language disorder (see also Kean (1985), Caramazza and Berndt (1985)).

The extract in [11.36] in which an aphasic explains how he returned to the hospital for treatment of his gums is borrowed from Goodglass (1976: 238). It is from the speech of a 28-year-old man. Goodglass points out that not only is this patient's speech syntactically odd, it is also prosodically bizarre (of course, you cannot see that from the transcript). Each chunk followed by a row of dots or by a period is uttered with falling intonation, as though it were a complete utterance.

[11.36] Ah . . . Monday . . . ah, Dad and Paul Haney [referring to himself by his full name] and Dad . . . hospital. Two . . . ah, doctors . . . , and ah . . . thirty minutes . . . and yes . . . ah . . . hospital. And, er Wednesday . . . nine o'clock. And er Thursday, ten o'clock . . . doctors. Two doctors . . . and ah . . . teeth. Yeah, . . . fine.

The impoverishment of the grammar can be examined systematically by getting patients to describe a picture where the task involves manipulating certain grammatical constructions. The examiner can then probe the extent of the disintegration of their control of grammar. Here is an example from Schwartz *et al.* (1985: 85) where five patients referred to by their initials attempt to describe what is going on in a picture of a boy giving a girl a Valentine:

[11.37] *D.E.*: The boy is gave. . . . The boy is gave the card.

H.T.: The boy show a Valentine's day. . . . The boy and the girl is Valentine.

V.S.: The girl . . . the boy is giving a . . . giving is girl friend. The boy Valentine the girl. The boy givin' Valentine to girl.

P.W.: The boy is Valentine the girl. The boy is giving the Valentine the girl and girl pleased.

M.W.: Valentine's day and candy. I think Valentine's day. Girl is Valentine's day. . . . Boy is getting with the girl Valentine's candy.

As you can see, these patients cannot produce the dative construction correctly and say *The boy is giving the girl a Valentine*. They also have difficulties with inflectional morphemes. Often, they are either absent (e.g. *The boy show*), or incorrectly used (e.g. *The boy is gave*).

Broca's aphasia lends further support to the claim made by linguists that in morphology and the lexicon it is necessary to distinguish between lexical items (roughly, content words) and grammatical morphemes (function words and inflectional affixes). In morphology this is the motivation for the separation of derivational morphemes which are used to create vocabulary items from inflectional morphemes and grammatical function words whose presence is required by the rules of the syntax. Broca's aphasia shows clearly that damage to the section of the mental lexicon in which grammatical morphemes are kept need not have implications for the storage and retrieval of content words.

11.4.2 Wernicke's aphasia

As you can see in the figure on p. 250 WERNICKE'S APHASIA (also called RECEPTIVE APHASIA) is a result of damage to Wernicke's area of the brain. Aphasics who suffer from this disorder show these symptoms:

(i) They have very fluent, rapid-fire speech – no production problem.

(ii) But they have great difficulty in understanding speech.

(iii) They find it very difficult, though not totally impossible, to match word meanings with the right phonological representations.

(iv) Often patients either utter plain nonsense or produce circumlocutions.

These patients very often experience something like an acute version of the tip-of-the-tongue phenomenon we saw earlier. They know the meaning they want to convey but are incapable of finding the right sound envelope for it. They can find reasonably near synonyms, but not the word they want. So they get into horrendously convoluted circumlocutions to paraphrase their intended meaning (e.g. 'what you sleep in' meaning 'bed' or 'something in the mouth that you chew with' meaning 'teeth'. Their speech is generally incoherent, as you can see from this typical example:

[11.38] Examiner: Do you like it here in Kansas City?
          Aphasic: Yes, I am.
        Examiner: I'd like to have you tell me something about your problem.
          Aphasic: Yes, I ugh can't hill all of my way. I can't talk all of the things I do, and part of the part I can go alright, but I can't tell from the other people. I usually most of my things. I know what I can talk and know what they are, but I can't always come back even though I know they should be in, and I know I should something eely I should know what I'm doing . . .

(from Bissantz *et al.* 1985)

A word of caution is in order here. Any evidence from language disorders must be handled with care since the workings of a malfunctioning brain may not mirror accurately the operation of a normal healthy one. None the less, the difficulties experienced by this type of aphasic are attested in a milder form in the tip-of-the-tongue phenomenon in normal speakers.

To sum up, the tip-of-the-tongue phenomenon and the circumlocution of aphasics with symptoms of Wernicke's aphasia suggest that the meaning of a word and the phonological shape that represents it are stored separately in the mental lexicon. Related meanings are stored together as in a thesaurus and they are not associated with their phonological representations initially. Further, the difficulties, if not total inability, that sufferers from Broca's aphasia have in forming grammatical words (i.e. words where roots have inflectional morphemes) show that grammatical forms are put together at a different stage from content words. Retrieval is successful only if all these facets of the word click into place at the right point.

11.5 FREUDIAN SLIPS

Linguists do not have a monopoly of interest in speech errors. The study of speech errors has interested not only linguists but also neurologists. We will now turn to a third group of scientists who study these phenomena: the psychologists.

Following Freud, many psychologists regard as FREUDIAN SLIPS the speech errors arising from making the wrong lexical choice from an array of alternative words that are looked up in the mental lexicon (cf. section (11.3.1)). Freud claimed that lexical substitutions reflect an underlying tension between the intentions of the speaker's conscious mind and what the subconscious mind wishes to say. Normally, the conscious mind wins and things the unconscious mind would like to put us up to are not allowed to surface. But occasionally something unintended does slip through, with embarrassing consequences. Freudian slips of this kind cause a few sniggers or raised eyebrows:

[11.39] a. The psychology of success – sex
b. (from a politician) I like Heath. He's tough – like Hitler. (Shocked silence from reporters) – Did I say Hitler? I meant Churchill.

(from Ellis 1980)

In successful word retrieval, embarrassment of this kind is avoided. Only the word with the intended meaning, which is selected by the conscious mind, is slotted into the sentence. Any other words that are looked up are suppressed.

11.6 THE SPREADING ACTIVATION MODEL

We have established that the mental lexicon has a number of distinct modules in which different bits of lexical information are kept. There are separate components for (i) the meaning and (ii) the phonological representation. Further, with respect to meaning, content words are kept separate from grammatical function words and inflectional affixes. We have seen that errors in speech processing give us an insight into the workings of the mental lexicon.

The question we will now consider is how is all this information retrieved successfully? One possibility could be that the speaker retrieves words going in a straight line, doing one thing at a time: (i) selecting the meaning; (ii) selecting the inflectional morphemes and grammatical function words; and (iii) finally mapping the morphemes making up the word on to a phonological representation. But this is unlikely to be correct. Evidence from speech errors, like blends where semantic confusion seems to be triggered by phonological resemblance, suggests that retrieval does not go step by step – pronunciation is not considered in isolation from semantic choices.

A superior model that has been proposed is the SPREADING ACTI-VATION MODEL (cf. Dell and Reich (1980), Hörmann (1986), Aitchison (1987)). In this model, the starting point is the broad area of meaning that the speaker intends to convey. Initially, the SEMANTIC FIELD targeted may be very broad and a lot more words may be activated than the speaker actually needs. Any promising candidate is considered before the choice is eventually narrowed to a word whose meaning and phonological shape have the best fit (cf. Aitchison (1987), Matthei and Roeper (1983), Marslen-Wilson (1989b)).

For instance, one may target people, then children, then one's children, then one's daughters. I know a mother who, when at all agitated, goes through the names of her daughters before she eventually finds the name of the right girl to give a good telling off. Often, if she wants to scold *Louise* she will say, '*Barbara – eh, Jane – eh, Louise*'. She knows the child, she sees her right in front of her, but in her fury she cannot locate the child's name in the mental lexicon. Similarly, a student might say, '*I haven't finished my history – English essay*'. Obviously, here the chosen topic of the sentence is school subjects. What is not zeroed in on initially is the exact subject. And the first attempt to zero in on a subject is unsuccessful.

Psychologists have developed the spreading activation model to account for the way in which words are represented in the mental lexicon. The representation they have put forward is much richer than the typical dictionary definitions of words. They have proposed that encyclopaedic information is stored in the form of an interlocking hierarchical network (cf. Aitchison (1987), Hörmann (1986) and Lipka (1990) and references cited there). The dominance relation in the hierarchy is expressed in terms of 'X is a Y' e.g. 'a mammal is an animal'; 'the cow is a mammal', 'the Friesian is a cow', and 'the Jersey is a cow'. This 'X is a Y' relation is called a relation of INCLUSION. So, we can say that the class of animals includes mammals; the class of mammals includes cows and the class of cows includes Friesians and Jerseys, etc.

In addition to inclusion, there are many other semantic relations in the network, e.g. 'X has Y', 'X contains Y', 'X is offspring of Y', etc. An example of a simplified version of the representation of the meanings of *cow* and *tortoise* in the mental lexicon is given in the figure on p. 257.

We can say that the nodes of the tree that have been activated

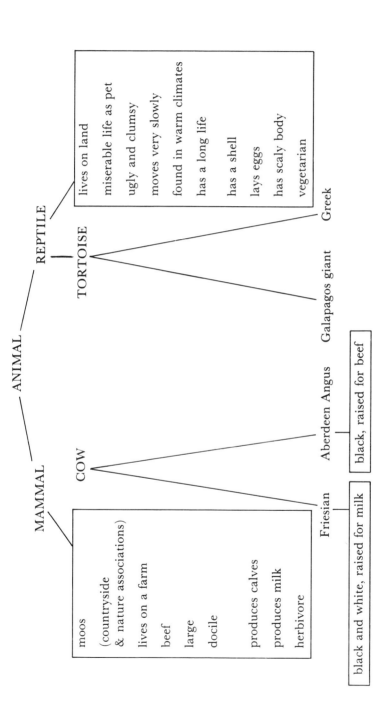

SPREADING ACTIVATION NETWORK

are, metaphorically speaking, 'hot'. The greater the amount of active consideration a node receives from the speaker, the greater is its degree of activation – hence the 'hotter' it is. A hot node transfers its heat to nearby nodes that are linked to it. But a node 'cools' as attention shifts elsewhere to activated nodes that are remotely, or not at all, linked to it. In short, the zeroing in on the meaning of a word on a particular active node is a crucial step. A large number of words are activated but few are considered actively. Then most of these are suppressed and, if all goes well, only one word is eventually selected.

WORD FREQUENCY is a very important factor that affects the speed of retrieval. Savin (1963) showed that it is easier to recognise frequently used words when they are presented in less than optimum conditions where they are difficult to see or hear. Even in optimum conditions when subjects are presented with both frequent and rare words, they find it easier to identify and classify the more frequent words (cf. Frederiksen and Kroll 1976). You would expect that. Assuming that words are listed, those that are used very rarely (e.g. *gazebo*, *zymotic*) are put at the bottom of the stack and words that are used several hundred times a day (e.g. *the*, *I*, *am*) are put at the top of the stack for easy access. Frequently used words are more active; they are hot in terms of the spreading activation model; they are always available for use.

The spreading activation model is not one-directional, going in a straight line one step at a time. It allows constant movement to and fro between the different sub-components. After having activated a range of words with the desired meaning, the speaker can look up pronunciations then zip back to the meanings and narrow the selection of words, then look up the pronunciation again. In between, the speaker may also be sorting out the inflectional morphemes to attach to the stems selected. And remember, at any time the speaker may peep back at aspects of the representation of a word and revise them in the light of new information. Alternatively, the speaker may look forward to see what choices are on offer later on, if a particular path is selected. What is amazing, as we saw in section (11.2.1) is that all this processing happens in a flash.

It is assumed that at first, when a whole lot of words are activated, the matching of meaning with phonological representation is done very sketchily. For instance, a vague phonological outline of a word may be all that is attempted – just an indication of the number of syllables, the stress pattern and the initial segment. As a decision about meaning firms up, the phonological representation is also gradually fleshed out. Progress through the lexicon is never linear. There is a close interplay between the meaning, the sounds and the grammatical properties of a word. Hence, at any point during the process of forming words or retrieving them from memory, the model allows decisions about one aspect of a word to impinge on decisions about other aspects.

11.7 SUMMARY

In this chapter we have explored the nature of the mental lexicon. We have seen that people store tens of thousands of words in the mind and are able to retrieve them instantaneously both as speakers and as listeners. This achievement is facilitated by the fact that the storage system is highly structured. Lexical items are listed in the mental lexicon with the information about their meaning, pronunciation and grammatical and morphological properties stored as separate sub-components. When retrieval is successful, all these facets of a word are recalled in a perfectly synchronised manner. However, in both normal and pathological speech, the recalling may break down at one or more points, resulting in speech errors.

Much of the discussion has been devoted to the nature of speech errors. We have seen that errors confirm theoretical linguists' ideas about words having distinct phonological, grammatical and semantic representations in the dictionary. The errors also confirm the theoretical distinction between, on the one hand, lexical items (roughly, content words, e.g. those formed by derivational processes in morphology), and, on the other hand, grammatical function words and inflectional affixes. This is important because a basic task of linguistic theory is to characterise the nature of linguistic knowledge that underlies people's ability to use language.

We have seen how various models, some focusing on speech perception and others on speech production, attempt to characterise how words are stored and retrieved from the mental lexicon – and how the errors attested arise. Anomalous utterances produced in ordinary speech by normal individuals and language disorders in the speech of aphasics have been shown to throw light on the nature of the mental lexicon.

The chapter ended with an account of the spreading activation model which offers an integrated view of lexical storage and retrieval. Because the model allows us to go to and fro between sound and meaning as well as look back or glance forward and anticipate stages, it is capable of accounting for any type of lexical error involving a confusion of meaning, grammar or phonology. It recognises that things may go wrong at any point in the word retrieval process.

When observation of how people process language seems to lend support to our theoretical models, we are encouraged to believe that we are on the right track.

EXERCISES

1. What are the main similarities and differences between the organisation of the mental lexicon and that of the dictionaries sold in bookshops?

2. Explain in detail how the meaning of *it* and *his* is inferred in the following sentence which you might encounter next time you read a detective story:

    The murderer put the arsenic in his glass and took *it* to his table.

3. Identify the malapropisms in the following passage and suggest how each of them might have arisen:

    'Observe me, Sir Anthony. – I would by no means wish a daughter of mine to be a progeny of learning: I don't think so much learning becomes a young woman . . . I would send her, at nine years old, to a boarding school, in order to learn a little ingenuity and artifice. – Then, Sir, she should have a supercilious knowledge in accounts; – and as she grew up, I would have her instructed in geometry, that she might know something of the contagious countries; – but above all, Sir Anthony, she should be mistress of orthodoxy, that she might not mis-spell, and mis-pronounce words so shamefully as girls usually do; and likewise she might reprehend the true meaning of what she is saying. – This, Sir Anthony, is what I would have a woman know; – and I don't think there is a superstitious article in it.'

    (Sheridan, *The Rivals*, I, ii)

4. Identify the kinds of error in these sentences. Explain what went wrong in each case.

   a. Utterance: Don't hide your light under a bush.
       Target: Don't hide your light under a bushel.

   b. Utterance: It was a very enjoyful performance.
       Target: It was a very enjoyable performance.

   c. Utterance: Prosecutors will be trespassed.
       Target: Trespassers will be prosecuted.

5. Account for the errors involving negative morphemes in the data below. What inferences can we make about the mental lexicon on the basis of such errors?

   a. Utterance: I tell you he's not crazy – I mean, he's insane.
       Target: I tell you he is insane.

   b. Utterance: The bonsai didn't die because I watered it.
       Target: The bonsai died because I didn't water it.

   c. Utterance: The vowels are not stricted – are unrestricted.
       Target: The vowels are unrestricted.

                                  (data from Fromkin 1973)

6. Many people cannot spell certain words correctly although they can read them correctly. They confuse *their* with *there*, *weather* with *whether*, they are not sure if *independent* ends in -*ent* or -*ant* (**independant*). What does this tell us about the relation between the production and perception of words in speech and in writing?

7. Show how the spreading activation model can be used to represent in the mental lexicon the meaning of *tulip, palm (tree), desk* and *chair*.

Glossary

Ablaut A change in a vowel in the root of a word that is used to show a grammatical difference. e.g. *sing* (verb) ~ *song* (noun); *shrink* (present tense) ~ *shrank* (past tense).

Accusative A case marking for the object of a transitive verb, e.g. *them* in *We ate them.*

Active voice If the doer of the action is also the subject of the verb the sentence is said to be in the active voice (e.g. The dog bit the man.) *see also* **Voice**.

Adjectival phrase A phrase the head of which is an adjective e.g. *much quieter.*

Adverbial phrase A phrase the head of which is an adverb e.g. *very quietly.*

Affix A bound morpheme that must occur together with a root to form a word, e.g. *re-, un-, -ing, -ed, -ise.* No word can contain affixes only.

Agent(ive) The noun phrase indicating who or what brings about the action, state etc. indicated by the verb.

Agglutinating language A language where words are typically formed by stringing together several morphemes one after the other.

Agrammatism Loss of the control of some inflectional affixes and syntactic function words usually found in patients suffering from Broca's aphasia. Their speech is like a telegram.

Agreement A grammatical requirement for words that are in the same syntactic construction to share some morphological marking e.g. *I am She is* (not **I is and she am*).

Allomorph A variant of a morpheme, i.e. one of the morphs that represent a particular morpheme.

Allophone A sound representing a given phoneme in certain contexts. Allophones of the same phoneme cannot be used to distinguish the meaning of words, e.g. [ɫ] and [l] are allophones of the phoneme /l/ in English.

Alphabet A system of writing where letters represent the phonemes of the langauge.

Alveolar A speech sound made by raising the tongue so that it makes contact with the alveolar ridge (i.e. teeth ridge), e.g. [d] in *dog.*

Analytic language *see* **Isolating language**.

Anaphora The use of a grammatical device to refer back to something mentioned earlier. Typically this is done using pronouns, e.g. *they* anaphorically refers back to *mice* in *Three blind mice, see how they run*.

Antonym If words have opposite meanings, they are called antonyms, e.g. *good* and *bad*.

Aphasia Impairment or loss of the ability to use language caused by damage to the areas of the brain that handle language.

Articulators Parts of the lips, tongue and throat that play a role in the production of a sound in speech.

Aspect A grammatical marking in the verb that indicates whether the action or state denoted by a verb is still in progress or completed.

Assimiliation The adjustment in the way a sound is made so that it becomes similar to some other sound or sounds near it.

Asterisk (*) A linguistic form is asterisked (i.e. 'starred') to show that it is not allowed.

Back-formation Word-formation involving the dropping of a peripheral part of a word which is wrongly analysed as a suffix, e.g. *lazy*, (Adj.) → *laze* (Verb).

Base Any form to which affixes are appended in word-formation *see also* **Root** and **Stem**.

Base form *see* **Underlying form**.

Bilabial A phonetic term for sounds like *m, b, p* which are made with the two lips.

Blend A word formed by joining together chunks of two pre-existing words, e.g. *channel + tunnel → chunnel*.

Borrowing Adoption of linguistic elements, such as morphemes or words of another language, e.g. English borrowed the word *malaria* from Italian.

Bound morpheme A morpheme which is always appended to some other item because it is incapable of being used on its own as a word, e.g. *-ing* in *coming*.

Broca's area The lower part of the frontal lobe of the brain responsible for speech.

Calque *see* **Loan translation**

Case Marking used to indicate the grammatical function of a nominal word, i.e. a noun, pronoun or adjective as in *she/her* and *he/him* in *She saw him* vs. *He saw her*.

Cliché A hackneyed expression, e.g. *at this point in time*; *that remains to be seen*; *in any shape or form*; *in this day and age*.

Clipping Word-formation where a long word is shortened to one or two syllables, e.g. *discotheque → disco*.

Cognates Words of different languages which are to some degree related in meaning and pronunciation because they come from a common historical source.

Competence Tacit knowledge of language that lies behind our ability to produce and understand an indefinitely large number of things that can be said or written.

Complementary distribution If two elements are in complementary distribution, they never occur in identical contexts. So it is not possible to use the difference between them as the sole indicator of a difference in meaning.

Compound word A word made of two or more words, e.g. *rail* + *way* → *railway*.

Content word *see* **Lexical item** and **Function word**.

Denominal A word 'derived from a noun', e.g. *bookish* (from the noun *book*) is a denominal adjective.

Dental A consonant made with the tip of the tongue against the upper front teeth, e.g. [t] in French *théâtre* 'theatre'.

Derivation A word-formation process that is used to create new vocabulary items, e.g. by adding suffixes as in *walk* → *walker*.

Deverbal A word 'derived from a verb', e.g. *teacher* (from the verb *teach*) is a deverbal noun.

Diagraph A combination of letters representing a single sound e.g. *ea* represents [e] in *bread*, *sh* represents [ʃ] in *shin*, etc.

Distribution The distribution of a linguistic item refers to all contexts where a linguistic form occurs taken together.

Environment Refers to the context where a linguistic element occurs.

Epenthesis The insertion of a sound inside a word.

Free morpheme A morpheme capable of occurring on its own (i.e. a word).

Fricative A consonant produced by narrowing the gap between the articulators so that there is audible turbulence as the air squeezes through the narrow gap left for it, e.g. [s] in *see*.

Function word A word mainly serving a grammatical function in a sentence e.g. *the*, *with*, *to* and *a*, as in *The man with a beard gave the milk to the baby*.

Fusional language *see* **Inflecting language**.

Generative rule A rule that specifies an indefinitely large set of the structures that are well-formed members of a class of linguistic structures, e.g. S → NP VP. (A structure where a noun phrase is followed by a verb phrase is a permissible sentence.)

Genitive A marking in noun phrases used to show grammatical subordination. The meaning of genitive constructions includes possession e.g. *Jane's money*, duration e.g. *a day's journey* etc.

Glottal stop A consonant produced with a narrowed or closed glottis.

Glottis The space between the vocal cords in the larynx.

Grammatical word This refers to the word as a morphological and syntactic entity, e.g. we can say that '*sat* is the past tense form of the verb *sit*' *see also* **Function word**.

Head The principal, obligatory element of a construction.

Homonyms Words that are in all ways identical in speech and writing but have unrelated meanings, e.g. *bat* 'little flying mammal', and *bat* 'wooden implement for hitting cricket balls'.

Homophones Words that sound the same but have different meanings, e.g *male* and *mail*.

Icon A sign which mirrors to some degree the object that it stands for:

the link between an iconic sign and whatever it stands for it not totally arbitrary.

Incorporating language A type of language that has very long words, many of them formed by syntactic processes which insert one word inside another or in some way involve compounding, e.g. the object of a verb may be inserted in the verb itself.

Indo-European The language reconstructed by linguists which is assumed to be the ancestor of most European languages (e.g. English, Latin, French, German, Russian) and some Asian languages (e.g. Sanskrit, Hindi, Persian).

Infix An affix placed inside a root.

Inflecting language A language where an inflectional affix typically represents several morphemes.

Inflection Affixation that modifies a word to give it the appropriate form when it occurs in some grammatical context.

Instrument The noun phrase referring to the entity used to carry out the action indicated by the verb.

Isolating language Normally in an isolating language (e.g. Vietnamese) a word is realised by just one morph. There are virtually no bound morphemes. Typically, words do not contain several meaningful units.

Labial An articulation involving one or both the lips.

Latinate This refers to words borrowed from classical languages and from Romance languages, especially French.

Lexeme A word in the sense of an item of vocabulary that can be listed in the dictionary. A lexeme is a lexical item *see* **Lexical item**.

Lexical item A word belonging to one of the major word-classes (i.e. noun, adjective, verb, adverb) which is listable in the dictionary with an identifiable meaning and is capable of occurring independently e.g. *girl*, *think*, *quick*, etc. (Syntactically, prepositions are also lexical items since they function as lexical heads of prepositional phrases *see also* **Phrase**.)

Lexicon The part of the grammar that contains the rules of word-formation and a list of lexical items *see also* **Mental lexicon**.

Loan translation A concept is borrowed but is rendered using the words of the language doing the borrowing (e.g. *ça va sans dire* → *it goes without saying*).

Loanword A word adopted from another language, e.g. *garage* from French.

Macron A short straight line placed above a vowel to indicate that it is pronounced long.

Malapropism Use of the wrong word which resembles phonologically the intended word, e.g. the use of *progeny* instead of *prodigy* in 'I would by no means wish a daughter of mine to be a progeny of learning' (Sheridan, *The Rivals*).

Mental lexicon The dictionary in the speaker's mind. It contains a list of words as well as rules for generating words that are not listed.

Morph A physical form that represents some morpheme.

Morphophonemic Having to do with the interaction of phonology and morphology.

Morphophonological *see* **Morphophonemic**.

Nasal A sound like [m] [n] [ŋ] which is made with the soft palate lowered so that air goes out through the nose.

Nonce word A word that is coined and used just one time.

Noun phrase A phrase whose head is a noun (or pronoun), e.g. *The new students*, *They*.

Onomatopoeia A word that mirrors an aspect of its meaning, e.g. *cuckoo*, *bang* is onomatopoeic.

Orthographic word This refers to the word in the written language which appears with a space on either side of it.

Orthography The conventional way of writing a language.

Parsing Analysing a sentence (or word) into its grammatical elements and providing a label for each element identified.

Passive voice If the individual that 'suffers' the action indicated by the verb functions as the subject of the verb, the sentence is said to be in the passive voice (e.g. *The man was bitten by the dog*).

Patient The noun phrase referring to the individual or thing that undergoes the action indicated by the verb.

Perfective aspect A form of the verb indicating completed action.

Person A grammatical form indicating a participant's role in a conversation or in writing. First person (*I*) is the speaker, second person (*you*) is the addressee and third person (*he/she/it*) is neither speaker nor addressee.

Phoneme A sound that is used to distinguish the meaning of words in a particular language. E.g. /t/ and /d/ are different phonemes of English. They distinguish *ten* /ten/ from *den* /den/.

Phonemic transcription A representation of speech showing the vowel and consonant sounds that are used to distinguish word meaning.

Phonological word The word in the spoken language which can be potentially preceded and followed by a pause.

Phonology The branch of linguistics concerned with the study of the properties, patterns, functions and representations of speech sounds in a particular language and in language in general.

Phonotactics The sub-domain of phonology concerned with constraints on the combination of speech sounds.

Phrase A syntactic constituent headed by a lexical category, i.e. a noun, adjective, verb, adverb or preposition *see also* **Noun phrase**, **Adjectival phrase** etc.

Place of articulation The position in the mouth or throat where the obstruction involved in the producing of a consonant takes place *see also* **Bilabial**, **Velar**.

Polysemy A word in the dictionary is said to be polysemous if it has more than one sense, i.e. if it has several related meanings e.g. *bridge* meaning (i) a structure forming or carrying a road over a river, a ravine etc.; (ii) a raised platform extending from side to side of a ship, for the officer in command; (iii) the curved central part of spectacles; (iv) in a violin, etc.: a thin upright piece of wood over which the strings are stretched (definitions based on *OED*).

Polysynthetic language *see* **Incorporating language**.

Portmanteau morph A morph that simultaneously represents several morphemes.

Prefix An affix that goes before the stem, e.g. *re-* in *re-write see also* **Affix**.

Prepositional phrase A phrase headed by a preposition, e.g. *on the table*.

Productivity The capacity of language users to produce and understand a limitless number of words and sentences, many of them novel, in their language.

Progressive aspect A form of the verb indicating that an action is still continuing.

Received Pronunciation The prestige accent of spoken British English.

Root The morpheme at the core of a word to which affixes are added. Such a morpheme is always a member of a lexical category, i.e. noun, verb etc. *see also* **Base** and **Stem**.

Schwa The vowel represented by the symbol [ə].

Semantic field An area of meaning containing words with interlocking senses such that normally you cannot understand one properly without understanding at least some of the others, e.g. the kinship terms (father, mother, sister, daughter, son, uncle, aunt, grandmother, grandfather, cousin etc.) constitute a semantic field.

Spoonerism A type of speech error where by accident (or sometimes by design, one suspects) initial sounds in syllables of neighbouring words swap places, e.g. *The Lord is a shoving leopard to his flock* (Revd William Spooner).

Stem Any form to which *inflectional affixes* can be attached *see also* **Root** and **Base**.

Stop A consonant made by closing the path of the airstream at the place where the articulators meet so that air is not allowed to go through the centre of the mouth past the obstruction, e.g. [p], [b].

Stress The relative auditory prominence of a syllable.

Subject The part of the sentence containing a noun phrase which precedes the verb and agrees with the verb in number, e.g. '*Her daughter* is a firefighter' vs. '*Her daughters* are brilliant'. Typically, the rest of the sentence (called the predicate) says something about the subject.

Suffix An affix that goes after the stem e.g. *-er* in *tall-er see also* **Affix**.

Suppletion A case of morphological alternation where forms representing the root morpheme bear no phonological resemblance to each other, e.g. *good ~ better*.

Syllabic consonant A consonant which functions as a syllable nucleus as though it were a vowel, e.g. the [n̩] in *cotton* or the final [l̩] of *metal*.

Synonymy If two words are synonymous they have the same meaning (in some specific situations) e.g. *big, large*.

Synthetic language *see* **Inflecting language**.

Tense Inflectional marking on the verb used to show the time when some action, event or state takes place (e.g. as 'past', 'present' or 'future') in relation to the moment of speaking.

Transitive verb A verb that takes a direct object, e.g. *kick*, in *She kicked the ball*.

Typology The comparative study of significant structural similarities and differences among languages which is done without implying that the similarities are inherited from a common ancestor.

Underlying form A form entered in the lexicon from which actual phonetic forms heard in speech are derived.

Velar A sound is articulated using the back of the tongue and the soft palate or velum. Consonants like [k] (as in *kayak*) and [g] (as in *go*) are velar.

Verb phrase A phrase headed by a verb, e.g. They *might have been going*.

Voice A marking in grammar (usually done by inflectional endings) that indicates the relation of the subject and verb in the action indicated by the verb *see also* **Active voice** and **Passive voice**.

Voiced A sound produced with the vocal cords vibrating. In English, all the vowels as well as some consonants like [l m d z] are voiced.

Voiceless A sound produced without vibration of the vocal cords. Consonants like [f s t h ʔ] are voiceless.

Wernicke's area The part of the brain that deals with understanding speech and finding vocabulary items for use in sentence production.

Word The smallest linguistic unit capable of standing meaningfully on its own in the grammar of a language *see also* **Lexical item**, **Grammatical word** and **Word-form**.

Word-class This refers to what is more traditionally called 'parts of speech', i.e. a set of words that can occupy the same syntactic positions, e.g. determiners, nouns, verbs, adjectives, adverbs, prepositions.

Word-form A form realising a word in speech (*see* **Phonological word**) or writing *see* **Orthographic word**.

References

Adams, V. (1973) *An Introduction to Modern English Word-formation.* London: Longman.

Aitchison, J. (1987) *Words in the Mind.* Oxford: Basil Blackwell.

Albrow, K. H. (1972) *The English Writing System: Notes towards a Description.* London: Longman.

Algeo, J. (1972) *Problems in the Origins and Development of the English Language.* New York: Harcourt, Brace Jovanovich, 2nd edn.

Allen, M. (1978) 'Morphological investigations'. Doctoral dissertation. University of Connecticut.

Aronoff, M. (1976) *Word-formation in Generative Grammar.* Cambridge, Mass.: MIT Press.

Barber, C. (1964) *Linguistic Change in Present-day English.* London: Oliver & Boyd.

Bauer, L. (1983) *English Word-formation.* Cambridge: Cambridge University Press.

Bauer, L. M. (1988) *Introducing Morphology.* Edinburgh: Edinburgh University Press.

Baugh, A. C and Cable, T. (1978) *A History of the English Language.* London: Routledge & Kegan Paul.

Beale, P. (1985) *Eric Partridge: A Dictionary of Catch-Phrases.* London: Routledge & Kegan Paul, 2nd edn.

Bissantz, A. S., Johnson, K. A., Godby, C. J., Wallace, R., Jolley, C., Schaffer, D. B., Perkins, J. W., Latta, F. C. and Geoghegan, S. G. (1985) *Language Files. Materials for an Introduction to Language.* Department of Linguistics, Ohio State University, Reynoldsburg, Ohio: Advocate Publishing Group, 3rd edn.

Bliss, A. J. (1966) *Dictionary of Foreign Words and Phrases in Current English.* London: Routledge & Kegan Paul.

Bloomfield, L. (1926) 'A set of postulates for the science of language'. *Language* 2: 142–64.

Bloomfield, L. (1933) *Language.* New York: Holt, Rinehart & Winston.

Bolinger, D. (1968) *Aspects of Language.* New York: Harcourt Brace & World.

Boomer, D. S. and Laver, J. (1968) 'Slips of the tongue'. *British Journal of Disorders of Communication* 3: 1–12.

Bradley, D. C. (1978) 'Computational distinctions of vocabulary type'. Doctoral dissertation, Cambridge, Mass: MIT.

Bradley, D. C. (1980) 'Lexical representation of derivational relation'. In M. Aronoff and M.-L. Kean (eds) *Juncture*. Saratoga, Calif.: Anima Libri.

Bresnan, J. (1982a) 'The passive in lexical theory'. In Bresnan (1982b).

Bresnan, J. (ed.) (1982b) *The Mental Representation of Grammatical Relations*. Cambridge, Mass.: MIT Press.

Butterworth, B. L. (1983) 'Lexical representation'. In B. L. Butterworth, (ed.) *Language Production, Vol. 2: Development, Writing and Other Language Processes*. London: Academic Press.

Butterworth, B. L. (1989) 'Lexical access in speech production'. In Marslen-Wilson (1989a).

Bybee, J. L. (1987) *Morphology as Lexical Organisation*. (Working Papers in Linguistics). Buffalo: State University of New York.

Caplan, D. (1987) *Neurolinguistics and Linguistic Aphasiology: An Introduction*. Cambridge: Cambridge University Press.

Caramazza, A. and Berndt, R. S. (1985) 'A multicomponent deficit view of agrammatic Broca's aphasia'. In Kean (1985).

Carroll, L. (1982) *Alice's Adventures in Wonderland and Through the Looking-Glass*. Harmondsworth: Penguin Books. First published in 1865 and 1872 respectively.

Cherry, E. C. (1953) 'Some experiments on the recognition of speech, with one and with two ears', *Journal of the Acoustic Society of America* 25: 975–9.

Chirol, L. (1973) *Les 'mots français' et le mythe de la France en anglais contemporain*. Paris: Éditions Klincksieck.

Chomsky, N. (1965) *Aspects of the Theory of Syntax*. Cambridge, Mass.: MIT Press.

Chomsky, N. (1986) *Knowledge of Language*. New York: Praeger.

Chomsky, N. and Halle, M. (1968) *The Sound Pattern of English*. New York: Harper & Row.

Clark, H. H. and Clark, E. V. (1977) *Psychology of Language*. New York: Harcourt, Brace Jovanovich.

Copley, J. (1961) *Shift of Meaning*. London: Oxford University Press.

Crystal, D. (1987) *The Cambridge Encyclopaedia of Language*. Cambridge: Cambridge University Press.

Crystal, D. (1988) *The English Language*. Harmondsworth: Penguin Books.

Crystal, D. (1991) *A Dictionary of Linguistics and Phonetics*. Oxford: Blackwell.

Cutler, A. and Isard, S. (1980) 'The production of prosody'. In B. L. Butterworth (ed.) (1980) *Language Production, Vol. 1: Speech and Talk*. London: Academic Press.

DeFrancis, J. (1989) *Visible Speech: The Diverse Oneness of Writing Systems*. Honolulu: University of Hawaii Press.

Dell, G. S. and Reich, P. A. (1980) 'Toward a unified model of slips of the tongue'. In Fromkin (1980).

Diller, K. C. (1978) *The Language Teaching Controversy*. Rowley, Mass.: Newbury House.

Diringer, D. (1968) *The Alphabet. A Key to the History of Mankind*. London: Hutchinson, 3rd edn.

Di Sciullo, A.-M. and Williams, E. (1987) *On Defining the Word*. Cambridge, Mass.: MIT Press.

Eliot, T. S. (1963) *Selected Poems*. London: Faber & Faber.

Ellis, A. (1980) 'On the Freudian theory of speech errors'. In Fromkin (1980).

Fantoni, B. (1984) *Private Eye's Colemanballs 2*. London: *Private Eye*/André Deutsch.

Fodor, J. A. (1981) *Representations: Philosophical Essays on the Foundations of Cognitive Science*. Cambridge, Mass.: MIT Press.

Fortescue, M. (1984) *West Greenlandic Eskimo*. London: Croom Helm.

Franklin, J. (1960) *A Dictionary of Rhyming Slang*. London: Routledge & Kegan Paul.

Frederiksen, J. and Kroll, J. (1976) 'Spelling and sound: approaches to the internal lexicon'. *Journal of Experimental Psychology: Human Perception and Performance*, 2: 361–79.

Fromkin, V. (1971) 'The nonanomalous nature of anomalous utterances'. *Language* 47: 27–52.

Fromkin, V. (ed.) (1973) *Speech Errors as Linguistic Evidence*. The Hague: Mouton.

Fromkin, V. (1980) *Errors in Linguistic Performance: Slips of the Tongue, Ear, Pen, and Hand*. New York: Academic Press.

Gairdner, J. (ed.) (1983) *The Paston Letters*. Gloucester: Alan Sutton.

Garrett, M. F. (1980) 'Levels of processing in sentence production'. In B. L. Butterworth (ed.) (1980) *Language Production, Vol. 1: Speech and Talk*. London: Academic Press.

Geipel, J. (1971) *The Viking Legacy: The Scandinavian Influence on the English and Gaelic Languages*. Newton Abbot: David & Charles.

Gelb. I. J. (1963) *A Study of Writing*. Chicago: University of Chicago Press, 2nd edn.

Gleason, H. A. (1961) *An Introduction to Descriptive Linguistics*. New York: Holt, Rinehart & Winston, 2nd edn.

Goldsmith, J. (1990) *Autosegmental and Metrical Phonology*. Oxford: Basil Blackwell.

Goodglass, H. (1976) 'Agrammatism'. in H. Whitaker and H. A. Whitaker (eds) *Studies in Neurolinguistics*. New York: Academic Press.

Green, J. (1987) *Dictionary of Jargon*. London: Routledge & Kegan Paul.

Gregg, V. H. (1986) *An Introduction to Human Memory*. London: Routledge & Kegan Paul.

Haber, L. (1970) *Black Pioneers of Science and Invention*. New York: Harcourt, Brace Jovanovich.

Halle, M. and Mohanan, K. P. (1985) 'Segmental phonology of modern English'. *Linguistic Inquiry* 16: 57–116.

Halle, M. and Stevens, K. (1962) 'Speech recognition: a model and a program for research'. *IRE Transactions of the Professional Group on Information Theory, IT–8*, 155–9.

Hankamer, J. (1989) 'Morphological parsing and the lexicon'. In Marslen-Wilson (1989a).

Harris, Z. (1951) *Methods in Structural Linguistics*. Chicago: University of Chicago Press.

Haugen, E. (1950) 'The analysis of linguistic borrowing'. *Language* 26: 210–35.

Holder, R. W. (1987) *The Faber Dictionary of Euphemisms*. London: Faber & Faber.

Hörmann, H. (1986) 'Meaning and context: an introduction to the psychology of language'. In R. E. Innis (ed.) *Cognition and Language*. New York: Plenum.

Huddleston, R. (1984) *Introduction to the Grammar of English*. Cambridge: Cambridge University Press.

Hudson, R. (1984) *Word Grammar*. Oxford: Basil Blackwell.

Hulst, van der, H. and Smith, N. (1982a) *The Structure of Phonological Representations, Part I*. Dordrecht: Foris.

Hulst, van der, H. and Smith, N. (1982b) *The Structure of Phonological Representations, Part II*. Dordrecht, Foris.

Hulst, van der, H. and Smith, N. (1982c) 'Introduction'. In van der Hulst and Smith (1982a).

Jackson, H. (1988) *Words and their Meaning*. London: Longman.

James, H. (1881) *The Portrait of a Lady*. Harmondsworth: Penguin Books.

Katamba, F. (1989) *An Introduction to Phonology*. London: Longman.

Katamba, F. (1993) *Morphology*. London: Macmillan.

Kean, M.-L. (ed.) (1985) *Agrammatism*. New York: Academic Press.

Kiparsky, P. (1982a) 'From cyclic phonology to lexical phonology'. In van der Hulst and Smith (1982a).

Kiparsky, P. (1982b) 'Lexical morphology and phonology'. In Yang, I.-S. (ed.) *Linguistics in the Morning Calm*. Seoul: Hanshin.

Kiparsky, P. (1983) 'Word formation and the lexicon'. In Ingemnn, F. (ed.) *Proceedings of the 1982 mid-America Linguistics Conference*. Lawrence, Kan.: University of Kansas.

Kiparsky, P. (1985) 'Some consequences of lexical phonology'. *Phonology Yearbook* 2: 83–136.

Klavans, J. (1985) 'The independence of syntax and phonology in cliticisation'. *Language* 61: 95–120.

Knowles, G. (1987) *Patterns of Spoken English*. London: Longman.

Lass, R. (1987) *The Shape of English: Structure and History*. London: J. M. Dent.

Lawrence, D. H. (1960) 'Love among the Haystacks' (1930). In *Love among the Haystacks and Other Stories*. Harmondsworth: Penguin.

Lecors, A. R. and Lhermitte, F. (1983) 'Clinical forms of aphasia'. In Lecours *et al*. (1983).

Lecours, A. R., Lhermitte, F. and Bryans, B. (eds) (1983) *Aphasiology*. London: Baillière, Tindall.

Lieber, (1983) 'Argument linking and compounding in English'. *Linguistic Inquiry* 14: 251–86.

Lipka, L. (1990) *An Outline of English Lexicology*. Tübingen: Max Niemeyer.

Lyons, J. (1968) *Theoretical Linguistics*. Cambridge: Cambridge University Press.

McCarthy, J. and Prince, A. S. (1990) 'Foot and word in the Arabic broken plural'. *Natural Language and Linguistic Theory* 8: 209–83.

M & S Magazine, The (Autumn 1992) London: Marks & Spencer PLC.

Marchand, H. (1969) *The Categories and Types of Present-day English Word-formation*. Munich: C. H. Beck.

Marslen-Wilson, W. (1987) 'Functional parallelism in spoken word-recognition'. *Cognition* 25: 71–102.

Marslen-Wilson, W. (1989a) *Lexical Representation and Process*. Cambridge, Mass.: MIT Press.

Marslen-Wilson, W. (1989b) 'Access and integration: projecting sound on to meaning'. In Marslen-Wilson (1989a).

Matthei, E. and Roeper, T. (1983) *Understanding and Producing Speech*. London: Fontana.

Matthews, P. (1991) *Morphology*. Cambridge: Cambridge University Press, 2nd edn. First published in 1974.

Mohanan, K. (1986) *The Theory of Lexical Phonology*. Reidel: Dordrecht.

Oldfield, R. C. (1963) 'Individual vocabulary and semantic currency: A preliminary study'. *British Journal of Social and Clinical Psychology* 2: 122–30.

Opie, I. and Opie, P. (1980) *A Nursery Companion*. Oxford: Oxford University Press.

Partridge, E. (1933) *Slang: Today and Yesterday*. London: Routledge.

Phillips, M. (1993) 'Another day, another scandal'. In *The Guardian*, 16 January: 24.

Phythian, B. A. (1982) *A Concise Dictionary of Foreign Expressions*. London: Hodder & Stoughton.

Pulleyblank, D. (1986) *Tone in Lexical Phonology*. Dordrecht: Reidel.

Pyles, T. and Alego, J. (1971) *The Origins and Development of the English Language*. New York: Harcourt, Brace Jovanovich, 3rd edn.

Pyles, T. and Algeo, J. (1982) *The Origins and Development of the English Language*. New York: Harcourt, Brace Jovanovich.

Quirk, R. and Greenbaum, S. (1973) *A University Grammar of English*. London: Longman.

Rao, S. G. (1954) *Indian Words in English*. Oxford: Clarendon Press.

Roeper, T. and Siegel, D. (1978) 'A lexical transformation for verbal compounds'. *Linguistic Inquiry* 9: 199–260.

Room, A. (1986) *Dictionary of Changes in Meaning*. London: Routledge & Kegan Paul.

Rubach, J. (1984) *Cyclic and Lexical Phonology*. Dordrecht: Foris.

Sagan, C. (1985) *Cosmos*. New York: Ballantine.

Salzman, L. F. (1952) *Building in England down to 1540: A Documentary History*. Oxford: Clarendon Press.

Sampson, G. (1985) *Writing Systems: A Linguistic Approach*. London: Hutchinson.

Sapir, L. (1921) *Language*. New York: Harcourt Brace & World.

Saussure, F. (1916) *Cours de linguistique générale*. Paris: Payot. English translation: *A Course in General Linguistics*. London: Duckworth.

Savin, H. (1963) 'Word-frequency effect and errors in the perception of speech'. *Journal of the Acoustical Society of America* 35: 200–6.

Schwartz, M. F., Linebarger, M. C. and Saffran, E. M. (1985) 'The status of the syntactic deficit in agrammatism'. In Kean (1985).

Scragg, D. G. (1973) *Spelling.* London: André Deutsch. (Revised version of G. H. Vallins, *Spelling,* 1954).

Seashore, R. H. and Eckerson, L. D. (1940) 'The measurement of individual differences in general English vocabularies'. *Journal of Educational Psychology* 31: 14–38.

Selkirk, E. O. (1982) *The Syntax of Words.* Cambridge, Mass.: MIT Press.

Sheridan, R. B. *The Rivals* (1775) In C. Price (ed.) (1975) *Sheridan Plays.* London: Oxford University Press.

Siegel, D. (1971) 'Some lexical transderivational constraints in English'. Unpublished MS, Department of Linguistics, MIT, Cambridge, Mass.

Siegel, D. (1974) 'Topics in English morphology'. PhD dissertation, MIT, Cambridge, Mass. (Published by Garland, New York, 1979.)

Skeat, W. W. (1892) *Principles of English Etymology.* Oxford: Clarendon Press.

Spencer, A. (1991) *Morphological Theory.* Oxford: Basil Blackwell.

Stanners, R. F., Neiser, J. J., Hernon, W. P. and Hall, R. (1979) 'Memory representation for morphologically related words'. *Journal of Verbal Learning and Behaviour* 18: 399–412.

Stevens, K. and House, A. S. (1972) 'Speech perception'. In J. V. Tobias (ed.) *Foundations of Modern Auditory Theory, Vol. 2.* New York: Academic Press: 3–62.

Strang, B. M. H. (1970) *A History of English.* London: Methuen.

Stubbs, M. (1980) *Language and Literacy: The Sociolinguistics of Reading and Writing.* London: Routledge & Kegan Paul.

Studdert-Kennedy, M. (1974) 'The perception of speech'. In T. A. Sebeok (ed.) *Current Trends in Linguistics, Vol. 12: Linguistics and Adjacent Arts and Sciences.* The Hague: Mouton: 2349–85.

Studdert-Kennedy, M. (1976) 'Speech perception'. In N. Lass (ed.) *Contemporary Issues in Experimental Phonetics.* New York: Academic Press.

Swadesh, M. and Voeglin, C. F. (1939) 'A problem in phonological alternation'. *Language* 15: 1–10. Reprinted in M. Joos (ed.) (1957) *Readings in Linguistics 1.* Chicago: University of Chicago Press.

Taft, M. (1979) 'Recognition of affixed words and the word frequency effect'. *Memory and Cognition* 7: 263–72.

Taft, M. (1981) 'Prefix stripping revisited'. *Journal of Verbal Learning and Behaviour* 20: 289–97.

Taft, M. and Foster, K. (1975) 'Lexical storage and retrieval of prefixed words'. *Journal of Verbal Learning and Behaviour* 14: 638–47.

Thun, N. (1963) *Reduplicative Words in English.* Uppsala: Carl Bloms.

Trevelyan, G. M. (1949) *Illustrated English Social History, Vol. 1, Chaucer's England and the Early Tudors.* London: Longman.

Vachek, J. (1973) *Written Language: General Problems and Problems of English.* The Hague: Mouton.

Vidal, J. (1992) 'The big chill'. *The Guardian* (London), 19 November.

Wells, J. C. (1982) *Accents of English I: An Introduction.* Cambridge: Cambridge University Press.

Young, J. and Young, P. (1981) *The Ladybird Book of Jokes, Riddles and Rhymes*. Loughborough: Ladybird Books.

Zijderveld, C. (1979) *On Clichés: The Supersedure of Meaning by Function*. London: Routledge & Kegan Paul.

Zwicky, A. (1985) 'Clitics and particles'. *Language* 61: 283–305.

Zwicky, A. and Pullum, G. (1983) 'Cliticisation vs. inflection: English *n't*'. *Language* 59: 502–13.

Indexes

Wernicke, C. 250, 253–4
Wijk, A. 142
Winchester, S. 13

Young, J. and Young, P. 21–2
Yves Saint Laurent 214

Zijderveld, C. 168
Zwicky, A. 164; and Pullum, G. 164

SUBJECT INDEX